JOURNAL OF MORAL THEOLOGY

Volume 2, Number 2 ~ June 2013

THE CHURCH AND THE WORLD

Edited by Christopher P. Vogt

Westphalia and Back:
   Complexifying the Church-World Duality in Catholic Thought 1
      William T. Cavanaugh

The "Signs of the Times" and their Readers in Wartime and in Peace 21
      Laurie Johnston

Time Poverty, Women's Labor, and Catholic Social Teaching:
   A Practical Theological Exploration 40
      Claire E. Wolfteich

Between Inculturation and Natural Law:
   Comparative Method in Catholic Moral Theology 60
      David M. Lantigua and David A. Clairmont

Syncretism: Why Latin American and Caribbean Theologians
Want to Replace a "Fighting Word" in Theology 89
      Ramón Luzárraga

The World in the Theology of Joseph Ratzinger/Benedict XVI 109
      Tracey Rowland

Mapping a Method for Dialogue: Exploring the Tensions between
   Razian Autonomy and Catholic Solidarity as Applied to Euthanasia 133
      Amelia J. Uelmen

Review Essay
Locating the Church in the World:
   Ethnography, Christian Ethics, and the Global Church 158
      Christopher P. Vogt

JOURNAL OF MORAL THEOLOGY

EDITOR
David M. McCarthy, *Mount St. Mary's University*

EDITORIAL BOARD
Melanie Barrett, *University of St. Mary of the Lake/Mundelein Seminary*
Jana M. Bennett, *University of Dayton*
Joseph Capizzi, *The Catholic University of America*
David Cloutier, *Mount St. Mary's University*
Kelly Johnson, *University of Dayton*
Jason King, *St. Vincent College*
M. Therese Lysaught, *Marquette University*
Ramón Luzárraga, *University of Dayton*
Rev. Bryan Massingale, *Marquette University*
William C. Mattison III, *The Catholic University of America*
Jeanne Heffernan Schindler, *Villanova University*
Msgr. Stuart W. Swetland, *Mount St. Mary's University*
Christopher P. Vogt, *St. John's University*
Brian Volck, *Cincinnati Children's Hospital Medical Center
University of Cincinnati College of Medicine*

Journal of Moral Theology is a peer-reviewed scholarly journal focusing on Catholic moral theology. It is concerned with contemporary issues as well as our deeply rooted tradition of inquiry about the moral life. Our mission is to publish scholarly articles in the field of moral theology, as well as theological treatments of related topics in philosophy, economics, political philosophy, and psychology. *Journal of Moral Theology* is published semiannually, with January and July issues.

The journal's articles are open-access, available at www.msmary.edu/jmt. Bound print issues are available by request through our website.

Articles published in the *Journal of Moral Theology* will undergo at least two peer reviews. Authors are asked to submit articles electronically to jmt@msmary.edu and will be informed about the review process by e-mail. Submissions should be prepared for blind review and conform to *Chicago Manual of Style*. Microsoft Word format preferred. Editors assume that submissions are not being simultaneously considered for publication in another venue.

ISSN 2166-2851 (print), ISSN 2166-2118 (online). *Journal of Moral Theology* is published by Mount St. Mary's University, 16300 Old Emmitsburg Road, Emmitsburg, MD 21727. Copyright © 2013 individual authors and Mount St. Mary's University. All rights reserved.

Except for brief quotations in critical publications or reviews, no part of this book may be reproduced in any manner without prior written permission from the publisher. Write: Permissions. Wipf and Stock Publishers, 199 W. 8th Ave., Suite 3, Eugene, OR 97401.

Pickwick Publications, An Imprint of Wipf and Stock Publishers, 199 W. 8th Ave., Suite 3, Eugene, OR 97401. www.wipfandstock.com. ISBN 13: 978-1-62564-453-4

A NOTE FROM THE ISSUE EDITOR

I am very grateful to all of the contributors to this issue who responded so generously to my invitation to share their particular expertise and theological perspective on the church and the world. Their good work has made this a rich collection of essays that address this fundamental theological question from a wide variety of interesting angles.

This issue begins with an essay by William Cavanaugh who asks us to reconsider the conventional wisdom that the Second Vatican Council led the Roman Catholic Church in the United States to grow from a world-fearing, ghettoized sect into a church very much at home in American society. Using the town of Westphalia, Iowa (a utopian Catholic community established before Vatican II) as a focal point for examining the church/world relationship in the concrete, he argues for a more complex understanding than the conventional narrative of historical progress or Ernst Troeltsch's categories of sect and church will allow.

Laurie Johnston's essay takes up the pressing question of how contemporary Christians should go about reading the signs of the times. She observes that since the Second Vatican Council, what the signs of the times are has been a matter of constant dispute as have the questions of how, by whom, and according to what criteria they should be discerned. Johnston illuminates both the difficulty and the necessity of reading the signs of the times, expanding upon Yves Congar's wisdom that Christians must strive to live as pilgrims not tourists in the world. Drawing from historical and contemporary examples, she points to solidarity, experience in humanity, and humility as keys to discernment.

Moral theology and practical theology share much in common. Each of these specialties seeks (among other things) to explain how spirituality and the demands of discipleship should shape the way that Christians live in the world. Claire Wolfteich employs a practical theological method to provide a rich description of the reality of time-poverty that many women (and men) face today. She goes on to develop a compelling theology of time, teasing out the critical, countercultural, and justice implications of Catholic teaching on labor, the Sabbath, and the domestic church.

Two essays in this issue address the challenges of inculturation. First, David Clairmont and David Lantigua bring Catholic moral theology into dialogue with the comparative study of religion as they consider two specific contexts in which Catholics have grappled with questions about the status of indigenous people and their religious beliefs: Colonial Latin America and Post-colonial Africa. Their study illuminates new ways of thinking about the relationship between the gospel, natural law, and culture. Second, Ramon Luzárraga explores how the Christian faith inculturates itself with popular religious practices in Latin America and the Caribbean. He describes the complex process of discernment behind efforts to name and support appropriate forms of inculturated worship and practice.

Tracey Rowland debunks superficial characterizations of Joseph Ratzinger/Benedict XVI's theology of the church and the world. By offering a careful examination of the influences that shaped Ratzinger's thought, and by providing an attentive analysis of his work as a theologian, Rowland sketches a nuanced church/world theology that is neither neo-Manichean nor hostile toward the world. Rowland illustrates the consistency between Benedict XVI's recent writings about the church and the world and Ratzinger's earlier theological work.

Dialogue is an important dimension of theological work on the church and the world. Amelia Uelmen explores the possibilities and limits of dialogue between Catholics and people of good will who have profoundly different cultural assumptions. Uelmen's essay centers on a careful analysis of Cathleen Kaveny's efforts to engage the thought of philosopher and legal scholar Joseph Raz. Uelmen sketches some of the methodological implications that emerge from her analysis of Kaveny's work, focusing in particular on the limits of abstract concepts as a basis for building bridges across difference and the promise of personal narrative for dialogue.

Finally, my own essay offers a review of two significant developments in the field. First, I survey some recent work by ecclesiologists and moral theologians who integrate ethnographic research into their writing, and I assess their claims about the indispensability of field research. Second, I survey the work of theologians associated with the "Catholic Theological Ethics in the World Church" organization, and I analyze some of the methodological claims being put forward by this movement.

When I agreed to serve as editor for this issue of the *Journal of Moral Theology*, I must confess that I did not fully realize the magnitude of the task. I would like to offer my thanks to everyone who contributed time and talent to this issue. I am particularly grateful to Samantha Deliso, who served as my graduate assistant at St. John's University this year. She provided considerable help with the initial review of the first draft of each article and assisted me again later with the difficult task of proof-reading. I am grateful to the members of the editorial board of the *Journal of Moral Theology* for their work in reviewing all of articles in this issue. I would like to offer special thanks to Jana Bennett who provided extremely helpful comments and feedback.

Very special thanks go to David Matzko McCarthy for the support and assistance he provided to me at all stages of the development and production of this issue. He consistently gave very helpful editorial advice while always allowing me the freedom to shape the issue. He was very patient in all of his dealings with me as I struggled through some of the difficulties that went along with being a first-time editor. David and his colleagues at Mount Saint Mary's University handled the work of formatting the issue, providing proofreading assistance, and dealing with other details of production. I would like to extend my gratitude to Ericka Dixon, Mackenzie Sullivan, Hannah Clinton, Gloria Balsley, and the members of the theology faculty of Mount Saint Mary's University for all of their work.

— Christopher P. Vogt

Westphalia and Back:
Complexifying the Church-World Duality in Catholic Thought

William T. Cavanaugh

SOME YEARS AGO, I was staying with an aunt and uncle in Winona, Minnesota when I came upon an old Catholic primary school geography textbook in a spare bedroom that had previously been occupied by a now grown-up cousin. The book is entitled *World Neighbors*; it was published in 1952 by William H. Sadlier, Inc., still today a major publisher of educational materials for public and non-public schools, as well as catechetical materials for Catholic schools. The book's foreword announced "the beginning of an era in Catholic education," but to contemporary eyes it looks more like a relic from the far distant past. Particularly fascinating is the depiction of a small town in Iowa called Westphalia, presented in a section entitled "A Study of a Community." It is an entirely Catholic town, settled by German immigrants, where the social and economic life of the community is organized through the parish, whose pastor reigns like a benevolent despot. It seems to belong to a much earlier era: the Middle Ages. The fact that it is mid-twentieth century America seems to mark it as an anachronism, a last-ditch effort to keep the modern world at bay. As we know with the benefit of hindsight, the life represented by Westphalia, Iowa, was not the beginning of an era, but the end of one. The insular Catholic universe it represented was about to be swept away by the changes of Vatican II and, more generally, the 1960s. Rather than huddling together and trying to protect the church from the world, the church would throw its arms open to the world and embrace modernity. Instead of seeing the world as one big opportunity for sin from which the church must stand apart, we would recognize the essential goodness of the world and seek to locate the church in the world, always trying to transform the world from within.

So goes the familiar story. As a broad characterization of changes in the Catholic orbit in the late twentieth century, it is not entirely inaccurate. And as a cautionary tale against nostalgia for a lost world, it is salutary. Those who want to return to a lost world usually end up making a mess of this one. Nevertheless, as a neatly progressive tale, the familiar story is incomplete and oversimplified. It fails to appreciate the efforts, sometimes successful, to bring the gospel to bear on material life in quite sophisticated ways. In dismissing these efforts, it fails to recognize what the past has to teach us today as we negotiate our way through the postmodern world.

I will begin with the story of Westphalia, circa 1952, then turn to the way that social milieu is narrated by the standard understanding of the church-world duality after Vatican II. I will argue that "world" has multiple meanings, and that the standard narrative does not do justice to the way that Westphalia engaged with the world. I will, finally, suggest some things that can be learned from complexifying the church-world dualism. I intend this paper as a bridge-building exercise; rather than siding with factions who would either dismiss or romanticize the pre-Vatican II Church in America, I will argue that we can attain a more nuanced view of that Church by attending to a more nuanced view of the church/world relationship.

JOURNEY TO WESTPHALIA

World Neighbors makes clear on page 1 that Catholics do not study geography out of idle curiosity. We need to know the land where God has put us and know about our fellow children of God in order that we may love them, and thus "do our part in helping God's Kingdom come."[1] The first section of the book deals with the land of the United States—rivers, lakes, climate, etc.—and the second deals with the people of the United States, "a Nation of Many Peoples." Within this second section is a subsection on community life in the U.S., in which Westphalia is featured as a kind of ideal. "In this community there are no poor people, no very rich, but all are comfortable, prosperous, hard-working, most of them farmers. There is no crime, no jail, no police force. The Ten Commandments are the Law here, says the Pastor, Father Hubert Duren. The Community and the Parish are here one and the same."[2] Although there are only a hundred families, Westphalia boasts "15 of its sons in the priesthood, 96 girls are nuns, 17 boys monks or Brothers, and 18 boys are in the armed forces."[3] The town's year is organized around the liturgical calendar and special occasions such as the blessing of fields by the Pastor each spring.

Westphalia was not always such a happy place, the textbook reports. "When Father Duren came to Westphalia years ago, he found the people poor, all their earnings draining out to the big towns where they bought supplies. There was no good school, no way of marketing produce for fair returns, no amusement for young people.

---

[1] Sister M. Juliana Bedier, *World Neighbors* (New York: W. H. Sadlier, Inc., 1952), 1.
[2] Bedier, *World Neighbors*, 64.
[3] Bedier, *World Neighbors*, 64.

Families were breaking up, drifting away. He taught the people the principles of co-operation and organized a credit union, thus keeping money in the community and providing a fund to improve farms and livestock. He set up a co-op store where farmers buy supplies."[4] The co-operative store gave the farmers control over processing and marketing their own meat and dairy products, and returned the profits to them, since they were its owners. In turn, the community built a co-operative beauty parlor and a co-operative garage. They used the profits from these ventures to build a school "where children are taught to co-operate, to esteem rural life, to live as happy, productive members of the Community, following the Church's social teaching and the liturgy through the year."[5] The community also built a recreation hall for dances, shows, and parties, a clubhouse with a soda fountain and billiard tables, and a baseball field. The people of Westphalia are shown enjoying these amenities in a gallery of pictures that accompanies the text. The pictures concentrate on the Zimmerman family, various of whose 14 children are shown shoveling alfalfa, repairing a hog feeder, receiving communion at daily Mass, visiting the soda fountain and the credit union, and relaxing at home, where Don and Jerry pop corn, Joey and Celia wash dishes, and Michael makes rosaries.

    Residents of Westphalia who remember it from that time speak of constant social activity surrounding the parish. Movies followed Sunday night devotions. There were plays, band concerts, baseball games, monthly meetings of the Rosary Society for women and the Holy Name Society for men, parish picnics, bingo nights, and special processions on feast days with townspeople carrying a large rosary, each bead as large as a softball. As one longtime resident says, "Religion was woven into our everyday life at that time."[6] There were no sharp distinctions between religious, social, and economic life. Support for the local businesses—"People knew that if the community was to prosper one had to support the businesses"—was a religious duty as much as it was a social pleasure; "Saturday nights people would come to the Co-op Grocery store to buy groceries for the week. This gave everyone a chance to visit with friends."

    The center of the community was, without question, Father Duren, shown in the textbook chomping a cigar and playing billiards at the clubhouse. Longtime residents remember Fr. Duren as a tall man,

---

[4] Bedier, *World Neighbors*, 65.
[5] Bedier, *World Neighbors*, 66.
[6] A dozen residents of Westphalia who remember the time to which the textbook refers were kind enough to complete questionnaires that I sent them. I am extremely grateful to Lorene Kaufmann, parish secretary of St. Boniface Church in Westphalia, for all her kindnesses and help in soliciting responses from people in Westphalia. All subsequent quotes from residents of Westphalia are taken from these completed questionnaires.

"demanding, but gentle," who composed music, painted, hand carved furniture, and built his own home with an energy-saving cooling system of his own design. In addition to the feats mentioned in the textbook, Fr. Duren also built and stocked an artificial lake for the community to fish and built two shrines, one to Our Lady and the other to St. Isidore, patron saint of farmers. The success of the community did not happen by accident, the textbook reports. Father Duren "follows a 5-point program in which religion, education, recreation, commerce, and credit are organized with the Church as the center of life in community and family. He calls it the Complete Life, Christian, American, and democratic. He believes Americans should rebuild their small communities. We should all unite under God and move in the direction of security on earth and in eternity. Westphalia shows it can be done."[7] The textbook reports that young people no longer wish to leave the small town, but it does not mention what some old timers in the community have told me: the young people had to ask Fr. Duren's permission to go to a dance in another town. As one resident reports, "Mostly everything that went on went through him." Not everyone was pleased. Though most reminisce fondly about Fr. Duren, one says, "He had his favorites, people who were brainwashed to his program. If not, he didn't care much for you."

NARRATING WESTPHALIA

It is easy for a contemporary reader to laugh and shake one's head at such a neat and tidy Catholic enclave. The account in the textbook is doubtlessly somewhat romanticized; people surely chafed at Fr. Duren's authority. Recent revelations of priestly abuse of authority cannot help but make contemporary readers wary of such 40-year reigns in which the pastor's leadership is unquestioned. Even if the textbook's account of life in Westphalia circa 1952 is essentially accurate, however, few Catholics today would wish to return to such a time and place. Attempts like that of Ave Maria, Florida, to recreate a kind of cohesive Catholic culture in Catholic enclaves have been marginal efforts and marred with controversy.

The standard way to narrate communities like Westphalia centers on the church-world dualism and pivots around the Second Vatican Council.[8] In brief, the story goes like this: once Catholics huddled in all-Catholic ghettos, at odds with the world. After Vatican II, Catho-

---

[7] Bedier, *World Neighbors*, 67.
[8] For example see Jay P. Dolan, *The American Catholic Experience: A History from Colonial Times to the Present* (Notre Dame: University of Notre Dame, 1992); Richard Gula, *Reason Informed by Faith: Foundations of Catholic Morality* (Mahwah: Paulist, 1989); and James McEvoy, "Church and World at the Second Vatican Council: The Significance of *Gaudium et Spes*," *Pacifica* 19 (Feb. 2006): 37-57.

lics came confidently to embrace the world, and became leaven in a pluralistic society. A typical account is that of Charles Curran's recent book *The Social Mission of the U.S. Catholic Church: A Theological Perspective*. Curran makes clear that his book is not simply a history of the social mission of the Catholic Church in America, but is a theological interpretation of that history.[9] Chapter one, entitled "Early Historical Context and Taking Care of Our Own," is a brief overview of the history of the immigrant Catholic Church in the nineteenth century. The title of the chapter tells the story. Poor and unwashed immigrants from Catholic homelands in Europe flooded the United States over the course of the nineteenth century, often incurring the hostility of the native Protestants, both for social reasons—the poor and foreigners are often disdained—and for theological reasons: "The greatest problem many Americans had with the Catholic Church was its failure to accept religious freedom and the basic principles of the U.S. Constitution."[10] Catholics tended to think that religious freedom was acceptable only if it was impracticable to offer official recognition to the Catholic Church as the bearer of truth. Error, after all, had no rights. The erroneous tended to disapprove of this view of the world, and nativist reactions against Catholicism sometimes turned violent. The Catholic reaction was to form their own parochial schools, since public schools were essentially Protestant schools. Extensive efforts at poor relief undertaken by Catholic religious orders were in part motivated by the desire to keep Catholic children out of the care of publicly-funded efforts, run by Protestant groups, to reform and improve the poor. Catholic laborers banded together into Catholic labor unions, beginning in 1869, and Catholic religious orders founded an extensive system of Catholic hospitals, which did minister to non-Catholics in times of crisis.[11] Catholic efforts before World War I, according to Curran, were largely directed to "taking care of our own" and not addressing "the reform of U.S. social institutions."[12] In addition to dealing with the hordes of poor Catholic immigrants, however, Catholics did try to present themselves as good, patriotic Americans, to lessen the stigma of foreigner with which they were often associated.

Curran's second chapter tells the story of the social mission of the Church from World War I to the Second Vatican Council, the period in which the *World Neighbors* textbook was produced. After the bishops formed the National Catholic War Council to show Catholic support for the American cause in World War I, the bishops—

---

[9] Charles E. Curran, *The Social Mission of the U.S. Catholic Church: A Theological Perspective* (Washington, DC: Georgetown University, 2011), x-xi.
[10] Curran, *The Social Mission*, 5.
[11] Curran, *The Social Mission*, 5-11.
[12] Curran, *The Social Mission*, 6.

through the later-renamed National Catholic Welfare Conference—began to address public policy issues under the leadership of John A. Ryan, who directed the NCWC Social Action Department from 1920 to 1945. Curran calls Ryan's efforts "the first attempts by the U.S. Catholic Church to develop its social mission."[13] All the previous efforts do not count as "social mission" for Curran because they do not address American society as a whole. Ryan saw the Church as a hierarchical institution whose primary business was the saving of souls. In this sense, as Curran points out, his thought obeyed the Neo-Scholastic distinction between natural and supernatural orders. But Ryan thought that the moral law necessary to the salvation of souls also included social and economic issues such as a living wage. The other key figure in Curran's pre-Vatican II narrative is John Courtney Murray, though in many ways Murray was ahead of his time, laying the groundwork for Vatican II. Murray was in the vanguard of emphasizing the independence of the laity from direct obedience to the hierarchy in social matters. Rather than the Catholic Action model, in which laypeople addressed social issues from within an organization juridically subject to the bishops, Murray called for Catholic action, with a small "a," in which laity played a direct role in the secular institutions of civil society to bring about a more just society. Murray also defended inter-creedal cooperation with non-Catholics for a better world. [14]

Curran provides an overview of the different kinds of Catholic groups working in the pre-Vatican II period: organizations of Catholic labor unionists, sociologists, and economists; the Legion of Decency; the Catholic Association for International Peace; the Catholic Worker; efforts to promote anti-communism and fight racism; community organizing efforts in collaboration with Saul Alinsky; the Catholic Family Movement, and others. The 1930s through the 1950s were, Curran says, "a golden period of Catholic action."[15] As immigration slowed and Catholics moved toward the American mainstream, Catholic attention moved from taking care of Catholic immigrants to the concerns of the broader society. There was an impressive range of Catholic organizations hard at work to bring Catholic social teaching to fruition in America, from organizations like the Legion of Decency that looked to the hierarchy for guidance to the majority of efforts which were led by laypeople. There were large Catholic organizations dedicated to bringing Catholic teaching directly to bear on labor, war, economy, racism, poverty, and family—all the great issues of the day.

---

[13] Curran, *The Social Mission*, 15.
[14] Curran, *The Social Mission*, 17-18.
[15] Curran, *The Social Mission*, 36.

Most of these organizations collapsed in the 1960s. Curran explains the collapse in part sociologically: Catholics went to college on the G.I. Bill after World War II, became affluent, and moved to the suburbs, away from tight-knit parish units. The newly prosperous and more Americanized Catholics were less likely to look to the Church for guidance. But beyond sociology, Curran is more interested in giving a theological account of the changes in Catholic social action. In chapters three and four of his book, he narrates the changes as an effect of the changes in the way the Catholic Church viewed itself and its own relationship to the world in the wake of Vatican II. According to Curran, pre-Vatican II treatises on the Church were defensive, concerned to protect the Church from Protestantism and secularism. The institutional and hierarchical aspects of the Church were emphasized, and the Church itself tended to be identified with the Kingdom of God. There was a two-tiered division of labor between those called to leave the world for the perfection of the religious life, and those laity called to live in the world. Vatican II, on the other hand, tended to present the Church as a mystery, a sacrament in and to the world, rather than a bulwark against the world. The call of the laity to perfection was emphasized, and the Church was seen not as the Kingdom, but as a pilgrim community called to witness to the Kingdom as it journeys through the world.[16]

Curran writes that the Church's ecclesiology changed in Vatican II, but he also wants to claim a "significant continuity in the understanding of the Catholic Church throughout the centuries."[17] Rather than turn to some classical Catholic theological sources, however, he turns instead to Protestant sociology of the twentieth century, that of Ernst Troeltsch and Max Weber. Weber's distinction between church and sect was developed by Troeltsch into a three-part typology of church, sect, and mysticism. The last term goes unused by Curran, who adopts the basic contrast between church and sect as the framework for analyzing Catholic social action in the U.S. Those Christians who follow the sect type, as exemplified by the Amish and other Anabaptist groups, see themselves as a small minority who follow the Sermon on the Mount strictly; they see "themselves in opposition to the world around them… if one does not detach from the rest of the world one ultimately has to compromise these Christian tenets. Sectarians believe themselves to be called as faithful witnesses to the Gospel message, not called to transform society."[18] The church type, exemplified by the Catholic Church, is a large group "that exists within the world and works to influence existing cultural, political, and economic structures. The church type moderates the radical eth-

---

[16] Curran, *The Social Mission*, 41-2.
[17] Curran, *The Social Mission*, 42.
[18] Curran, *The Social Mission*, 42.

ic of Jesus."[19] The basic contrast between sect and church is between those who detach themselves from the world and those who work within the world.

Curran comments that Troeltsch used the term "sect" as descriptive, not evaluative. But he adds, "Troeltsch's approach is sociological and descriptive but it points to aspects that are normative for the Catholic Church."[20] The Catholic Church in Curran's view clearly conforms to Troeltsch's church type, not only descriptively but normatively. Curran then goes on to parse this normative judgment about the Catholic Church into four related types of inclusivity: in relation to Church membership, in its concern for all of reality, in its basic approach to theology ("both-and" not "either-or"), and in recognizing different levels of morality with different degrees of certitude. The second mark of inclusivity is especially relevant to the relationship of church to world, and according to Curran clearly distinguishes the church type from the sect type. The church does not withdraw from the world, but is concerned about the world as a whole. At the same time, the church recognizes that the world has its own autonomy that must be respected; but this cannot mean that God's wishes for creation can be ignored. With regard to the relationship of church and state, after Vatican II the Catholic Church no longer seeks to subordinate the state to itself, but rather seeks to work for justice within the structures of the state. The theological justification for this embrace of all of reality is the fact that creation is the good gift of a good God. "The created, the natural, and the human are not evil"[21] but rather mediate the presence of God to us. The sacraments of the Church display this embrace of mediation:

> The Eucharist is basically a celebratory meal recalling the many meals Jesus celebrated with his disciples, including what we call the Last Supper. The celebratory meal is the primary way in which human families and friends gather together to celebrate their love and friendship for one another.... So the liturgy takes over the fundamental sharing inherent in a meal and makes the meal the primary

---

[19] Curran, *The Social Mission*, 43.
[20] Curran, *The Social Mission*. After discussing the various types of inclusivity that come with being a church, not a sect, Curran returns to sociology and cites various surveys indicating that the number of committed Catholics has dropped in the U.S. over the past several decades, and that many American Catholics are looking to individual conscience rather than to the Church for guidance on moral issues. Curran concludes, "Sociological surveys by their very nature can never be normative or prescriptive, but they indicate in their own way that the Catholic Church is a big church, inclusive of saints and sinners and of the more or less committed, in which there is both unity on core issues and diversity on more peripheral issues" (53).
[21] Curran, *The Social Mission* 47.

way in which Christians celebrate God's love and their commitment to love God and neighbor.[22]

In the following chapter, Curran takes this post-Vatican II understanding of the Catholic Church and shows its effects on the social mission of the Church. According to Curran, in the pre-Vatican II Church, the mission of the Church was seen as twofold. Divinization, the work of sanctifying the people, was the job of the clergy and religious. Humanization, working for the betterment of the world, was the role of the laity. The main development in the wake of Vatican II, according to Curran, has been the integration of the two missions into one.[23] Now the transformation of the world is seen as an integral aspect of the preaching of the gospel. This is a direct result of the Vatican II emphasis on the dialogue between the Church and the world.[24] As a result of this breaking down of the supernatural/natural dichotomy, the roles of clergy, religious, and the laity have changed as well. The full gospel dignity of the laity's work in the world has been recognized, while the clergy and religious have come out of their confinement in the supernatural sphere to become actively involved in working for the transformation of the world. The Leadership Conference of Women Religious, for example, has claimed working for a more just and peaceful world as integral to its calling.[25] An important manifestation of this active embrace of the world has been the breaking down of the triumphalism and separatism of the Catholic Church. We have moved out of the "Catholic Ghetto."[26] The Church no longer seeks to foster specifically Catholic social organizations, but rather encourages Catholics to work together with all people of goodwill, of another religion or none at all, to foster justice in a pluralistic society. At the same time, Catholics now work with others through the mechanism of the state. Structural change through public policy is the most important way the Church works to transform the world. "From a theoretical perspective, there is no doubt that structural change is a very effective way to correct injustice, which explains the Church's present-day emphasis on change in public policy on a number of issues."[27] At the same time, Curran gives a nod to the principle of subsidiarity, which shows the coherence of Catholic social teaching with the limited constitutional government of American democracy. Government should only intervene to do what voluntary associations cannot do on their own.[28]

---

[22] Curran, *The Social Mission*, 47.
[23] Curran, *The Social Mission*, 57-8.
[24] Curran, *The Social Mission*, 58-9.
[25] Curran, *The Social Mission*, 66.
[26] Curran, *The Social Mission*, 76.
[27] Curran, *The Social Mission*, 71.
[28] Curran, *The Social Mission*, 72-3.

Overall, Curran's narration of changes in Catholic social mission in America is a progressive tale. We have moved from huddling together in Catholic ghettos like Westphalia to embracing the world in all its plurality. Catholic Charities and Catholic health care institutions now receive significant government funding and mostly resemble secular institutions, but this is simply a flowering of the Catholic emphasis on mediation and the desire to avoid being a "sect."[29] The death of most Catholic social action movements in the United States is attributed to Vatican II, and celebrated. "The very concept of Catholic Action no longer made sense after Vatican II, when action on behalf of justice and the transformation of the world were seen as the constitutive dimension of the preaching of the Gospel and the mission of the Church."[30] Why Catholic Action does not qualify for this conception of "action on behalf of justice and the transformation of the world" is not clear, except that, in Curran's view, the more justice and transformation of the world are seen as constitutive of the Church, the more the Church should come to be constituted by the world. Curran explains that we have moved beyond hierarchical Church documents that

> see the Church and the world as two previously constituted entities that then enter into dialogue and relationship with one another. But political and liberation theologians do not understand faith as an independently constituted reality illuminating the political or economic sphere. The prior question is how the commitment to struggle for the poor and against injustice affects faith itself. Commitment to this struggle is the horizon that shapes our understanding of faith itself and of the Church.[31]

Curran mentions no reciprocal relationship whereby the world is constituted by the Church. The world is simply out there, a reality with which the Church must reckon.

CHURCH AND WORLD

Curran's tale is attractive because, like all progressive narratives, it allows us to see our current situation as superior to what came before. Once we were huddled against the world, and now we have turned toward the world and embraced it in order to transform it. Who beside sociopaths want to go back to such a negative and defensive attitude toward the world? I think Curran's narrative is problematic—not because I wish to return to the pre-Vatican II Church, but because it oversimplifies the relationship of the Church to the world by reading it through the church/sect dualism, and in doing so

---

[29] Curran, *The Social Mission*, 81-5.
[30] Curran, *The Social Mission*, 92.
[31] Curran, *The Social Mission*, 59.

too easily dismisses the relevance of pre-Vatican II efforts to conform the world to the gospel.

The problem begins with the fact that Curran—without recognizing the difference among them—uses the church/world duality in at least three different ways:

A. It follows the Catholic/non-Catholic binary, such that embrace of the world means the embrace of non-Catholics.

B. It follows the God/creation or supernatural/natural binary, such that embrace of the world means recognizing the goodness of the created order and the way it mediates God's presence to us.

C. It follows the Christ/culture or faith/daily life or religious/social binary, such that embrace of the world means integrating the gospel with economic and political and social realities.

Conflating these three meanings of church/world leaves Curran without sufficient nuance to recognize more than two different approaches to the church/world question. We are left with a choice between church type and sect type—or to question the very categories with which he is operating.

The breaking down of barriers between non-Catholics and Catholics in the post-Vatican II era should be recognized as an unqualified gain. To describe this movement as an embrace of the world by the Church, however, is misleading. The ecumenical movement, from the Catholic point of view, is rather a recognition that those who were previously anathematized as belonging to the realm of perdition and not to the Church are now recognized as belonging to the one church of Christ, even though not yet in full communion with the Catholic Church. The "realm of perdition"—those whose salvation is in serious jeopardy by reason of their obstinate refusal to recognize Christ—corresponds to the Johannine use of "world" (*kosmos*) to mean that part of creation which is still in rebellion against Christ's definitive rule (see, e.g., John 12:31, 16:11, 18:36). This use of the church/world duality as corresponding to those who follow Christ/those who are in rebellion against Christ—let's call this sense D—is not employed by Curran at all, despite its biblical pedigree.

Sense D is the primary way the Gospel of John uses the term "world," but John also uses it secondarily as in B to denote the created order.[32] In this case, however, the world is not located in a duality

---

[32] The marginal comment on John 1:10 in The New Oxford Annotated Bible notes, "The primary meaning of *world* in the Fourth Gospel is the fallible social systems and social relations created by humanity… but it also denotes physical creation, including humanity."

with the church; the church is part of the created order. Curran, of course, would agree. But he thinks that there is a type of Christian—the sect type—that overlooks the goodness of the created order that came into being through Christ (John 1:10), and thus turns its back on the world, trying to maintain its own purity against the evils of the created order. For Curran, then, the two different uses of the term "world" in the Gospel of John reflect not two quite different meanings of the word *kosmos*—used by the author of the Fourth Gospel in two quite distinct contexts—but rather two different types of being church, one that has a positive view of creation and one that has a negative view. The church/world relation then becomes a matter of the church's attitude toward the world, whether one shuns it or embraces it. But the choice that is being presented to the readers of the Gospel of John is not yes or no to creation, as the Gnostics thought, but yes or no to Christ's reign. The corresponding light/dark and ascending/descending dualities in John do not correspond to spirit/matter—which would be a Gnostic reading—but rather to those who accept Christ's kingdom/those who reject it. The Gospel of John is not trying to get the reader to say yes to creation (the secondary use of *kosmos*) but to say no to sin (the primary use of *kosmos*), although of course creation is assumed to be good, as the echoes of Genesis 1:1-5 in John 1:1-5 make obvious.

Troeltsch's church/sect distinction is equally distorting if it is the lens through which one approaches the relationship between the gospel and economic, political, and social life (option C). For Curran, the church/world duality corresponds to the religious/social or Christ/culture duality. The sect type of Christians consists of those who detach themselves from the world, by which is meant the larger surrounding culture and its economic, political, and social life. The church type embraces the world by participating in that life, thus breaking down all of these dichotomies and helping to spread the Kingdom of God by transforming the world from within. If presented in these terms, who would not want to be church type rather than sectarian? When B and C are conflated, it seems especially obvious that the church does not want to turn its back on God's good creation, but rather to embrace the grace found in all natural things, and thus to participate fully in the world in all its dimensions, economic, political, and social.

But there are good reasons to reject the choice between church and sect, because of their distorting effect on church/world discourse. To begin, Troeltsch's typology fits awkwardly in Curran's own narrative. If the Catholic Church is normatively church type and not sect type, why did the pre-Vatican II Catholic Church refuse to embrace the world in the way that Curran narrates? Curran fails to explain why, if the church type is in the Catholic Church's DNA, it took until after Vatican II to realize it. It may be that the immigrant experience in America produced a particularly long-lasting collective amnesia in the American Catholic community, one that was righted only when Catholics entered the mainstream of American society in the 1960s. It may be, on the other hand, that the very terms of Troeltsch's typology are insufficient to understand the experience of the Catholic Church in America.

In traditional Catholic usage, the distinction between church and sect was determined not by a particular group's attitude toward the world, but by that group's attitude toward the Church. A sect was a group that rejected Church authority. From the Catholic point of view, what made the Waldensians a sect and their contemporaries, the Franciscans, a religious order within the Church had nothing to do with differences in their attitudes toward the "world." Both were equally "unworldly" in the sense of D above—rejecting, through evangelical poverty and the renunciation of violence, the powers and principalities of the *kosmos*—and both were equally "worldly" in the sense of B above, embracing the natural world as God's good creation.[33] With regard to C, both were either shunning the world or seeking to transform the world's attitudes toward power and material goods, depending on how one narrates it. But the key difference, what made the Waldensians a sect in Catholic eyes, was not their attitude toward the world, but their rejection of Church authority, in sharp contrast with the Franciscans.

For Troeltsch, on the other hand, "The Franciscan movement belonged originally to the sect-type of lay religion."[34] Eventually, Troeltsch says, the Franciscans split into two factions, one that remained true to the sect type (the various kinds of Franciscan "Spirituals") and those who were domesticated into the church-type system. What marks the original Franciscan (and Waldensian) spirit as sectarian was its rigid adherence to what Troeltsch calls the "Law of Jesus."[35] According to Troeltsch, Jesus' message was purely religious, and did not, at first, produce a social ethic; "in the whole range of the Early Christian literature—missionary and devotional—both within and without the New Testament, there is no hint of any formulation of the 'Social' question; the central problem is always purely religious."[36] Because it shuns the social, Troeltsch writes of the "Gospel Ethic,"

---

[33] The followers of Francis are well-known for their positive regard for the natural world, as in Francis' Canticle of the Sun, and I can find no evidence of any dualism amongst the Waldensians, despite their proximity to the Cathars. Reinarius Saccho's 1254 list of accusations against the Waldensians contains no hint of ontological dualism or a negative attitude toward material creation. Saccho's list can be found at www.fordham.edu/halsall/source/waldo2.html.

[34] Ernst Troeltsch, *The Social Teaching of the Christian Churches*, trans. Olive Wyon (New York: Harper & Row, 1960), 355.

[35] Troeltsch, *The Social Teaching*, 355-8.

[36] Troeltsch, *The Social Teaching*, 39.

"Its first outstanding characteristic is an unlimited, unqualified individualism."[37] The Sermon on the Mount was not intended to provide an ethics or a politics by which the social order could be maintained; it was instead a manifesto for the pure, who would await the Parousia in isolation from the mainstream of society. When the Roman emperor converted to Christianity in the fourth century, the church type came to the fore, in which the teachings of Jesus were moderated to accommodate the realities of the social world, which simultaneously created the opportunity for clearly defined sects within the Christian movement to separate themselves out from the world. Just as Curran does not consider the Catholic Church to have had a "social mission" until it was ready to address the whole of society, so Troeltsch uses the term "social" to refer only to an ethic that is directed at governing society as a whole. In other words, the very terms in which Troeltsch casts his supposedly descriptive analysis are dictated from the point of view of the church type. Troeltsch assumes that, even in the ancient and medieval worlds, there was such a thing as "society" as a whole. He assumes, furthermore, that religious/social, religious/political, and religious/economic are binaries that are not simply modern but apply to the pre-modern world as well.

All of these assumptions are dubious. As the ferment of political theologies of the last few decades has made abundantly clear, Jesus' message was not inherently apolitical or asocial; the Kingdom of God was directly relevant to the kingdoms of the world. The Kingdom of God did not have to come to resemble the kingdoms of this world in order to become social or political. There is no good reason to assume that Jesus' teachings must be adjusted to address society as a whole in order to move from the purely religious to the social. Firstly, "society as a whole" is a modern Western concept; secondly, religion as something separate from political and social life is also modern. Indeed, as historian John Bossy notes, the modern concepts of religion and society are like twins, both created when the early modern state was creating a unitary society governed by a sovereign out of the medieval patchwork of *societates*, semi-autonomous guilds, clans, cities and other organic associations with overlapping jurisdictions and loyalties. Bossy writes that the development of the modern idea of society was "a successor effect of the transition in 'religion', whose history it reproduced. One cannot therefore exactly call Religion and Society twins; but in other respects they are like the sexes according to Aristophanes, effects of the fission of a primitive whole, yearning towards one another across a great divide."[38] The "primitive whole"

---

[37] Troeltsch, *The Social Teaching*, 55.
[38] John Bossy, *Christianity in the West 1400-1700* (Oxford: Oxford University, 1985), 171. The fact that such fission is commonly associated with the Treaty of Westphalia

of which Bossy writes is the pre-modern inseparability of "religion" from life as a whole. *Religio* in the pre-modern West was a sub-virtue of the cardinal—not theological—virtue of justice which did not belong to a separate, "supernatural" realm of activity; not until the dawn of the seventeenth century was *religio* identified as *supernaturalis*.[39] There was a division of labor between kings and priests, but not between "religion" and "politics." As Aquinas makes plain, both *religio* and acts of governance were directed toward the same end, the enjoyment of God, and right *religio* was necessary for good governance.[40]

Troeltsch, following Weber, attempted to resist the Marxist or Durkheimian reduction of religion to the social, and so defined religion as essentially asocial and belonging to the realm of value. Politics, on the other hand, is defined in terms of influencing the leadership of a state, that is, the one and only public realm, where instrumental rationality holds sway.[41] Religion, then, is an essentially interior impulse that can have an effect on society and the political, but if religion seeks to be influential, it must come to terms with, and accommodate itself to, the sphere of social life, which is a given and runs according to its own logic. Those who accept this process of accommodation are church types; those who reject it to maintain the purity of religion are sect types.

To accept Troeltsch's terms and to fit them into a church/world duality is to straightjacket the different possibilities of church engagement with the world. Contrary to Curran's contention that being church type is normative for Catholicism, Troeltsch's is a distinctly liberal Protestant project that locates the essence of religion in an asocial interiority, rather than in the daily engagement of the Christian with the material world that is penetrated by the grace of God. In

---

(1648) is an irony not lost on me. "Westphalia" is often used as shorthand for the system of nation-states that superseded Christendom.

[39] Ernst Feil, "From the Classical *Religio* to the Modern *Religion*: Elements of a Transformation between 1550 and 1650," in *Religion in History: The Word, the Idea, the Reality*, ed., Michel Despland and Gérard Vallée (Waterloo, ON: Wilfred Laurier University, 1992), 35.

[40] Thomas Aquinas, *On Kingship to the King of Cyprus*, trans. Gerald B. Phelan (Toronto: Pontifical Institute of Mediaeval Studies, 1949), 60 [Bk. II, ch. 3]; also Thomas Aquinas, *Summa Theologiae*, II-II. q.10, a.10. I treat the genealogy of the concept of religion at much greater length in my book *The Myth of Religious Violence: Secular Ideology and the Roots of Modern Conflict* (New York: Oxford University, 2009), ch. 2.

[41] Weber's famous essay, "Politics as a Vocation," defines politics this way: "We wish to understand by politics only the leadership, or the influencing of the leadership, of a political association, hence today, of a state." The state, in turn, is defined thus: "A state is a human community that (successfully) claims the monopoly of the legitimate use of physical force within a given territory." Max Weber, "Politics as a Vocation," http://anthropos-lab.net/wp/wp-content/uploads/2011/12/Weber-Pol-itics-as-a-Vocation.pdf.

Troeltsch's scheme, the social is equated with the one society bounded by the state, thus eliminating from view any other kind of social and political action that tries to imagine a plurality of social spaces. Thus Troeltch ignores everything from the complex medieval space of overlapping *societates*; to Catholic experiments in corporatism and distributism in the late 19th and early 20th centuries; to the English pluralism of John Neville Figgis and G.D.H. Cole in the 1920s and 1930s; to Rowan Williams' call for recognition of different spaces of law in Britain; to contemporary calls for "radical democracy," a recognition of a pluralism of grassroots experiments in self-governance that go beyond the dreary exercise of voting for one of two corporation-sponsored candidates once every four years. Rather than assuming that there is one "world" out there, one dominant culture that we must either embrace or reject, it is both more empirically correct and theologically faithful to see and imagine multiple ways of engaging with God's good creation while attempting to transform sin into the Kingdom of God.

Vatican II does not represent the embrace of the church type over the sect type, the turn from detachment from the world to living in the world. The treatment of the church/world relationship in the documents of Vatican II is carefully nuanced. All four of the above valences of the church/world duality can be found in *Gaudium et spes*, with different approaches to each. In the preface, the "world of men" is defined as "the whole human family along with the sum of those realities in the midst of which it lives; that world which is the theater of man's history, and the heir of his energies, his tragedies and his triumphs; that world which the Christian sees as created and sustained by its Maker's love, fallen indeed into the bondage of sin, yet emancipated now by Christ."[42] As in option B, the world is here the whole of creation, essentially good, fallen and redeemed. But *Gaudium et spes* also uses "world" to mean that part of creation that stands outside the Church (A): the Council "sets forth certain general principles for the proper fostering of this mutual exchange and assistance in concerns which are in some way common to the world and the Church."[43] In the same paragraph, the Council also expresses "high esteem" for the way that "other Christian Churches and ecclesial communities" are working toward the same goal, and expresses confidence that the Catholic Church can be "helped by the world" in preparing the ground for the gospel.[44] The "world" in *Gaudium et spes* is also used in sense C, as referring to the temporal activities of

---

[42] Vatican II, *Pastoral Constitution on the Church in the Modern World* (*Gaudium et spes*), no. 2, www.vatican.va/archive/hist_councils/ii_vatican_council/ docments/-vat-ii_cons_19651207_gaudium-et-spes_en.html.
[43] Vatican II, *Pastoral Constitution*, no. 40.
[44] Vatican II, *Pastoral Constitution*, no. 40.

economics, politics, and social life; this is what is meant when the Church appeals to those who live "in the world," as in "the Church requires the special help of those who live in the world, are versed in different institutions and specialties, and grasp their innermost significance in the eyes of both believers and unbelievers."[45] These temporal activities or "earthly affairs" possess a certain sort of autonomy. "If by the autonomy of earthly affairs we mean that created things and societies themselves enjoy their own laws and values which must be gradually deciphered, put to use, and regulated by men, then it is entirely right to demand that autonomy."[46] The document goes on to claim the "rightful independence of science" and deplores those who consider faith and science to be mutually opposed. The document is then careful to distinguish true autonomy from false, rejecting the idea that "created things do not depend on God, and that man can use them without any reference to their Creator."[47] This paragraph is then followed by an admonition to reject the world, in the sense of D. "That is why Christ's Church, trusting in the design of the Creator, acknowledges that human progress can serve man's true happiness, yet she cannot help echoing the Apostle's warning: 'Be not conformed to this world' (Rom 12:2). Here by the world is meant that spirit of vanity and malice which transforms into an instrument of sin those human energies intended for the service of God and man."[48] *Gaudium et spes* thus presents a nuanced approach to church and world. It calls us to recognize the goodness of creation, fallen and redeemed by Christ, and cooperate with non-Catholics to transform earthly affairs while resisting being conformed to the evils of the world.

The devil, of course, is in the details. What does it mean to say, "The council brings to mankind light kindled from the Gospel, and puts at its disposal those saving resources which the Church herself, under the guidance of the Holy Spirit, receives from her Founder"?[49] Are there Christian approaches to economics, for example, or do Christians learn economics from the "science" of economics the way everyone else does? Do Christians try to create different economies, or is there one "economy"—one "world"—in which we all participate, for better or for worse?

---

[45] Vatican II, *Pastoral Constitution*, no. 44.
[46] Vatican II, *Pastoral Constitution*, no. 36.
[47] Vatican II, *Pastoral Constitution*, no. 36.
[48] Vatican II, *Pastoral Constitution*, no. 37. The Latin text of *Gaudium et spes* has *saeculo* for "world" here, whereas the texts cited for senses A, B, and C all use a declension of *mundus*. Paul, in the cited text from Romans 12, uses a derivation of *aeon* instead of *kosmos*; the Gospel of John, on the other hand, uses *kosmos* for both the positive and negative senses of "world."
[49] Vatican II, *Pastoral Constitution*, no. 3.

Westphalia Today

Answering such questions in the abstract leads to distorting oversimplifications about the embrace or rejection of "the world." What interests me about Westphalia is that it provides an occasion for reflection on church and world in the concrete. The picture we see is complex. In 1952, there was not much contact with the non-Catholic world (A). There were no non-Catholics in Westphalia, and as in many other Catholic environments pre-Vatican II, Catholic identity was a source of pride, in both the positive and negative senses of the word. Clericalism and a stifling uniformity were often symptoms of this detachment from the non-Catholic world. Ecumenism and interreligious dialogue in the post-Vatican II Church are unqualified gains.

At the same time, Westphalia in 1952 was not at all disengaged from the natural world (B) or the temporal affairs of economic and social life (C). Indeed, in some ways Westphalia was more engaged with the world than are many Catholics post-Vatican II, when the collapse of Catholic social action organizations and the move to the suburbs limited the temporal engagement of many American Catholics to voting. Economics for the people of Westphalia in 1952 was not an abstruse discipline dominated by experts to whom one must defer; it was a community project of cooperative ventures that required the active participation of all the members of the body of Christ in Westphalia, their active involvement in each other's lives. "The economy" was not an abstract and incomprehensible unity of which Westphalia was a tiny and insignificant part, buffeted daily by decisions made far away by people of which one had no understanding and over which one had no control; economy was simply the sum of face-to-face transactions that one had with neighbors and fellow communicants. The people of Westphalia were profoundly engaged with the world. They grew food and/or knew where it came from. Commodities were not abstractions that appeared on shelves out of nowhere, and profits on services like the garage and the beauty parlor did not disappear into the ether of "the financial system" but circulated as credit among the members of the community, who had to earn each other's trust. For better and for worse, people were in each other's business, in all senses of that word. By no means were they "detached from the world."

Westphalia has changed, along with both the Church and rural America. The school is closed; the Credit Union moved to Harlan; the Co-op is gone. People shop at the Wal-Mart in Denison, and it is not an occasion for socializing. "We still have our church but young people grow up, graduate and move on because there are no jobs here. Large farms are becoming more prevalent. Not good for keeping a small town prosperous." According to another longtime resident, Fr. Duren predicted this. "He said back in the '50s how the family farms would be bought up by corporations and here it is today—it's a different world in all respects." St. Boniface Parish in Westphalia shares a priest with two other towns. In some ways, this is a gain. People appreciate the new role of the parish council, and one parishioner reports that now "the people of the parish have a say in what goes on—not only in parish life but in family life also." But all who responded to my questionnaire report some version of the following: "The feeling of community life is now very different with less cooperation from the members." "Religion is sort of on the back burner for a lot of the people." And this summary, "Most of what was gained by hard work and vision has been lost in this community. We have our church and clubhouse and ball park. I think as time progressed people didn't hold on to their vision of a prospering community and we lost it."

The causes of the decline that Westphalia shares with much of rural America are many. They include the enormous concentration of the power of agribusinesses and government policies that have, especially since the 1970s, favored corporate interests in agriculture.[50] Beyond rural America, consumerism has detached people from production and producers. We talk of "the global economy" increasing interaction among people, but the reality is of increasing detachment from the material world and from each other.[51] As Wendell Berry has written, we have given proxies to corporations to produce all of our food, clothing, and shelter, and are rapidly giving proxies to corporations and the state to provide education, health care, child care, and all sorts of services that local communities used to provide. As Berry says, "Our major economic practice, in short, is to delegate the practice to others."[52] The post-Vatican II era is, in this sense, characterized not by engagement but a profound disengagement with the world.

The recent movement to promote locally grown food and community-supported agriculture (CSA) shows that, in some ways, Westphalia was ahead of, not behind, the times. Nostalgia, however, is not the point. The solution today is not to try to recreate Westphalia in 1952. Westphalia can, nevertheless, contribute to the "vision" of a prospering community to which the resident last cited above referred. Ideas about how to engage the world will vary with each different context. But the church should not abandon the hope that the followers of Christ can contribute distinctive visions of how to en-

---

[50] See, for example, Michael Pollan, *The Omnivore's Dilemma: A Natural History of Four Meals* (New York: Penguin, 2006).

[51] I discuss this in more detail in my book *Being Consumed: Economics and Christian Desire* (Grand Rapids, MI: Eerdmans, 2008).

[52] Wendell Berry, *Citizenship Papers* (Washington, DC: Shoemaker & Hoard, 2003), 64.

gage the temporal order, how to create new spaces of engagement with earthly life that do not simply bow to the inevitability of "the world."

What matters about Westphalia, in other words, is not simply the town itself, but the fact that *World Neighbors* told the story. Today, the geography textbooks my children use in our Catholic school are the same as those used in public schools. They learn about "the economy" as if it were simply out there, a given fact obeying its own laws. *World Neighbors*, on the other hand, covers economics in a chapter entitled "Sharing Goods Through Trade." There, Catholic school students learned that God has distributed treasures and skills in different ways so that we must interact with each other to get what we need. Those engaged in trade should seek first to supply others' needs, and only take a reasonable profit. Advertisers should not lie. Prices should be set according to the principle of the Just Price, not supply and demand. The "Christian merchant" will pay good wages, allow fair working hours, let his workers have some say in the management of the business, and let them own shares in the business, for "Christ says that the hireling shepherd runs away when the sheep are in danger."[53] The text acknowledges the battle is uphill: "in American business life, religion is not a great power. Even Catholics have largely lost the sense of obeying Christ in everyday life. Church is too often thought to be for Sunday, and religion is limited to saying one's prayers."[54] But the text hopes to provide a vision of a different world, to spur the imaginations of young people to create economic spaces where the eternal breaks into the temporal, to resist simply passively accepting "the economy" as if it were fated and impervious to the impact of the gospel. The book's foreword announces that it was "designed to show the Church at work in the world, and to study human beings in their spiritual and religious aspects as well as in their ability to produce economic and material wealth."[55]

What it would mean to be "the Church at work in the world" today must surely include working alongside other people of good will from other faiths and none. But it also must mean overcoming the temptation to separate "religion" from everyday life and to accept dominant systems as given. Today's Christians can take inspiration from previous attempts, like that of Westphalia, to knit together our spiritual lives with our material lives, and thus become more "worldly." M

---

[53] Bedier, *World Neighbors*, 189-92.
[54] Bedier, *World Neighbors*, 190.
[55] Bedier, *World Neighbors*, ii.

The "Signs of the Times" and their Readers in Wartime and in Peace

Laurie Johnston

THOUGH THE PHRASE "THE SIGNS OF THE TIMES" appears only a few times in the documents of Vatican II, there is no doubt that the shift in theological method which it signifies has been profound and lasting. Yet the phrase has been controversial from the start, and the divisions in moral theology since the Council have often reflected competing understandings of *what* the signs of the times are and *how* and *by whom* they should be discerned, and according to what *criteria*. While there is consensus that fidelity to God's call requires Christians today to attend to the world around them in a deeper way than may have been recognized before the Council, the method of that discernment and the conclusions drawn from it are often sources of disagreement. In what sense might drone warfare be a sign of the times? What is the meaning of the lived experience of gay Christians for the development of the church's teaching on sexual ethics? Whose role is it to read the signs of the times and explain how just war teaching should be developed and applied today—politicians? theologians? bishops?[1] *Octogesima adveniens* explains that, for Catholic social teaching to function, "[i]t is up to the Christian communities to analyze with objectivity the situation which is proper to their own country, to shed on it the light of the Gospel's unalterable words and to draw principles of reflection, norms of judgment and directives for action from the social teaching of the Church."[2] But in a truly *catholic* church, surely the historical experiences of those local contexts must then filter back somehow to aid in the development of magisterial teaching? And how might the signs of the times function as calls for development in the teachings of the magisterium? Fundamentally, these are questions not just about the function of authority within the church, but also, on a deeper level, about the relationship of the church to the world

---

[1] For a discussion of the debate over how and by whom just war theory should have been applied in the case of the war in Iraq, see David Gushee, "Just war divide," *Christian Century* 119, no. 17 (August 14, 2002): 26-9.

[2] Paul VI, *Octogesima adveniens* (1971), no. 4, www.vatican.va/holy_father/paul_-vi/-apost_letters/documents/hf_p-vi_apl_19710514_octogesima-adveniens_en.html.

and how truth comes to be apprehended via both church and world. There is much to be examined when it comes to the question of how history and experience (and whose history and experience) are to be sources for theological reflection today.

After a brief discussion of the emergence of the phrase "the signs of the times" at the Second Vatican Council and its theological implications, this essay will examine a series of historical examples that illustrate the problem of bias in our attempts to read the signs of the times. I will then suggest that we are reading the signs of the times *well* when our efforts are marked by careful attention to human experience, informed by the tradition of the church, and leavened by *disponibilitá*, humility, and solidarity, especially with the most vulnerable. While history reveals many pitfalls in reading the signs of the times, there are realities of sin and suffering which we are called to *not ignore*. Faithfulness to the gospel in the world today requires attentiveness to what God is doing in both church and world, and it is this very attentiveness to the world which in turn deepens our understanding of the gospel itself.

SIGNS OF THE TIMES: ORIGINS AND DEVELOPMENT

At the Second Vatican Council, a recognition was emerging that despite the timeless character of revelation, the church itself lives within history and is responsible for helping to shape the history of *this world*; the church is the "people of God" who work not as powerful agents of empire, but as fellow humans sharing a responsibility for the common good here on earth. Whereas scholastic theology had emphasized the eternal character of the church as the perfect society, Vatican II recognized the human, history-bound nature of the church as well, and the ways in which our understanding of Christian discipleship must continually evolve in order to remain faithful. Pope John XXIII of course played a key role in this development—though he was not alone in sensing the need for it. His novel use of the phrase "the signs of the times" is first noted in *Humanae salutis*, the statement with which he convoked the Second Vatican Council. He wrote:

> While distrustful souls see nothing but darkness falling upon the face of the earth, we prefer to restate our confidence in our Savior, who has not left the world he redeemed. Indeed, making our own Jesus' recommendation that we learn to discern "the signs of the times" (Mt. 16:4), it seems to us that we can make out, in the midst of so much darkness, more than a few indications that enable us to have hope for the fate of the Church and humanity. The successive bloody wars of our times, the spiritual ruins caused by many ideologies, and

the fruits of so many bitter experiences have not been without useful lessons.[3]

Here Pope John, like some others who followed him, is using the phrase in a positive sense: The signs of the times are movements of providence within history, hopeful developments, marks of redemption in the midst of negative human experiences.[4] And though the pope's usage of this phrase was quickly embraced and came to play an important role at the Council, particularly in the drafting of *Gaudium et spes*, it also came in for some criticism rather quickly.[5] The most immediate critiques of the phrase "reading the signs of the times" dealt with the problematic of human sin. There are two ways in which this emerges: First, there is the problem that no matter how helpful a particular development in the world may appear, no sign of the times can be regarded as purely positive or unequivocally a sign of the presence of God's grace in the world. Second, there is the problem that even when God's revealing grace *is* at work in the world, our sin-blinded perception is always biased and flawed, and so we may miss it or misconstrue what it requires of us.

The meaning of the signs of the times was soon enlarged to refer not only to hopeful signs, but to any broad trends or movements in the world that seem to characterize a given historical period. Yet many felt that the phrase still contained far too much uncritical optimism. It is, of course, dangerous to identify any historical event or trend too closely with divine providence (apart, of course, from the Christ event) or to equate earthly "progress" with the kingdom of God. Conversely, while the Hebrew prophets readily interpreted negative events as signs of God's disfavor, few of us are qualified to so judge. Human history is ambiguous, so that even trends that may appear to be hopeful signs of the times can become deeply destructive; progress in justice is matched by progress in injustice; a hasty peace accord may plant the seeds for future conflicts; the fall of communism may pave the way for a re-emergence of violent ethnic conflicts. Any good, worthy accomplishment can become an idol, become skewed, and thus it is impossible, in the here and now, to really know which of the world's achievements are actually serving

---

[3] John XXIII, *Humanae salutis* (1961), http://jakomonchak.files.wordpress.com/20-11/-12/humanae-salutis.pdf.
[4] It is worth noting that this is not the original meaning of the text in Matthew, in which Jesus is referring to the signs of the coming apocalypse.
[5] Since there are a number of helpful accounts of the development of the phrase and its fate during and after the Council, I will discuss only a few aspects. See in particular Johan Verstraeten, ed., *Scrutinizing the signs of the times in the light of the Gospel* (Leuven: Peeters, 2007). Also, Anthony Cernera, "Reading the Signs of the Times: An Ongoing Task of the Church in the World," in *Vatican II: The Continuing Agenda*, ed. Anthony Cernera (Fairfield: Sacred Heart University, 1997), 249-74.

the kingdom and which are not. As Yves Congar has reminded us, in his writing on the relation of church and world, all of our achievements here on earth are relativized by the fact that everything must finally go "through the cross," for "there can be no higher life except on a foundation of renunciation and death" which is, of course, a stumbling-block for the world.[6] The kingdom of God cannot be attained within history because "the natures of things contain the energies necessary for their own operation as expressed by their bare definition, but they are ordered to something higher than themselves and they reach their fullness only by a means that comes from that 'something higher', namely, what Catholic theology calls the... supernatural."[7] Furthermore, "the world's work... is not holy by itself: it has to be hallowed by being put into relation, in a way that remains in a sense external to it, with the unique holiness of God and Jesus Christ."[8] A great deal of caution is in order then whenever we attempt to find meaning in contemporary history.

Not only is the history of the world itself deeply ambiguous, but humans are notorious for reading into history what they want to see there. Sin not only affects our ability to do good, but also to perceive the good accurately. And our ability to weigh competing goods and act accordingly is hampered by our inadequate development of the virtue of prudence. Thus, the problem of *bias* is a major one when it comes to reading the signs of the times, which is why a key phrase was added to the idea of the signs of the times in *Gaudium et spes*. Rather than just "reading" the signs of the times as if they were something self-evident, the church's task is described in this way:

> Inspired by no earthly ambition, the Church seeks but a solitary goal: to carry forward the work of Christ under the lead of the befriending Spirit. And Christ entered this world to give witness to the truth, to rescue and not to sit in judgment, to serve and not to be served. To carry out such a task, the Church has always had the duty of *scrutinizing the signs of the times and of interpreting them in the light of the Gospel*. Thus, in language intelligible to each generation, she can respond to the perennial questions which men ask about this present life and the life to come, and about the relationship of the one to the other. We must therefore recognize and understand the world in which we live, its explanations, its longings, and its often dramatic characteristics.[9]

---

[6] Yves Congar, *Lay People in the Church* (Westminster: Newman, 1965), 100-1. The book was originally published as *Jalons pour une théologie du laïcat* (Paris: Éditions du Cerf, 1954).
[7] Congar, *Lay People in the Church*, 102.
[8] Congar, *Lay People in the Church*, 421.
[9] *Gaudium et spes*, nos. 3-4 (emphasis added), www.vatican.va/archive/hist_councils/ii_vatican_council/documents/vat-ii_cons_19651207_gaudium-et-spes_en.html.

In other words, the signs must be carefully weighed, and the gospel is the answer to the problem of human bias because it provides a criterion of judgment. Yet this addition does not entirely resolve the problem of bias, because while the good news of Christ's death and resurrection unite Christians in faith, the relationship of this good news to the signs of the times around us remains something that we must interpret. And as Mary Catherine Hilkert explains,

> It is not as if the ambiguous signs of our times need interpretation in light of the clear meaning of the scriptures, a single reading of the classics of the tradition, unbiased preaching and catechesis, or liturgical celebrations that approximate the eschatological banquet. Rather there are aspects of our culture and other religious traditions that can reveal to us dimensions of our own heritage which we have not yet discovered. Likewise, dialogue with other cultures and religions can call into question and challenge long-accepted interpretations of what we name as our tradition.[10]

Thus it is also true that the signs of the times are themselves part of what can deepen our understanding of the gospel. Hilkert is arguing that we often require dialogue with those outside our own particular context in order to fully understand not only what the signs of the times mean, but also how the gospel is calling us to respond in any given situation. Thus, we cannot assume the gospel provides a simple norm by which may then sit back and evaluate whatever signs present themselves to us. Instead, it is precisely in scrutinizing the signs of the times and learning from the experiences of all of humanity that we come to deepen our understanding of the gospel and its call on our lives. This, then, requires a deep openness to the experiences of others both now and in history.

A HISTORICAL INTERLUDE: READING THE SIGNS IN WARTIME

To illuminate precisely how difficult it can be for us to carry out this task of discernment, I want to first provide a few cautionary examples. One of the human experiences which has most frequently prompted Christians to reflect on the meaning of human history is the experience of war. Perhaps because war tends to invigorate what Niebuhr called "ideological taint," our responses to war often seem to highlight Christians' failures at moral discernment. Furthermore, questions about violence and its proper role remain among the most vigorous debates in moral theology, and divergences there are often clear markers of broader divergences in church-world theology. Reading the "signs of wartime" is therefore a particularly vital and important task.

---

[10] Mary Catherine Hilkert, "Presidential Address," *CTSA Proceedings* 61 (2006): 97.

One hundred fifty years ago, in the midst of the Civil War, white Christian preachers in the South were attempting to divine the will of God in the midst of a difficult situation. Many of them, it seems, were telling their congregations that the war between the states was a sign of the times. More specifically, it was a sign of God's judgment on them, and if they wanted to prevail in the war, God was calling white Christians in the south to one key moral task: They needed to *reform* the institution of slavery. Too many southern Christians, the preachers complained, were not living up to the biblical standards for how one ought to treat one's slaves. This, they argued, was deeply displeasing to God. Adopting a more humane form of slavery—for example one that would respect slave marriages and permit slaves to learn to read so that they could at least read the Bible—would garner God's favor and ensure victory over the northern states.[11] While these preachers were correct to think that war was an invitation to Christians to re-examine their consciences—as it always is—the moral prescriptions they offered were profoundly misguided.

More recently and notoriously, just after the attacks of September 11, Jerry Falwell and Pat Robertson made headlines by claiming that those attacks were a punishment from God upon the people of America. Specifically, Falwell argued that abortions in the US had "made God mad," and he also suggested a long list of people—including pagans, gays and lesbians, the ACLU, and feminists—who "helped this happen."[12] While September 11 could certainly be read as an occasion in which American Christians ought to be doing some soul-searching, and perhaps even passing some judgments on the evils of our day,[13] Falwell's view seems hopelessly misguided and simplistic, and smacking of hubris in his attempt to locate sin only in the "other." Such attempts—especially in wartime—to equate the will of God with one's own political agenda are nothing new, of course; Eusebius of Caesarea, writing in the 4th century, attributed the emperor Constantine's successes in battle directly to God's favor:

> God, the defender of the lives of his own people... caused a great light to shine forth as in the midst of a dark and gloomy night, and raised up a deliverer for all, leading into those regions with a lofty arm, his servant, Constantine... [and so] the protector of the virtu-

---

[11] See Eugene Genovese, *Consuming Fire: The Fall of the Confederacy in the mind of the white Christian South* (Athens: University of Georgia, 1998).

[12] These remarks were made during a broadcast of The *700 Club* and were widely reported. See, for example, John Harris, "God Gave U.S. 'What We Deserve', Falwell Says," *The Washington Post* (September 14, 2001): C3.

[13] Matthias Nebel, who writes about reading the signs of the times as sharing in the judgment of Christ over history, would agree here. See his "Signs of the Times and Structures of Sin," available in summary form at www.stthomas.edu/cathstudies/cst-/conferences/gaudium/5page.html or at full length in Johan Verstraeten, ed., *Scrutinizing the Signs of the Times in the Light of the Gospel*, 99-120.

ous, mingling hatred for evil with love for good, went forth with his son Crispus, a most beneficent prince, and extended a saving right hand to all that were perishing. Both of them, father and son, under the protection, as it were, of God, the universal King, with the Son of God, the Savior of all, as their leader and ally, drew up their forces on all sides against the enemies of the Deity and won an easy victory; God having prospered them in the battle in all respects according to their wish.[14]

While Eusebius' readers ought to know that this is panegyric, and perhaps not much more excessive than some of the compositions of today's political speechwriters, it is nevertheless deeply problematic, verging upon the idolatrous: For Eusebius, it seems that the Roman Empire really could be regarded as the kingdom of God on earth. Certainly reading the signs of the times must be more complex than equating victory with God's favor and defeat with God's punishment—particularly for followers of a Christ who brought victory out of defeat.

Of course there are numerous historical examples of Christians throughout history who have resisted an easy equation of God's will and their own limited interpretations. A few centuries later, Patriarch Sophronius of Jerusalem responded to the signs of his times in a more nuanced way. Unlike some contemporaries who hoped for salvation from a revived Byzantine empire, Sophronius eventually rejected the imperial ideologies of his day (in a way which would certainly please those modern-day theologians concerned about "neo-Constantinianism"). His insights were hard-fought: First, he lived through the sack of Jerusalem by the Persians in 614. Then in 638—just a few years after the death of Muhammad—Jerusalem was surrounded by an Arab army. But this time, Sophronius negotiated a peaceful surrender of the city. Sophronius had responded to that first invasion much like Eusebius or the Civil War era preachers would have: He urged Christians to repent so that they might once again enjoy God's favor—i.e., military victory. But his later writings, writes scholar David Olster, display "ever greater skepticism that imperial success was the barometer of God's favor."[15] Instead, after 638, he reminds his flock that what matters is spiritual victory in Christ. After all, "Christ has chained Satan's armies" and "peacefully raised invisible war against those warring against us" (i.e. demons). For Sophronius, Christians' true citizenship was to be found in "Christ's uncircumscribable empire… an Empire that cannot be destroyed."[16]

---

[14] Eusebius, *Ecclesiastical History*, trans. Kirsopp Lake (Cambridge: Harvard, 1965), Bk. 10.8-9.
[15] David Michael Olster, *Roman Defeat, Christian Response and the Literary Construction of the Jew* (Philadelphia: University of Pennsylvania, 2004).
[16] Olster, *Roman Defeat*, 102.

Christians have access to this empire by experiencing union with Christ through the liturgy—and the real threat to that union would be if they allowed fear of the Saracens to distract them from the truth of their victory in Christ.[17] While Sophronius' response is much to be preferred in comparison to Falwell's, it remains unsatisfactory if the "liturgy" to which he refers is limited to that which takes place inside a physical building. Surely the signs of the times are calling us to more.

A focus on heavenly citizenship in a time when the earthly empire is under duress is, of course, something Sophronius shares with St. Augustine. Augustine's *City of God* is fundamentally an attempt to interpret God's will in the light of contemporary history. Shortly after the sack of Rome, many Roman pagans were blaming Christians for that event, arguing that their abandonment of Roman religion had displeased the gods. Christians, too, were concerned, and confused about why God would allow the Pax Romana, which had helped with the spread of Christianity so much, to be threatened. Augustine responds with some solid historical realism, pointing out that any attempts to discern the action of God in contemporary history should be treated with great skepticism. Yes, there will be both punishments and rewards after death, but in this life, as the gospel says and Augustine reminds us, God "makes his sun rise on the evil and on the good, and sends rain on the righteous and on the unrighteous."[18] He points out that while in some cases it appears that God permits good rulers to have a long reign, in other cases they die young. And so the sack of Rome was not necessarily a sign of God's particular desire to punish the Romans; nevertheless, it provides an excellent opportunity for Christians to be reminded of Christ's injunction to "lay up for yourselves treasures in heaven."[19] So while a defeat in war may offer an opportunity for the Christian community to repent and be reminded that we are merely pilgrims on this earth, calamities should not be read as a direct revelation of God's will. Nor is the enjoyment of peace a sign of God's particular favor or the holiness of a nation. Whether we experience the perils of war or the calm of peace, what God cares about most is that we respond in a holy way. As Augustine puts it in a clear call for the development of moral character, "what is important then, is not what is suffered, but by whom."[20]

Sophronius calls us to focus on the liturgy and Augustine invites us to attend first and foremost to the state of our souls, rather than the state of the earthly city. But experiencing union with Christ

---

[17] Olster, *Roman Defeat*, 106.
[18] Augustine, *City of God*, trans. Marcus Dods (New York: Modern Library, 1950), Bk. I.8, citing Matthew 5:45.
[19] Augustine, *City of God*, Bk. I.10, citing Matthew 6:19-21.
[20] Augustine, *City of God*, Bk. I.8.

through the liturgy also has implications for that "liturgy" or work of Christian living that the formal liturgy prepares us for; insensitivity to the plight of those suffering in the earthly city is certainly a threat to our souls. Augustine tells Christians that we are pilgrims in this world, but Congar points out that being a pilgrim is not the same thing as being a tourist.[21] Whatever the meaning of the historical events taking place around us, we are never absolved from responsibility for the world and are clearly called to attend to those who are bearing the brunt of those events—the victims of history.

THE ROLE OF HUMAN EXPERIENCE IN READING THE SIGNS OF THE TIMES, WITH CONTEMPORARY ILLUSTRATIONS

How, then, can we read the signs of the times and respond as pilgrims, not tourists? Clearly it means we must be more than spectators, and reading the signs of the times must be more than an intellectual activity that can be carried on without commitment.[22] The signs of the times are not merely there to satisfy our curiosity, but are a call on our lives that demands a response. Juan Luis Segundo held that just as with all other forms of revelation, "the intent [of reading the signs of the times] is not that we know something that otherwise would be impossible or difficult for us to know, but rather that we be different, and act better."[23] As Johan Verstraeten explains it,

> Scrutinizing and understanding the signs of the times does not start from an abstract or apparently "neutral" perspective, because social discernment is based on a commitment: being linked "with humankind and its history by the deepest of bonds" (*Gaudium et Spes* 1), the people of God are called to contribute to the humanization of the world in view of the coming of the kingdom of God. But this is not an easy task, since it confronts the Church with the real ambivalence of history.[24]

Reading the signs of the times, then, requires solidarity with and immersion in the world. And though the idea that we must be immersed in the world if we are to understand it is one which receives new emphasis in *Gaudium et spes,* it is certainly not novel. One might see a precursor to it in Aquinas' discussion of prudence, that key virtue of moral discernment. He says that the virtue of prudence requires *experience* and *memory* to be developed. While he is speaking on the individual level, this can also apply to the way that the

---

[21] This memorable turn of phrase is from Congar, *Lay People in the Church*, 432.
[22] Cernera, "Reading the Signs of the Times," 272.
[23] Juan Luis Segundo, "Revelation, Faith, Signs of the Times," in *Mysterium Liberationis,* ed. Ignacio Ellacuria and Jon Sobrino (Maryknoll: Orbis, 1993), 332.
[24] Johan Verstraeten,"Catholic Social Thought as Discernment," in *Scrutinizing the signs of the times in the light of the Gospel,* 99.

study of others' experiences and memories, through history as well as contemporary reality, can help us to read the signs of the times and respond appropriately.[25]

In fact, the importance of experience as key to our individual and communal development of moral discernment is also an idea which is present in another controversial phrase—the assertion in *Populorum progressio* that the Church speaks with authority precisely because it is "*iam rerum humanarum peritissima*."[26] While this phrase is often translated as "expert in humanity," the translation "experienced in humanity" would be just as legitimate, and, I think, more to the point. The official English translation speaks of "The Church, which has long experience in human affairs..." To claim to be an expert in humanity is certainly bold, and has come in for criticism (especially from some women who find it implausible that a male-dominated magisterium could be truly expert on what it means to be a human woman[27]). Still there is no question that the core of Christian faith is a fundamental set of understandings about who we are as humans created in the image of God, marked by sin, and called to redemption through the God-human who reveals what humans are meant to be. Nevertheless, we also come to understand *through experience* what it means to live out our humanity. This is evident in both our successes and failures at reading the signs of the times. Sophronius and Augustine both clearly learned from painful experience not to place too much faith in earthly powers. The Civil War era preachers, though they were attempting to scrutinize the signs of the times in the light of the gospel, were not sufficiently attentive to the experiences of slaves, and so arrived at a flawed reading of the Bible. This bears out Catherine Hilkert's point that the experiences of others are vital in coming to understand what the truth of the gospel means in our own context. Reading the signs of the times must be a communal undertaking, carried out by the entire people of God and informed by experiences outside the church as well. To be truly "*rerum humanarum peritissima*" requires attention to all of humanity, but, I would argue, especially those that are most vulnerable.

A brief paragraph written recently by a member of the Community of Sant'Egidio illustrates beautifully the kind of experience—or expertise?—in humanity that can result from sustained attention to the poor and marginalized. In addition, it serves as a reminder that the moral challenges of wartime cannot be conceived as radically dif-

---

[25] *Summa Theologica* II-II, q. 47, q. 3, *ad.* 3.
[26] Paul VI, *Populorum progressio* (1967), no. 13, www.vatican.va/holy_father/paul_-vi/encyclicals/documents/hf_p-vi_enc_19670326_populorum_lt.html.
[27] Such critiques were widespread in response to the "Letter to the Bishops of the Catholic Church on the Collaboration of Men and Women in the Church and the World," issued by the Congregation for the Doctrine of the Faith in 2004. Also, see Tina Beattie, *New Catholic Feminism* (New York: Routledge 2006), 1-14.

ferent from the challenges we face in our attempts to live out the virtue of solidarity in the everyday. Mario Giro writes,

> An old woman barricades herself in a dilapidated building in the slums of an Italian city. She refuses to open her door. Her neighbours are convinced she's becoming a derelict. A member of the Sant'Egidio community knocks at her door and starts to speak to her. She replies in monosyllables. He leaves but comes back later to continue a dialogue that may go on for months, even a year, until she agrees to open the door and let him in and finally start getting some help. Using these skills in patient communication based on friendship, the community later made contact with a guerrilla chieftain hidden away for years in the heart of Africa, brought him out of his isolation and persuaded him to negotiate instead of fight.[28]

Giro is attempting to explain how a group of people without formal diplomatic training were nevertheless successful at mediating a peace accord that brought an end to a thirty-year civil war in Mozambique, garnering Sant'Egidio a nomination for the Nobel Peace Prize. Giro continues,

> The community reluctantly saw it had no choice but to act as a mediator. Lacking experience, it had to learn what to do as it went along. It invented a "language of reconciliation" whose syntax it picked up as a humanitarian organization working for the poor. Sant'Egidio had discovered how to talk to all kinds of people from its compassionate work in a wide variety of constantly changing situations in which its members related to the poor, shared their lives, spoke their language, went to the same places they did and regarded them not as welfare cases but as full members of society.[29]

For Giro, it is clear that experience with the poor is the teacher which allows Christians to become "experts" in peacemaking as well and perceive the opportunities to share in Christ's reconciling mission in the world. Sant'Egidio members had developed this expertise with the poor directly in response to their reading of the gospels, and yet here was a reality which invited them to realize that the call of the gospel on their community was not just to respond to the immediate needs of the poor but also to become involved in the more messy, political work of diplomacy. In this way they came to understand their vocation in the world in a new way because of their ongoing experience with the poor at home and abroad.

Giro's explanation clearly shows a willingness to reconceive one's own vocation in response to the signs of the times and an ability to

---

[28] Mario Giro, "Sant'Egidio's diplomacy of friendship," *UNESCO Courier* (January 2000), 33.
[29] Giro, "Sant'Egidio's diplomacy of friendship," 33.

draw on expertise in humanity to do so. Andrea Riccardi, the founder of the Community of Sant'Egidio, expresses a similar sentiment when he explains that he has sought to be an "organic Catholic."[30] Riccardi is referring explicitly to the idea of an "organic intellectual" developed by Antonio Gramsci, the great Italian communist thinker and opponent of Mussolini. As Gramsci discusses in *The Prison Notebooks,* an organic intellectual is not a person who exists above or separate from society, concerned with abstract ideas only. Rather, an organic intellectual emerges from a particular social class and represents the experiences (and interests) of that class.[31] Yet by calling himself an "organic Catholic," Riccardi is not only reiterating Gramsci's focus on the importance of learning from experience (particularly the experience of the poor or working classes), but Riccardi also expresses a sense of rootedness in the Catholic tradition (which Gramsci of course did not share). For Riccardi, it is the dialogue between the tradition of the church and direct experience of the poor which allows us to understand our vocation. And this is never a merely abstract understanding of vocation and reading the signs of the times. The peace accord in Mozambique became possible because the members of Sant'Egidio were reading the signs of the times in Mozambique, not as disinterested observers, but from a stance of deep commitment and what is called in Italian *disponibilitá*—a willingness to be available, involved, engaged. Thus experience alone is not a sufficient teacher; experience must be leavened by the virtue of solidarity or *disponibilitá*.

Yet even experience leavened by solidarity can prove insufficient when it comes to reading the signs of the times. In recent years, Catholic Relief Services, an organization with a great deal of experience with the poor around the globe and a demonstrated sense of commitment, still found that it had simply failed to adequately read the signs of the times in Rwanda. Two staff members of CRS have described the experience thus:

> Armed conflicts of various sorts, from Biafra to Vietnam, Afghanistan to Sri Lanka, have taught CRS hard lessons. No single war experience after World War II, however, so affected the direction of the agency as the genocide in Rwanda. Prior to the genocide in 1994, CRS had served the people of Rwanda through its relief and development programs for more than thirty years. Staff saw the ethnic tensions and knew their origins but simply learned to work around them. CRS followed "best practices" in development, establishing excellent programs in agriculture, health, education, and a number of other areas. The genocide destroyed these carefully cultivated pro-

---

[30] Personal Interview with Andrea Riccardi (Convent of Sant'Egidio, Rome, November 24, 2006), digital recording.
[31] Antonio Gramsci, *Prison Notebooks* (New York: Columbia University, 1992).

grams. While CRS had done its development work well, it was not prepared to help Rwandans name the animosities and roots of conflict or to spur efforts for peace.[32]

Though CRS had missed the earlier signs, its response as an organization to the terrible "sign" of the genocide has been truly remarkable. In a process which could be seen as a practical vision of what it means to read the signs of the times *in the light of the gospel*, CRS "initiated an agency-wide process in which every office around the world considered how Catholic social teaching could be integrated into all aspects of its work."[33] New attention to integral human development, the option for the poor, justice, subsidiarity, and solidarity led to a significant deepening and transformation of its programming, and has resulted in an explicit commitment to strategic peacebuilding as part of its work. Perhaps this case shows that reading of the signs of the times calls for not just experience and commitment, but humility in examining how those signs are calling us to change. What is clear is that CRS has been open to examine what it could no longer ignore: By keeping its distance from questions of ethnic rivalry, it helped allow that rivalry to ultimately destroy all of its other good work. As complicated as it might be to attempt to build peace while also providing aid and development services, CRS now sees that it must embrace a more holistic form of engagement, shaped by the resources of Catholic social teaching. Recently, this has meant undertaking complex projects such as raising awareness about the ways that extractive industries are driving violent conflict in Congo and elsewhere, advocating for fair allocation of oil revenues in Chad, and promoting peaceful elections in Southern Sudan through collaboration with churches there.[34] Many resources are still devoted to more typical development projects like sanitation, agriculture, and microfinance; nevertheless, peacebuilding efforts from the grassroots levels on up have become a more significant part of CRS's programming. These might include community meetings to resolve local conflicts, peace education for children, or relationship-building between refugees and the communities hosting them. Previously, these activities might have been seen as beyond the scope of CRS's mandate. Its experience of reading the signs of the times has prompted it to reorient itself as an organization with deeper attention to the gospel and the tradition as guides for practical action. Thus it illustrates my contention that we must not only scrutinize the signs of the times in the

---

[32] William R. Headley, CSSp, and Reina C. Neufeldt, "Catholic Relief Services: Catholic Peacebuilding in Practice." in *Peacebuilding: Catholic Theology, Ethics, and Praxis,* ed. Robert Schreiter, R. Scott Appleby, and Gerard F. Powers (Maryknoll: Orbis, 2010), 128.
[33] Headley and Neufeldt, "Catholic Relief Services," 129.
[34] These and many other activities are documented at www.crs.org.

light of the gospel, but we must cultivate the humility to allow the signs of the times to deepen our understanding of the gospel and our tradition.

READING THE SIGNS AS FLAWED AND FINITE READERS IN A FLAWED AND COMPLEX WORLD

While I have thus far pointed to some key markers of what might be required from us as we attempt to read the signs of the times—solidarity, experience in humanity, and humility—a key question remains: How can we arrive at a hermeneutic of the signs of the times? Among the many events in the world, which ones merit our careful attention and response, and why? Certainly experience helps us to discern, but to say that we must learn from experience *how* to learn from experience is, of course, circular. Perhaps one way to articulate what it means to read the signs of the times would be to define it in a negative way: The signs of the times are *those things taking place in the world around us which we ignore only at our moral peril.* This is still circular—we should not ignore what we should not ignore—but it does illuminate some aspects of the moral failings which often prevent us from reading the signs of the times. We always know only partially what is going on in the world and what it means for our vocation, but it is precisely the sin of being *content* with that partial knowledge that concerns me most.[35] Christians are called to a kind of *moral curiosity* about the world. This is difficult, though—we are finite creatures and the unending quest to understand what is going on is exhausting because of the sheer complexity of the world; particularly today, our ability to take in complexity is challenged by the many sources of information that assault us. And even in situations where injustice is clear and obvious, and there is no question that there is a need for a prophetic stance on it, the way to deal with that injustice without perpetuating further injustices is rarely obvious.

Still, by defining the signs of the times as *those things taking place in the world around us which we ignore only at our moral peril*, we leave room for both the role of individual conscience and also communal discernment; after all, *Gaudium et spes* is clear that discerning the signs of the times is the task of the entire church as the people of God. What I myself am called to *not ignore* is partly a function of my own particular vocation and location: I must not ignore those evils to which I am personally linked, nor those examples of fidelity which hold wisdom for how I ought to respond to my own particular cir-

---

[35] This is similar, I think, to James Keenan's assertion that sin is best understood now as a "failure to bother to love." Perhaps what I am describing is sin as a failure to bother to find out. See Keenan's *Moral Wisdom* (Lanham: Rowman & Littlefield, 2004), 57.

cumstance. What we as a church are called to *not ignore* is that evil in which we are implicated and that good which we are particularly positioned to carry out. But in fact, what both my community and I must *not ignore* is the entire world, and all of history, because it is God's history. Yet my own finitude prevents me from comprehending the deeply complex reality of what is taking place in the world at this moment, much less at other moments. I cannot even comprehend the many ways in which my own life is ensnared in networks of evil and injustice, complicit in social sin. And yet the call to read the signs of the times is essentially a call to not be content with our ignorance, nor to be content with simple answers about what it means to follow the gospel today.

But in the midst of this complex and chaotic world, there is a deep longing for fixed, unchanging truth. Indeed, the testimony to a God whose love is unending, whose forgiveness is limitless, and whose being is eternal is a source of great consolation in head-spinning times. Yet some theologians today seem concerned that reading the signs of the times might detract from the church's task of safeguarding and transmitting eternal, divinely revealed truths. One senses a desire to return to a vision of the church as *societas perfecta*, an impermeable bulwark against the error of the world outside that is tossed on the waves of history and human sinfulness. In the light of these concerns, Nicholas Lash's reflection on the meaning of history for theology is to the point:

> The attempt... to discern the truth from nowhere in particular, is now known to be doomed to fail. "An imperfect past is," ever and again, "appraised by an imperfect present." There is no "privileged position, no Archimedean point from which we can, timelessly and neutrally" survey debates in science or philosophy, in politics, or ethics, or theology. And Archimedes' name reminds us that what is at issue here is never merely knowledge "for its own sake," but is always also power.
>
> But what if that "imperfect past" contains a perfect utterance? What if, in all the darkness and confusion that is human history, a Word was spoken which announced, for every future time and distant, unfamiliar place, the promise of God's healing peace? How might we hope to keep the hearing of that utterance pure?[36]

Here is the paradox of what it means to read the signs of the times in the light of the gospel: Christians must read *in* history a *revelation* whose source is beyond history. We are flawed humans, responding

---

[36] Nicholas Lash, "Remembering our future," *The Month* 34 (January 2001), 1, citing P.J. Fitzpatrick, *In Breaking of Bread: The Eucharist and Ritual* (Cambridge: Cambridge University, 1993).

to flawed history, in the hope that the Word of grace will redeem flaws and transcend finitude.

Human flaws and finitude extend, as well, to the church itself in its human aspect, and this means that reading the signs of the times cannot be something which only applies to the world outside the church. We must read the signs of the times not just for the sake of the church's mission to the world, but to be the church itself—precisely for the sake of reform, to "keep the hearing of that utterance pure." This means that faithful discipleship means *learning* from the world and even from the church's critics. In *True and False Reform in the Church*, Congar writes,

> It might… happen that underneath the questions which the world poses to the Church, there is God interrogating his own, standing at the door and knocking with the blows of realities and events, those teachers to whom he sometimes hands us over…. There is a movement of things which the Church cannot refuse to undergo without neglecting her proper duty towards the world, or, if you prefer, towards God in the subject of the world.[37]

Gaudium et spes expresses a similar sentiment when it acknowledges that the "Church herself knows how richly she has profited by the history and development of humanity."[38] For now, at least, the fate of the church is deeply intertwined with the fate of the world around it, and any theology of church and world which attempts to bifurcate the two too severely can benefit from the insight of Massimo Faggioli, who writes that:

> In the Catholic Church of today it seems very easy to make a judgment on the signs of the times in secular culture, but *Gaudium et Spes* can and must play a role also in the discernment of the signs of the times *in the Church*…. We cannot live out of the simplistic assumption that the institutional Church is an island of grace surrounded by evil. *Gaudium et Spes* is a critical tool for a moral judgment on the worldly matters, but also for our way to be a Church.[39]

---

[37] "Il peut même arriver que… sous les questions que le monde pose à l'Eglise, ce soit Dieu qui interroge les siens, se tenant à la porte et frappant a coups de faits et d'événements, ces maîtres qu'il nous donne parfois de sa main… L'Eglise doit écouter de semblables appels et, sous réserve du jugement qu'il lui revient de porter, accepter certaines mises en question. Il y a un mouvement des choses qu'elle ne refuserait pas de suivre sans manquer à son propre devoir envers le monde ou, si l'on préfère, envers Dieu au sujet de monde." *Vrai et fausse réforme dans l'Eglise*. Paris: Éditions du Cerf, 1950, 1968 (my translation).
[38] *Gaudium et spes*, no. 44.
[39] Massimo Faggioli, "The Battle over '*Gaudium et Spes*' Then and Now: Dialogue with the Modern World after Vatican II," Presented at the conference "Vatican II at 50," Georgetown University (Oct. 12, 2012), www.georgetown.edu/Faggioli-Gaudium-et-Spes/document/1242773362770/Faggioli-034+Vatican+II+Georgetown2.pdf.

We read the signs of the times, therefore, not only to understand what God is doing in the world, but to discern what God is doing in the life of the church itself.

Of course, in our efforts to understand what God is doing in the church and how it may be called to reform, human bias once again raises its head. Recent history reveals many shortcomings within the church that are clear failures of moral discernment, whether it is the complicity of its members in violence, the replication of broader ethnic or racial divides within the church itself, or preaching that mimics prevailing political ideologies. So here it is helpful to return to the insights of Mary Catherine Hilkert, who reminds us:

> The possibility of biased judgment on the part of a group as well as by individuals clearly needs to be acknowledged. The problem is that that same dilemma faces all members in the Body of Christ, regardless of our roles. Just as "secular feminist ideology," for example, can be a form of bias affecting the judgment of believers on questions of women's roles in the Church and ministry, so too are patriarchy and clericalism forms of bias. We all remain finite and sinful, both as individuals and as communities of faith.[40]

But while no group is beyond bias, there is no question that reading the signs of the times is bound to take place with greater accuracy when it is done communally, and the perspectives and concerns of all the people of God inform the effort. Still, bias is always a problem and there is no hermeneutic for reading the signs of the times that can allow us to escape it. We have only the faith that God will not leave his church completely bereft of the guidance of the Spirit.

SOME POSSIBLE SIGNS TODAY

A discussion of the signs of the times would not be complete without at least some small attempt to suggest where a few of those signs might be evident today. And so to return to the words of Congar, what are some of the "blows and realities of events" that deserve our attention now? It is worth noting that the very first sign of the times ever mentioned by Pope John XXIII was modern warfare.[41] While the threat of nuclear annihilation has faded somewhat since then, there is no question that the most dramatic signs of our times continue to be the ever-changing dynamics of violence: drone warfare, cluster bombs, conflict minerals, rape as a weapon of war. These are clear blows on our doors which demand a response. But there are also more hopeful signs of the times when it comes to war and peace. The Arab Spring, to the extent that it represents widespread and of-

---

[40] Hilkert, "Presidential Address," 91.
[41] John XXIII, *Humanae Salutis* (Libreria Editrice Vaticana, 1961), no. 6.

ten nonviolent demands for democracy, can be seen as an assertion of human dignity. What is more, nonviolence as a political strategy is being taken more and more seriously even by hard-core security experts.[42] Another sign of hope could be the emerging practice of peacebuilding. The concept behind peacebuilding is that political peace is something which can actually be cultivated in an active way, from the grass roots up to the highest echelons of society. This is a recognition that has emerged partly from the field of conflict resolution, through a systematic study of the social dynamics that contribute to the aggravation or diminishment of conflict. Many nongovernment organizations as well as government and international actors have come to embrace a wide range of possible interventions to minimize violent conflict—from providing relief aid in a way which forces warring parties to cooperate to get it to their people, to setting up early warning and monitoring mechanisms, to facilitating grass-roots dialogues, to organizing programs to deal with post-conflict reconciliation. The previously discussed reorientation of Catholic Relief Services can, in some ways, be located in the context of a broader shift—that has taken place in many organizations—towards addressing conflict directly.[43]

Yet nonviolent resistance movements and peacebuilding efforts are not only contemporary signs of the times, but they themselves could be seen in part at least as a fruit of Christians' efforts to read the signs of the times in the light of the gospel. These movements are not necessarily religious in nature, but there is no question that many Christian communities and organizations have contributed substantially to the theory and practice of both, and a Christian conception of reconciliation has been particularly influential when it comes to peacebuilding. One can see some of the roots of this development in *Gaudium et spes*. The document describes peace as an organic reality that is the fruit of right relationships. Rather than just the province of statesmen, in *Gaudium et spes* peace is something which depends upon all of us to build it, and therefore activism for peace is an essential element of Christian vocation. This is new: For all of their wisdom, Augustine and Sophronius had little to say about what Christians could do to actually promote a tangible—though certainly imperfect—earthly peace. Here we have an example, then, of how human experiences of conflict and conflict resolution have deepened Christians' understandings of the gospel of peace. As *Pacem in terris* reminds us, mere desire for peace is not enough: "It is not enough for

---

[42] See, for instance, Maria Stephan and Erica Chenoweth, *Why Civil Resistance Works: The Strategic Logic of Nonviolent Conflict* (New York: Columbia University, 2011).

[43] See, for example, Mary B. Anderson, *Do No Harm: How Aid Can Support Peace—Or War* (Boulder: Lynne Rienner, 1999).

Our sons to be illumined by the heavenly light of faith and to be fired with enthusiasm for a cause."[44] Real-world expertise, gained through careful social analysis, is key to peacemaking. But at the same time, the evangelical vision of the perfect peace that comes only from God has served as a challenge to and corrective of the partial forms of peace which the world knows, challenging convention wisdom about the necessity of war and violence. The gospel has helped illuminate alternatives.

CONCLUSION

"Scrutinizing the signs of the times in light of the gospel"—in essence, this is a shorthand for several important theological ideas: The form which Christian discipleship takes in the world depends at least partly upon our context, and historical events are a locus of God's continuing revelation, a revelation which invites response. Reading the signs of the times is not a one-way street, but a process of dialogue between Scripture, tradition, and human experience, potentially deepening not only our understanding of the world around us, but also our understanding of the gospel itself and how the church is called to embody it.

As believers in the scandalous notion that a God who is beyond history has chosen to make Godself known by an act of ultimate solidarity with human history, surely it is not strange to think we continue to be called to attend to historical events with diligence and openness. This is especially important today when there are many overlooked wars and victims in various corners of the world, and even the wars we are aware of fail to hold our attention or concern for very long. The signs of the times are the call of Christ to follow him in the world today, along its particular byways. They require careful observers, experienced in humanity, and full of *disponibilitá*. Yet there is no doubt that even such careful observers will often find themselves like the disciples on the road to Emmaus: We walk along, discussing the remarkable events taking place in these days and yet remain unable to understand their true meaning. Still, our faith in the risen Lord leads us to hope that even now he is accompanying us and, with the light of the Scriptures, helping us to understand. 🅼

---

[44]John XXIII, *Pacem in terris* (1963), no. 147, www.vatican.va/holy_father/john_-xxiii/encyclicals/documents/hf_j-xxiii_enc_11041963_pacem_en.html.

Time Poverty, Women's Labor and Catholic Social Teaching: A Practical Theological Exploration

Claire E. Wolfteich

Time given to Christ is never time lost, but is rather time gained, so that our relationships and indeed our whole life may become more profoundly human.
    John Paul II, *Dies Domini*, no. 7

You cannot get lost in the easy wind and downy flake of motherhood and then turn around, focus, and produce work. You have to be cunning, practical, and selfish. You have to steal time. Time is your enemy, your gift, your wanton desire, and you will never have enough of it.
    Stephanie Brown, poet and mother of two[1]

TIME IS THAT OFTEN UNNOTICED but ever present dimension of daily life. Is time an abundant gift or a scarce commodity? What are the ethical, spiritual, and ecclesial dimensions of how we live with time? As the contrast between the two opening quotes illustrates—with John Paul II's vision of time as a selfless, humanizing gift and Brown's hardnosed experience of time as an elusive object of selfish manipulation and desire—a gap exists between the church's theological vision of time and the day-to-day realities of women's experience with time, particularly at the work-family nexus. Reflection on that gap is a weak link—and a potentially rich area for development—in Catholic social teaching. Illustrating a practical theological method, this essay draws upon social scientific research on time use and feminist leisure studies for a thick description of the issue; it then brings this contemporary situation into dialogue with Catholic teaching on labor, Sabbath/Sunday, and the domestic church, with particular study of John Paul II's apostolic letter

---

[1] Stephanie Brown, "Not a Perfect Mother," in *The Grand Permission: New Writings on Poetics and Motherhood*, ed. Patricia Dienstfrey and Brenda Hillman (Middletown, CT: Wesleyan University, 2003), 31.

Dies Domini ("The Day of the Lord").[2] While this apostolic letter is not often referenced in discussions of Catholic social teaching, I argue that its teaching on time, Sabbath, and the Lord's Day complements more well-known texts on labor and can contribute a richer theological understanding of the ecclesial, spiritual, and ethical implications of time poverty. At the same time, the letter does not address "time poverty" or gender directly in any detail, and thus risks distancing the theology from women's concrete experience.

While there is sizable social scientific literature on time poverty and the work-family "time squeeze," there has not yet been sufficient attention given to the theological and spiritual dimensions of time poverty in women's lives. One can make a good case that this issue deserves serious attention, particularly in a tradition that understands time as the matrix of God's incarnational life with us, structures time according to the rhythms of the liturgy, elevates contemplative time as a cherished spiritual paradigm, advocates for just work, and celebrates the family as the "domestic church." Informed by social scientific research on time poverty, I will argue that time is a social justice issue with particular, though by no means exclusive, impact on women and families. The issue of time poverty should be addressed in ways that do not further cement the existing gender complementarity imbedded in Catholic social teaching and that do not accept wholesale the commodified assumptions about time imbedded in the social science research. Time poverty also is a spiritual issue with implications for ecclesial life and spiritual practice. The Catholic tradition offers rich theological resources for a spirituality of work, family, and time. So too we can look to women's own practices and autobiographical reflections to discern practical wisdom and an authentic lay spirituality in the midst of time poverty.

DIALOGUE BETWEEN PRACTICAL THEOLOGY AND MORAL THEOLOGY

In exploring the interrelated economic, political, social, ecclesial, and spiritual implications of time poverty, this essay aims to illustrate a practical theological contribution to Roman Catholic studies and to further dialogue between practical theology, moral theology, and spirituality studies. As "practical theology" has much in common with moral theology, and yet is less well known as a scholarly discipline in Catholic circles, some prefatory words will be useful. Practi-

---

[2] For related work that focuses more specifically on implications for theologies of the domestic church and practices of spiritual renewal, see Claire E. Wolfteich, "It's About Time: Rethinking Spirituality and the Domestic Church," in *The Household of God and Local Households*, ed. Thomas Knieps-Port le Roi, Gerard Mannion and Peter De Mey, Bibliotheca Ephemeridum Theologicarum Lovaniensium 254 (Leuven: Peeters, 2012), 127-44.

cal theology as an academic discipline has roots that are traced back at least to Friedrich Schleiermacher, who argued for the place of practical theology in the German university. As Edward Farley argues, Schleiermacher had strong influence on the shaping of the "theological encyclopedia" and the entrenchment of a "clerical paradigm" (focused on the training of pastors) for practical theology in Protestant contexts up to the present day.[3] While practical theology has not attained the same visibility in Catholic theological education, various forms of "practical theology" certainly can be found within Catholicism. Some of this work happens under the name "pastoral theology," though "practical theology" is increasingly accepted. Catholic scholars now are significant contributors to practical theology in local, national, and international levels of research and professional organization.[4]

Practical theology, shaped by earlier developments in European political and Latin American liberation theologies, underwent something of a resurgence in the 1980s, with a strong turn to a more public, church-world focus. Leading figures such as Don S. Browning, influenced by his University of Chicago colleague David Tracy, turned strongly to issues of ethics and public life in pluralistic societies, broadening the field beyond the so-called "clerical paradigm" or focus on training for church ministries. In fact, this move is already present in the Second Vatican Council's *Gaudium et spes* ("Pastoral Constitution on the Church in the Modern World"), which redefines "pastoral" to signify concern not only with the tasks of ordained clergy but more broadly with the church's engagement with the world. As Kathleen Cahalan observes: "the Council was pivotal in claiming 'pastoral' as an ecclesial discourse pertaining to the church's relationship to the world, most notably in *Gaudium et spes*."[5]

Indeed, the church-world question is quite central to the work of pastoral and practical theology. Just as the "pastoral" conciliar document moves toward more open ecclesial engagement with and inquiry into the modern world, so too practical theology as a discipline has moved in recent decades to highly complex, interdisciplinary forms of research on political, cultural, and economic issues seen in relationship to religious traditions and the life of faith communities. As Reformed theologian Richard Osmer writes: "Practical theologians carry out diverse research programs and make their own constructive, scholarly contribution to the theological enterprise as a

---

[3] Edward Farley, *Theologia: The Fragmentation and Unity of Theological Education* (Philadelphia: Fortress, 1983).
[4] For more information about international research and conversation in practical theology, see the International Academy of Practical Theology (www.ia-pt.org) and the *International Journal of Practical Theology*.
[5] Kathleen A. Cahalan, "Locating Practical Theology in Catholic Theological Discourse and Practice," *International Journal of Practical Theology* 15 (2011): 4.

whole.... The scope of this field includes matters of public importance beyond the church, and often is directed toward shaping public policy and social transformation."[6] British scholars John Swinton and Harriet Mowat also emphasize the church-world dynamic: "Practical theology is critical, theological reflection on the practices of the Church as they interact with the practices of the world, with a view to ensuring and enabling faithful participation in God's redemptive practices in, to, and for the world."[7] Thus, some speak of a "public paradigm" in practical theology,[8] strongly infused by theological ethics, committed to contextual analysis, attentive to practices, and engaged in church-world issues such as human rights, poverty, HIV-AIDS, and globalization.[9] With the heightened attention to "the world" or the "public" sphere, practical theologians have drawn heavily on ethics in defining the aims, foci, and methods of practical theology.

Moral theology and practical theology share many common features, particularly given the turn to a "public paradigm" in practical theology, the rise of "practice" as a salient category across theological disciplines, and movements toward more inductive, contextual, and "applied" approaches in moral theology. In their edited volume *Gathered for the Journey: Moral Theology in Catholic Perspective*, David Matzko McCarthy and M. Therese Lysaught, for example, point to the importance of practice in shaping moral reasoning: "Excellence in Christian moral living is a skill that can be acquired only over time, through ongoing practice (and with much grace)."[10] In their understanding, practice is learned through ongoing participation in a community, and they link practice closely to "formation" and bodily knowing: "[T]he practices of the Christian life—praying, attending Mass, confessing, loving one's enemy, eating with the

---

[6] Richard R. Osmer, *Practical Theology: An Introduction* (Grand Rapids: Eerdmans, 2008), ix-x.
[7] John Swinton and Harriet Mowat, *Practical Theology and Qualitative Research* (London: SCM, 2006), 6.
[8] See, for example, Gordon S. Mikoski, "Mainline Protestantism," in *The Wiley-Blackwell Companion in Practical Theology*, ed. B.J. Miller-McLemore (Oxford: Blackwell, 2012), 563.
[9] See, for example, several of the volumes that have resulted from the biennial conferences of the International Academy of Practical Theology, including: Edward Foley, ed., *Religion, Diversity, and Conflict* (Münster: LIT, 2011); Wilhelm Gräb and Lars Charbonnier, ed., *Secularization Theories, Religious Identity, and Practical Theology* (Münster: LIT, 2009); Elaine Graham and Anne Rowlands, ed., *Pathways to the Public Square* (Münster: LIT, 2005); and Pamela D. Couture and Bonnie J Miller-McLemore, ed., *Poverty, Suffering and HIV/AIDS* (Cardiff: Cardiff Academic, 2003).
[10] David Matzko McCarthy and M. Therese Lysaught, "Introduction," in McCarthy and Lysaught, ed., *Gathered for the Journey: Moral Theology in Catholic Perspective* (Grand Rapids: Eerdmans, 2007), 2.

poor—shape our bodies to act and respond."[11] Julie Hanlon Rubio structures her work on family ethics in terms of practices. Rubio draws upon Alasdair MacIntyre, Stanley Hauerwas, Craig Dykstra, and Dorothy Bass as she defines practice as "an intentional, shared action, situated in the context of a tradition, ordinary in outward appearances but transcendent in its association with fundamental human goods."[12] Such texts illustrate the common interests and cross-fertilization between moral theology and practical theology; practical theology's close work with diverse theories of practice could further enhance this turn to practice in moral theology. So too, the strongly contextual focus of practical theology resonates with some recent work in moral theology. In her introduction to *Applied Ethics in a World Church*, Linda Hogan describes the "changing idiom" of moral theology, evident in the "increasingly interdisciplinary character of moral theology, as well as in the manner in which it proceeds from local cultural contexts, inductively, in dialogue with the classic articulations of the tradition."[13] While practical theology and moral theology both are broad fields that include a range of methods and disciplinary debates, these fields have increasingly convergent interests in interdisciplinary and inductive methods, contextual theology, attention to practice, and public engagement.

So too discipleship or spirituality can be understood as a deeply related aspect of both moral and practical theology. As I have argued elsewhere, embrace of a public paradigm of practical theology should not mean diminished concern with personal and communal spirituality rooted in ecclesial life.[14] *Gaudium et spes* expresses well these more integrated dimensions of practical theology: "[T]he Church seeks but a solitary goal: to carry forward the work of Christ under the lead of the befriending Spirit.... To carry out such a task, the Church has always had the duty of scrutinizing the signs of the times and of interpreting them in the light of the Gospel."[15] This statement captures several important aspects of practical theology in my understanding—that is, theology as a hermeneutical project that involves interpretation of both contemporary culture and gospel with a pneumatological, ecclesiological, and missional dimension. I have

---

[11] McCarthy and Lysaught, "Introduction," 2.
[12] Julie Hanlon Rubio, *Family Ethics: Practices for Christians* (Washington, DC: Georgetown University, 2010), 99.
[13] Linda Hogan, ed., *Applied Ethics in a World Church: The Padua Conference* (Maryknoll: Orbis, 2008), 9.
[14] See, for example, Claire E. Wolfteich, "Spirituality," in *The Wiley-Blackwell Companion to Practical Theology*, 328-36, and Claire E. Wolfteich, "Animating Questions: Spirituality and Practical Theology," *International Journal of Practical Theology* 13 (2009): 121-43.
[15] *Gaudium et spes*, nos. 3-4, www.vatican.va/archive/hist_councils/ii_vatican_council/documents/vat-ii_const_19651207_gaudium-et-spes_en.html.

argued, building upon Gerben Heitink, for example, for renewed attention to the pneumatological dimensions of practical theology.[16] This would include developing theological theories of action that attend to the role of the Holy Spirit and turning to spiritual practice as an object of study and potential theological source.

Here I would point to resonances between discipleship-based approaches in practical theology and moral theology. Practical theologian Dorothy Bass, for example, focuses on practices as constituting a way of life and describes a "life-giving way of life" or a "way of life abundant" as the "telos of practical theology and Christian ministry."[17] Kathleen Cahalan and James Nieman claim that the basic task of practical theology is "the promotion of faithful discipleship."[18] So too, in his introduction to *A History of Catholic Moral Theology in the Twentieth Century*, James Keenan describes 20th century developments in moral theology as a move from defining moral theology as a "fixed science of action" to becoming a "guide" for discipleship. He writes: "[T]he nature of moral theology is to respond to the practical challenges of each period in history…. What we find in the twentieth century, then, is the enormously complex move from defining moral theology as the fixed science of human action to becoming a guide for the personal and communal development of the conscientious disciples of Christ."[19]

In my understanding, discipleship is a lifelong process of seeking to follow Christ shaped by concrete practices over time, rooted in prayerful intimacy (John 15), bearing fruit in just and loving acts, sustained by a community of believers in the companioning life of the Holy Spirit. In promoting faithful discipleship, moral theology and practical theology are best done in dialogue with spirituality studies and ecclesiology, with attention to issues of formation and transformation. This practical theological examination of time poverty and women's labor, then, puts into critical dialogue social scien-

---

[16] On these points, see Gerben Heitink, *Practical Theology: History, Theory, Action Domains* (Grand Rapids: Eerdmans, 1999), 193: "The central problem practical theology must face is the hermeneutical question about the way in which the divine reality and the human reality can be connected at the experiential level. This question focuses attention on the pneumatological basis of the theological theory of action. The fundamental choice to be made in this respect has its impact on the daily praxis in the church." See, too, my "Words and Fire, Deserts and Dwellings: Toward Mystical Practical Theologies," 2013 Presidential Address for the International Academy of Practical Theology (Toronto: April 12, 2013).

[17] Dorothy C. Bass, "Ways of Life Abundant," in *For Life Abundant: Practical Theology, Theological Education, and Christian Ministry*, ed. Dorothy C. Bass and Craig Dykstra (Grand Rapids: Eerdmans, 2008), 27.

[18] Kathleen Cahalan and James Nieman, "Mapping the Field of Practical Theology," in *For Life Abundant*, 66.

[19] James F. Keenan, *A History of Catholic Moral Theology in the Twentieth Century: From Confessing Sins to Liberating Consciences* (New York: Continuum, 2010), 6-7.

TIME POVERTY, WOMEN, WORK, AND FAMILY

In her discussion of the time-squeeze in American family life, Marin Clarkberg notes "a growing perception of a time famine.... Between 1965 and 1992, for example, the percent of respondents saying that they 'always feel rushed' increased almost 50%, so that now more than one in three Americans say that they *always* feel rushed."[20] David Maume describes the "overpaced American." Noting that the pace of work has increased in recent decades, Maume also suggests that the increased permeability of work-home boundaries and work-family conflict may increase perceptions of work intensification, particularly for women. As he concludes, the pacing of work has significant effects on family well-being.[21] In her book *No Time: Stress and the Crisis of Modern Work*, Canadian author Heather Menzies links time poverty, overwork, and an increased pace of life in highly technological societies that profoundly shapes identity and relationships.[22] The experience of time poverty is widespread, with multiple contributing factors and certainly affecting men, though the focus here will be its particular impact on women and families.

From an economic perspective, time poverty is an economic calculation—the difference between time requirements and time availability.[23] When there is less time available than time needed, there is time poverty. Time is an overlooked economic resource that should be counted, some have argued, in any measure of well-being or poverty. Economist Clair Vickery developed a model for calculating time poverty in 1977 as she argued that time—and not only income—must be factored into poverty indexes. Vickery emphasized the value of home production for the well-being of families and sought to estimate the "additional female-headed families who would be counted as poor because of a deficiency of nonmarket time."[24] Income measures of poverty fail to capture the value of work in the home.

---

[20] Marin Clarkberg, "The Time-Squeeze in American Families: From Causes to Solutions," in *Balancing Acts: Easing the Burdens and Improving the Options for Working Families*, ed. E. Applebaum (Washington, DC: Economic Policy Institute, 2000), 25.

[21] Maume, David J., "The 'Over-Paced' American: Recent Trends in the Intensification of Work," in *Research in the Sociology of Work* Vol. 17: *Workplace Temporalities* (Amsterdam: Elsevier, 2007), 251-83.

[22] Heather Menzies, *No Time: Stress and the Crisis of Modern Life* (Vancouver: Douglas & McIntyre, 2005).

[23] Andrew S. Harvey and Arun K. Mukhopadhyay, "When Twenty-Four Hours is Not Enough: Time Poverty of Working Parents," *Social Indicators Research* 82, no. 1 (2007): 57-77.

[24] Clair Vickery, "The Time Poor: A New Look at Poverty," *The Journal of Human Resources* 12, no. 1 (1977): 27-48.

Others have built on Vickery's work. Canadian economists Harvey and Mukhopadhyay, for example, continue to argue for a redefined poverty standard that accounts for the time deprivation of working parents, noting that time deficits require additional income to purchase goods and services such as child care, home maintenance, and meal preparation. They conclude that working parents, particularly single parents (who are overwhelmingly female), are "a severely time deprived group."[25] Similarly, a report given at a 1993 conference on feminist perspectives on poverty critiqued the American government for failing to account for time's economic value:

> Throughout its history, the U.S. government has neglected to explicitly recognize that families have basic personal time needs and that such time has value. Despite much political talk about the importance of family values and especially the need for parents to spend more quality time with their children, we neither attempt to estimate the value of such time in terms of gross domestic product nor account for it when establishing poverty guidelines.[26]

This report also finds that working parents, especially single parents, are more vulnerable to poverty due to lack of time. Feminist scholars also have argued that time is a form of political capital, and women are disadvantaged by their lack of it. Valerie Bryson writes: "Many feminist writers on citizenship see time as a scarce political resource that women have less of than men, and argue that 'time poverty' continues to act as a constraint on their citizenship.... Such problems are compounded in developing nations, where women's 'time poverty' is bound up with acute economic and educational disadvantage."[27]

How does women's market work impact time availability? How is work and leisure shared among dual earner parents? In her influential 1989 book *The Second Shift: Working Parents and the Revolution at Home*, sociologist Arlie Hochschild argued provocatively that within dual-earner households, women clock an additional month of work in unpaid domestic tasks (the "second shift") as compared to their partners.[28] Some researchers have disputed Hochschild's claim as exaggerated and based on dated data. One study found that when unpaid and paid work hours are combined, there is much less of a differential between men and women than Hochschild suggested, for

---

[25] Harvey and Mukhopadhyay, "When Twenty-Four Hours Is Not Enough," 57-77.
[26] Robin A. Douthitt, "Time to do the Chores?: Factoring Home Production Needs into Measures of Poverty," presented at the conference, "Poverty: Feminist Perspectives" (University of British Columbia, School of Social Work: November 18-20, 1993), 2.
[27] Valerie Bryson, "Time-Use Studies: A Potentially Feminist Tool," *International Feminist Journal of Politics* 10, no. 2 (June 2008): 135-6.
[28] Arlie Hochschild, *The Second Shift: Working Parents and the Revolution at Home* (New York: Viking Penguin, 1989).

while women do more unpaid work, men on average do more paid work hours.[29] Of course, women's disproportionate responsibility for unpaid labor impacts their ability to maintain paid work, attain pay equity, and seek professional advancement.

While the exact extent of the differential is a complicated question, the overall picture of a disproportionate time bind affecting employed mothers seems clear. In a study of 29 countries, Jonas Edlund notes: "It can be observed that the work–family time squeeze is in most countries a problem more pertinent to women than to men." Women in the United States had the most unequal work-family load as compared to any other country studied.[30] Australian time use data showed as of 2006 that motherhood "markedly intensifies gender inequities in time allocation by increasing specialization and women's workload." This study argues that any calculation of women's time use must attend to multi-tasking—e.g., women typically do more than one thing at a time, and women's time given to childcare alongside another "primary" activity such as shopping or recreation may be overlooked in time use research. And while men are doing more child care than in the past, they are not as often solely responsible for the children; women may be present as well. Hence, men's increased child care work does not necessarily free up mothers for leisure activities.[31] Indeed, a study that tested Hochschild's claims about the "second shift" found that employed mothers of preschoolers in the United States had nearly seven fewer hours of leisure per week compared to their employed partners: "In households with both parents employed fulltime, mothers enjoy less adult-only free time, less active leisure and watch less TV than fathers.... Full-time

---

[29] A team of researchers tested Hochschild's claim in their own study of American mothers of preschoolers, for example, finding that women employed full-time in dual-earner couples worked an extra week-and-a half per year, rather than a full extra month. See Melissa A. Milkie, Sara B. Raley, and Suzanne M. Bianchi, "Taking on the Second Shift: Time Allocations and Time Pressures of U.S. Parents with Preschoolers," *Social Forces* 88, no. 2 (2009): 487-518. See too Lyn Craig, "Is There Really a Second Shift, and If So, Who Does It? A Time of Diary Investigation," *Feminist Review* 86 (2007): 149-70. See also Suzanne M. Bianchi, John P. Robinson, and Melissa A. Milkie, *Changing Rhythms of American Family Life* (New York: Russell Sage Foundation, 2006).

[30] Jonas Edlund, "The Work-Family Time Squeeze: Conflicting Demands of Paid and Unpaid Work Among Working Couples in 29 Countries," *International Journal of Comparative Sociology* 48, no.6 (2007): 451-80.

[31] Lyn Craig, "Children and the Revolution: A Time-Diary Analysis of the Impact of Motherhood on Daily Workload," *Journal of Sociology* 42, no. 2 (2006): 125-43. On this point about father's involvement in child care, for a study in the American context see too M. J. Mattingly and S.M. Bianchi, "Gender Differences in the Quantity and Quality of Free Time: The U.S. Experience," *Social Forces* 81 (2003): 999-1031.

employed mothers also experience a large deficit in community and socializing activities."[32]

Working class families face particular issues, such as the impact of shift work on family life, the difficulty in synchronizing work schedules for shared leisure, less control over working hours, and fewer resources to pay for child care, elder care, and household maintenance.[33] Low-income families face distinct issues in managing time—for example, in organizing child care (often dependent on family members' schedules), medical visits, social service appointments, erratic employment, and urban transportation schedules.[34]

FEMINIST LEISURE STUDIES

Feminist leisure studies add to this picture a critical analysis of time use research methods and a more textured picture of women's subjective experiences of time. First, scholars argue that traditional methods used to record time use (e.g., time diary) fail to accurately capture women's multitasking and subjective experience of time. For example, women who are watching television may be recorded as enjoying leisure time, when in fact they simultaneously are supervising children and folding laundry; their labor and caretaking responsibilities go unrecorded. Rosemary Deem describes "the greater time fragmentation and time scarcity apparently experienced by some women in their experiences of leisure and their attempts to capture time and space free from work and household obligations. These attempts are often frustrated by the existence of responsibilities which do not disappear even when they are apparently engaged in leisure."[35] Indeed, women on vacation with their families report levels of labor and fatigue not typically noted in time use research. One study of women's experiences of vacations, for example, noted that some mothers came back "as tired and stressed as they had been before departure." Holidays entail sometimes more intensive time with

---

[32] Milkie, Raley, and Bianchi, "Taking on the Second Shift: Time Allocations and Time Pressures of U.S. Parents with Preschoolers," *Social Forces* 88, no. 2 (2009): 502-3. See too Kei M. Nomaguchi, Melissa A. Milkie, and Suzanne M. Bianchi, "Time Strains and Psychological Well-Being: Do Dual-Earner Mothers and Fathers Differ?" *Journal of Family Issues* 26, no. 6 (2005): 756-92.

[33] Tracey Warren, "Class-and Gender-Based Working Time? Time Poverty and the Division of Domestic Labor," *Sociology* 37, no. 4 (2003): 733-52.

[34] K. M. Roy, "Don't Have No Time: Daily Rhythms and the Organization of Time for the Low-Income Families," *Family Relations* 53, no. 2 (Mar 2004): 168-78. See too S. Jody Heymann, "Low-Income Parents and the Time Famine," in Hewlett, Rankin, and West, eds., *Taking Parenting Public: The Case for a New Social Movement* (Lanham, MD: Rowman & Littlefield, 2002), 103-16, and Peggy Kahn, "The Work-Family Time Binds of Low-Income Mothers: Nurse Aids Struggle to Care," *Journal of Women, Politics, and Policy* 27, nos. 3-4 (2005): 97-111.

[35] Rosemary Deem, "No Time for Rest? An Exploration of Women's Work, Engendered Leisure and Holidays," in *Time & Society* Vol. 5 (1996): 6.

children and partners, a hectic pace, and some degree of labor for preparing and facilitating the family's enjoyment. "The existence of time hierarchies often meant prioritizing the needs of some family members over others; this process rarely seemed to give high priority to mothers."[36] Women's roles in creating leisure time for others often means that women's labor goes under-noticed and their own leisure under-supported even in time demarcated as "leisure."

Mattingly and Bianchi use the language of "time contamination" (a phrase that calls out for theological response) to describe women's "triple burden:" "Women have less free time. The free time that they have is often contaminated by other activities or the presence of children, and their free time is not as beneficial to them as men's in terms of reducing feelings of time pressure."[37] The leisure gap is most accentuated for women who are both full-time workers and mothers, according to a Canadian study: These women "have the least time for leisure.... They feel the burden of their manifold responsibilities and have a hard time getting them off their mind long enough to enjoy leisure. Working mothers are the most fatigued among women because of their double-day."[38]

Feminist leisure scholars thus critique traditional methods of time use research, pointing out that this research fails to detail women's multi-tasking and to explore women's subjective experiences of time, work, and leisure. Women's distinctive experiences of time are intimately related to their multiple, overlapping work and their family responsibilities—with the resulting time deprivation and fatigue that accompanies their abiding "ethic of care."[39]

Catholic Social Teaching: Women's Labor, Time, and the Domestic Church

What emerges from this social science research is a picture of time poverty as a real economic and political disadvantage with gendered dimensions. This highly concrete analysis is lacking in Catholic social teaching around women, labor, and the domestic church. The full realization of Church teachings about just work and the dignity of labor and family require an understanding of time as economic and political resource with advocacy for structural changes to alleviate time poverty among those most vulnerable to its effects. For those most vulnerable, one could even consider this as an extension of the "preferential option for the poor."

---

[36] Deem, "No Time for Rest?," 17.
[37] Mattingly and Bianchi, "Gender Differences," 999-1031.
[38] Maureen Harrington, Don Dawson, and Pat Bolla, "Objective and Subjective Constraints on Women's Enjoyment of Leisure," *Society and Leisure* 15, no. 1 (1992): 217.
[39] Harrison, Dawson, and Bolla, "Objective and Subjective Constraints on Women's Enjoyment of Leisure," 217.

At the same time, while practical theology is informed by social science research to develop a "thick description" of an issue, social science also carries implicit and explicit norms and so must be incorporated critically. In this case, in light of Catholic theologies of labor and time, one must problematize the wholesale instrumentalization and commodification of time taken for granted in time use research. Time is not only economic commodity—but also, more fundamentally, a sacred gift offered to all by the Creator. Right relationship with the Creator entails a just enjoyment of that gift. Moreover, one would situate feminist leisure studies within a theological exploration of "Sabbath" and "Sunday," a liturgical participation in time, and an appreciation for contemplation as ancient spiritual practice. We are interested not only in gaining "leisure" but in accessing the full range of spiritual practice and theological knowing into which all human beings are graciously invited.

This section highlights several points of key documents on labor and family as it frames time poverty as social justice issue. The following section turns to the apostolic letter *Dies Domini* and articulations its related significance for a practical theology of time.

The Second Vatican Council revived an ancient understanding of domestic church—a key affirmation of the ecclesiological significance of the family and household practices. The family, "so to speak, the domestic church," is the matrix in which the people of God is nurtured, formed, and from which they are sent.[40] This explicit attention to the ecclesial dimension of the family is part of a larger move to affirm the lay apostolate as encompassing domestic, economic, and political spheres (see, for example, *Apostolicam actuositatem*, no. 7); laity from their ordinary contexts of family and social life are to sanctify the world "from within as a leaven" (*Lumen gentium*, no. 31). Conciliar documents such as *Gaudium et spes* and subsequent Catholic social teaching such as John Paul II's *Laborem exercens* (1981) affirm a high theology of work as constitutive of lay vocation and holiness, a calling, means of "humanization," and even a form of "co-creation." The dignity of work is linked to its significance for the family—particularly in supporting basic needs and education. Ideally, work and family together partner in developing persons in community who respond generously to God's calling and whose dignity also is protected.

---

[40] *Lumen gentium* ("Dogmatic Constitution on the Church") reads: The family is "so to speak, the domestic church. In it parents should, by their word and example, be the first preachers of the faith to their children; they should encourage them in the vocation which is proper to each of them" (no. 11), www.vatican.va/archive/hist_-councils/ii_vatican_council/documents/vat-ii_const_19641121_lumen-gentium-_en.html.

Catholic social teaching ascribes value to women's unpaid domestic labor and advocates for structures that accommodate market work to the needs of families. In many ways, there is a synchronicity here between the theological arguments of, for example, *Laborem exercens*, and the economists who advocate for measures of economic well-being that take time—and not only income—into account. Over-reliance on market measures of value obscures the value of time and labor in the home and risks undermining family well-being. At the same time, the valuing of unpaid labor and time in Catholic social teaching often is linked to essentialist assertions of mothers' special vocation to the home and family. *Gaudium et spes* asserts that work should be adapted to the needs of the person and domestic life, "especially in respect to mothers of families" (no. 67). John Paul II's *Laborem exercens* strongly affirms women's domestic (specifically, mothering) labor and asserts the primacy of mothering labor as compared to market work:

> Experience confirms that there must be a social re-evaluation of the mother's role, of the toil connected with it… It will redound to the credit of society to make it possible for a mother—without inhibiting her freedom, without psychological or practical discrimination, and without penalizing her as compared with other women—to devote herself to taking care of her children and educating them in accordance with their needs, which vary with age. Having to abandon these tasks in order to take up paid work outside the home is wrong from the point of view of the good of society and of the family when it contradicts or hinders these primary goals of the mission of a mother.[41]

The 1981 apostolic exhortation *Familiaris consortio* similarly prizes women's "maternal and family role" over all other public contributions and calls for a renewed theology of work that affirms women's domestic labor (no. 23).[42] This gendered theology of work and family is integral to assertions of the family's ecclesial task and significance as a "specific revelation and realization of ecclesial communion" (no. 21). In short, arguments for a just valuing of women's labor and arguments for the ecclesial nature of the family depends on a theology of complementarity that bounds a mother's mission or vocation as located first and foremost within the home, relies on women's time availability in the home for children's care and education, critiques social and economic structures that undercut

---

[41] *Lumen gentium*, no. 19.
[42] John Paul II, *Familiaris consortio*, www.vatican.va/holy_father/john_paul_ii/apost_exhortations/documents/hf_jp-ii_exh_19811122_familiaris-consortio_-en.html.

women's domestic roles, and only then offers a qualified affirmation of women's public work beyond the domestic sphere.

Moral theologians such as Barbara Hilkert Andolsen have made the case that women's unpaid domestic labor is a social justice issue.[43] So too time poverty can be framed more explicitly in Catholic social teaching as a social justice issue. The dignity of women's labor in market and domestic spheres is rightly affirmed by Catholic social teaching, and this teaching logically extends the "preferential option for the poor" to those women and families who are most vulnerable to the effects of time poverty. As the 1987 papal encyclical *Sollicitudo rei socialis* ("On Social Concern") notes: "[T]his love of preference for the poor, and the decisions which it inspires in us, cannot but embrace the immense multitudes of the hungry, the needy, the homeless, those without medical care" (no. 42). Poverty in this document is defined broadly, not simply as a lack of material goods:

> [I]n today's world there are many other forms of poverty.... The denial or the limitation of human rights - as for example the right to religious freedom, the right to share in the building of society, the freedom to organize and to form unions, or to take initiatives in economic matters - do these not impoverish the human person as much as, if not more than, the deprivation of material goods? (no. 15)[44]

So too one could include time poverty among the most vulnerable as a real form of poverty. I emphatically do not include here the time poverty that results from an overabundance of choice and opportunity; this time poverty too is a problem but in no way should be equated with the suffering of the poorest of the poor.

Moral theologian Christine Firer Hinze has argued that theories of gender complementarity are interwoven with Catholic social teaching on labor in ways that unnecessarily link the two and undercut the Church's agenda to promote social justice for workers.[45] Building on Hinze's argument, I would assert that the resolution of the problem of time poverty cannot restrict women's sphere of labor

---

[43] Barbara Hilkert Andolsen, "A Woman's Work is Never Done: Unpaid Household Labor as a Social Justice Issue," in *Women's Consciousness, Women's Conscience: A Reader in Feminist Ethics*, ed. Barbara Hilkert Andolsen, Christine E. Gudorf and Mary D. Pellauer (Minneapolis: Winston, 1985), 3-18. See too Barbara Hilkert Andolsen, *The New Job Contract: Economic Justice in an Age of Insecurity* (Cleveland: Pilgrim, 1998).

[44] John Paul II, *Sollicitudo rei socialis* ("On Social Concern"), nos. 15, 42, www.vatican.va/holy_father/john_paul_ii/encyclicals/documents/hf_jpii_enc_30121987_sollicitudo-rei-socialis_en.html.

[45] See Christine Firer Hinze, "U.S. Catholic Social Thought, Gender, and Economic Livelihood," *Theological Studies* 66 (2005): 568-91 and "Women, Families, and the Legacy of *Laborem Exercens*: An Unfinished Agenda," *Journal of Catholic Social Thought* 6, no. 1 (2009): 63-92.

to the home, based on essentialist gender theories— but rather needs to work for more just sharing of time between market and family spheres and between women and men. Economic arguments for redefined measures of poverty—ones that take into account the value of time and the serious impact of time poverty on families—go hand in hand with Catholic social teaching on the dignity of both domestic and market work as a dimension of full humanity and spiritual calling.

TIME, SABBATH, AND THE LORD'S DAY

As much as time use research usefully expands an understanding of the social and economic realities of time poverty, one also can bring a theological critique to some of the working assumptions and implicit theologies embedded in this social science literature. For example, the framing of time as economic commodity that can be "contaminated" by the presence of children works against a much richer understanding of time as sacred gift that is so central to many religious traditions and certainly seen in Catholic Christian liturgical and spiritual traditions. On the one hand, time must be seen as an economic and political resource in order to adequately measure well-being and ascribe value to unpaid labor. At the same time, as Catholic social teaching rejects the instrumentalization of the worker—insisting on the priority of the worker as subject—so too it rejects the reduction of time to money or any other instrument of exchange (nor does it see time as an "enemy," to return to the opening quote by Stephanie Brown). The practice of liturgy—the marking of the liturgical calendar, the liturgy of the hours, the celebration of Sunday—these shape the community's imagination of and, indeed, its bodily knowing of time as sacred arena of God's own creative and salvific work among us.

John Paul II's 1998 apostolic letter *Dies Domini* ("The Day of the Lord")[46] is seldom connected with Catholic social teaching on work and family, although theological reflection on time is highly relevant to theologies of labor and the domestic church—and certainly to the problem of time poverty. *Dies Domini* offers a vision of time that is liberative, contemplative, humanizing, and ecclesial. Rooted in Jewish Sabbath theology, the document moves to recover the "meaning of Sunday," the "Lord's Day." Sabbath is not only a remembrance of creation but in some sense a continuation of it: "The rest decreed in order to honour the day dedicated to God is not at all a burden imposed upon man, but rather an aid to help him to recognize his life-giving and liberating dependence upon the Creator, and at the same

---

[46] Quotations from *Dies Domini* taken from the following translation: www.vatican.va/holy_father/john_paul_ii/apost_letters/documents/hf_jpii_apl_05071998_dies-domini_en.html.

time his calling to cooperate in the Creator's work and to receive his grace. In honouring God's "rest," man [sic] fully discovers himself" (no. 61). *Dies Domini* describes the practice of Sabbath as a kind of contemplative, lingering (or leisurely) practice that imitates a creative God, who on the seventh day lingered "before the 'very good' work (Gn 1:31) which his hand has wrought, in order to cast upon it *a gaze full of joyous delight.* This is a 'contemplative' gaze which does not look to new accomplishments but enjoys the beauty of what has already been achieved" (no. 11).

These reflections further develop Catholic social teaching on the dignity of labor; theologies of work and theologies of Sabbath are necessarily interconnected and complementary. *Dies Domini* also offers tantalizing visions here of a theology of time that stands in stark contrast to the reality of time poverty. This is a liberative understanding of time as gift, rest as integral to humanization and authentic self-discovery, Sabbath as joyous, delighted contemplation in imitation of a creative God. The letter also focuses quite specifically on the theological/ecclesiological significance of time. "In Christianity time has a fundamental importance": that is, time is the arena of creation, Incarnation, salvation, and the eschaton. "In Jesus Christ… time becomes a dimension of God, who is himself eternal" (no. 74). "Christ is the Lord of time; he is its beginning and its end; every year, every day and every moment are embraced by his Incarnation and Resurrection, and thus become part of the 'fullness of time'" (no. 74). As the "weekly Easter," Sunday is the day that reveals the meaning of time (no. 75). The practical significance of time gets focused in this letter around one particular practice: celebration of the Eucharist on Sunday. Christians are exhorted to give time to Christ and to the Church through participation in the Eucharistic assembly on Sunday, for: "The Eucharist is not only a particularly intense expression of the reality of the Church's life, but also in a sense its 'fountain-head.' The Eucharist feeds and forms the Church" (no. 32). Indeed, "the *dies Domini* is also the *dies Ecclesiae*" (no. 35). Thus, the practice of "giving time" is essential to the church. To rediscover Sunday means that we "open our time to Christ, that he may cast light upon it and give it direction" (no. 7).

Dies Domini laments cultural forces that have weakened the meaning of Sunday in people's lives but does not provide a detailed analysis of changing economic, social, and cultural dynamics. Yet while gender complementarity features significantly in Catholic social teaching on labor, gender receives scant attention in Catholic teaching about time, Sabbath, and Sunday—even though it clearly plays a role in how time is practiced and experienced. John Paul II is not alone here; most Christian and Jewish authors (both male and female) writing on Sabbath—from Abraham Joshua Heschel to Marva Dawn, Dorothy Bass to Norman Wirzba—give little attention to women's labor and time poverty as they explore practices of Sabbath keeping.[47] Closer attention to the gendered dimensions of such religious practice is an important next step. Here the time use research and feminist leisure studies can fruitfully inform a fuller practical theological treatment of labor, family, and time.

SPIRITUAL PRACTICE IN TIME POVERTY

Clearly Catholic teaching on Sabbath and the Lord's Day seeks to announce "good news" about time and, by extension, about work. Time is sanctified as the arena for God's creative, redemptive, and sanctifying activity. Time is the liberative, humanizing, and contemplative gift of Shabbat—a gift given not only to the people of Israel, but to all. Christ is the "Alpha and the Omega," the "Lord of time;" time is not far from God but is the arena of God's life with us, even part of God's eternal self in Jesus Christ. Through our own gift of time back to Christ and through our ecclesial Eucharistic assembly on the day of the Lord, we are made one with the church as it feeds on Christ in the Eucharist, celebrates the Resurrection, and anticipates the "Sunday which will never end." This is abundant good news: It is about time.

Yet, a gap yawns between women's experience of time poverty and this magisterial theological vision, as we have seen through time use research and feminist leisure studies. Women's autobiographical reflections and devotional literature also reveals this gap and its implications for spiritual practice. In her book *The Busy Mom's Guide to Spiritual Survival*, Kelly Trujillo describes the effects of time poverty on her spiritual practice as a new mother. Upon opening a book about spiritual disciplines: "I was excited at first and so ready to deepen my spirituality life; yet as I turned each page, I felt worse and worse and worse. I can't do any of this, I realized, I don't have the time.... [T]he discouragement became overwhelming."[48] Similarly, in focus groups of Catholic women conducted by the United States Conference of Catholic Bishops in 50 American dioceses from 2002-2004, women described the spiritual effects of their being "stretched thin" when balancing the responsibilities of family and work life. A

---

[47] See, for example, Abraham Joshua Heschel, *The Sabbath* (New York: Farrar, Strauss, and Giroux, 1951); Marva Dawn, *Keeping the Sabbath Wholly: Ceasing, Resting, Embracing, Feasting* (Grand Rapids: Eerdmans, 1989); Dorothy C. Bass, *Receiving the Day: Christian Practices for Opening the Gift of Time* (San Francisco: Jossey Bass, 2000); and Norman Wirzba, *Living the Sabbath: Discovering the Rhythms of Rest and Delight* (Grand Rapids: Brazos, 1996). One text that does offer fascinating first-person reflections on Sabbath practice from an Orthodox Jewish woman's perspective is Blu Greenberg, *How to Run a Traditional Jewish Household* (New York: Simon & Schuster, 1983).

[48] Kelly Trujillo, *The Busy Mom's Guide to Spiritual Survival* (Indianapolis: Wesleyan, 2007), 15.

young Catholic mother noted: "I find it hard to commit time to prayer; I'm rushed in the mornings and tired at night."[49] Of course, this is not a new problem. Francis de Sales counsels many laywomen about the need to leave aside their spiritual disciplines with indifference when the needs of others in their household call.[50] Even Teresa of Avila struggled with time poverty as she tries to carve out time for writing amidst the busyness of her apostolic work: "I have to eat and sleep and carry on business and talk with everyone.... How is it that when there is so little time left over to enjoy Your presence You hide from me?"[51] Dialogue between spiritual classics (including women's spiritual autobiographies), Catholic social teaching, and social science research can open up new layers of theological reflection on women's experience and time poverty.

As Teresa well understood, the compression of time makes contemplative practice more difficult. This is important in a tradition that cherishes contemplation as spiritual practice and frames Sabbath as an imitation of God's delighted contemplation of creation.

Moreover, time poverty may impinge on women's (and their families') practices of Sunday observance, including Eucharistic assembly, and thus undercut the ecclesial significance of time that John Paul II so emphatically asserts. Freeing time from the "time bind" is an ecclesial imperative. This entails as well some internal church reflection: the church which relies on women's volunteer labor needs to take time poverty more seriously as it asks for women's "gifts" of time to fuel the work of the local church. To the extent that the time bind is chosen and/or culturally driven—reflecting consumerism, workaholism, avoidable overscheduling—then Catholic social teaching also calls here for countercultural conversion. The Catholic tradition and imagination proposes practices of resistance: observing Sabbath/Lord's Day, Eucharist as eschatological feast that re-members the body of Christ, contemplative practice, markings of alternative time rhythms through the liturgical year.

Without dulling the call for justice and reaffirmation of the sacrality of time, one also can look to women's lives for practical wisdom and theological knowing around time. What practical wisdom do women cultivate in the constant balancing of labors and care? Surely, there are involved here constant practices of discernment and

---

[49] Quotes are taken from the focus group reports of specific dioceses—here, from Rockville Center, New York. For a summary and interpretation of the first phase of the focus groups, see also Bishop Edward Cullen's article, "Women's Spirituality in the Workplace," *America* 189, no. 8 (September 22, 2003).

[50] See Francis de Sales and Jane de Chantal, *Letters of Spiritual Direction* (New York: Paulist, 1988) and Francis de Sales, *Introduction to the Devout Life* (New York: Random House, 2002).

[51] Teresa of Avila, *The Book of Her Life* (Washington, DC: Institute of Carmelite Studies, 1976), 327.

the development of virtues. Is there a spirituality of time asceticism—a new desert spirituality—to be seen not simply as lamentable but also in some cases as the fruitful outworking of women's fuller lay vocation? One might consider alternative theological visioning and practices of time which emerge from women's spiritual life in the midst of time poverty. The USCCB focus groups of Catholic women show that along with laments about loss of contemplative time, women also express great creativity in adapting prayer practices in the time bind. The experience of time as *abundant* gift offered to all persons, spoken of so eloquently in *Dies Domini*, is more elusive. Like Stephanie Brown in the opening quote, several women in these focus groups described time as sparse, sought after, desired. They "make" time and "catch pockets of time," and in those short moments, they adapt prayer to places such as subways, bathtubs, workplaces, and treadmills. Women's reflections reveal the diversity of ways in which they "give time to Christ" in their ordinary spheres of labor, including in the home. And some reflect how the practice of Eucharist yields new knowing. For Deborah Smith Douglas, for example, an employed mother struggling "against the entropic forces that regularly disintegrate her life," Eucharistic practice revealed grace in fragmentation: "As I watched, the priest... proceeded to break the consecrated wafer... into pieces... my life is like that, I realized... by a miracle of grace, by the grace of God—I can come to see myself not as meaninglessly disintegrated but as broken and given like bread, poured out like wine."[52] A practical theological reading of time poverty would look here too—to the embodied practice of Eucharistic spirituality in the quotidian—for "signs of the times" and for "good news."

Conclusion

Catholic social teaching can offer powerful and liberating theological visions of labor and time. A critical step is to harness the critical, countercultural and justice implications of such a vision for women and families—and to relate the vision to concrete practice and experience. Time poverty should be seen as a social justice issue to be addressed structurally and theologically, with a "preferential option for the poor" extended to the most vulnerable. Theologies of time—embodied in liturgical practice and Sabbath observance—can be interwoven with teachings on the dignity of labor and the imperatives of social justice to yield a powerful argument for better working conditions and family policies for women. All created beings are given the gift of time, to be stewarded, enjoyed, and shared with justice. All should be able to rest from their labors and worship. Shaped over time in the life of the faith community, religious practice can become

---

[52] Deborah Smith Douglas, "Broken Pieces," *Commonweal* 118 (May 3, 1991): 292.

a site of resistance, alternative imagination, new knowing, and creative fidelity in the midst of social change. 🅼

Between Inculturation and Natural Law: Comparative Method in Catholic Moral Theology

David M. Lantigua and David A. Clairmont

THE HISTORY OF CATHOLIC MORAL THEOLOGY may be understood as a developing conversation between the church and wider society that can be read in one of two ways. On the one hand, we can emphasize the distinctiveness of the church, drawing forth the moral implications of the creed to highlight differences between "church" and "world." On the other hand, we can focus on the nature of life in the church community, which will not only bring us into contact with the turbulence of its history but also its noble and beautiful struggles for love and truth. Depending on which line of emphasis one selects, the terms "church" and "world" will mean something different as will the conversation between them. In the following paper, we focus on the latter way of reading this conversation, and in doing so, we attempt to bring Catholic moral theology into dialogue with the comparative study of religion. We are concerned primarily with how religion has been understood in the pastoral life of the church.[1] We focus in particular

---

[1] As a community of study in the North American academy (which we assume to be the primary readership of this journal), Catholic moral theologians work in an ecumenical environment in conversation with others interested in Christian ethics and the wider field of religious ethics, which is itself affected by scholarship in the critical, comparative study of religion and the comparative philosophy of religions. These will not be our focus here, although we will have a few comments on possible intersections between Catholic moral theology and these fields at the conclusion of our essay. While each of the authors of this essay has written for the wider audience of religious ethics, both share the conviction that deep comparative thinking across religious and cultural traditions is both possible and necessary for contemporary Catholic moral theology. While David M. Lantigua emphasizes primarily the accessibility of contemporary narratives of cross-culturally recognized moral exemplars, in conversation with historical-contextual approaches to understanding the meaning of basic moral concepts, David A. Clairmont emphasizes the trans-temporal and cross-cultural appeal of moral and intellectual struggle within religious traditions, revealed in historical studies of the relationship between a community's moral concepts and moral practices. See Darrell J. Fasching, Dell DeChant, and David M. Lantigua, *Comparative Religious Ethics: A Narrative Approach to Global Ethics*, 2nd Ed. (Oxford: Wiley-Blackwell, 2011); and David A. Clairmont, *Moral Struggle and Reli-*

upon two periods of church history—one more distant and one more recent—when the comparative study of religion was pastorally necessary for particular church communities interacting with local communities in the global South. We find that when the comparative study of religion interacted with the operative categories of moral theology during those periods, useful insights emerged for moral thinking in the tradition more broadly. Moreover, during those same periods there existed, in some instances, a spirit of theological openness and goodwill that characterized the analysis of similarities and differences among various religiously informed ways of life. We characterize this theological spirit as a play between remembering the historical witness of the tradition and creating the tradition anew from the challenges of the day and the experiences of the faithful who were pressed to meet those challenges. The theologians involved allowed time for their traditional vocabulary of moral theology to be tested, refined, and further articulated in response to the pastoral situations in which these comparisons emerged.

The remainder of our paper will proceed chronologically to treat two central themes in moral theology: first, *natural law*, and second, the *relationship between the gospel and culture*. In the first part of the paper, we examine the case of the 16th century debates among Spanish theologians and jurists about the lifestyles of Amerindian civilizations; our central theological figure will be the Dominican bishop, Bartolomé de las Casas (1484-1566). We specifically consider the place that natural law held in debates about Amerindian freedom in religious matters regarding Christian missionary activities. In the discussions between Las Casas and the other theologians of Salamanca, the status of religion as what we would now call (following Clifford Geertz) a "cultural system" was central to understanding how the natural law ought to be interpreted in light of the moral practices of Amerindian peoples. We show the place that natural law and culture played in the missionaries' debates about religious coercion and suggest that the close connection between natural law and virtue in Catholic theology was one of the reasons why it was difficult to separate moral judgments about particular religious practices from the wider cultural contexts in which those practices took place.

In the second part of the paper, we turn to more contemporary conversations currently underway among African Catholic theologians about how to articulate basic moral concepts and formulate moral judgments in a way that does justice to the African cultural milieu, while maintaining a privileged place for the gospel in the missionary efforts of the church. In recent African Catholic theology, important debates about inculturation are ongoing wherein the faith communi-

---

gious Ethics: On the Person as Classic in Comparative Theological Contexts (Oxford: Wiley-Blackwell, 2011).

ty sorts through the truth of the gospel as it is lived in the truths of indigenous cultures. Although the postcolonial African context differs markedly from the colonial Latin American missionary context, a recurring debate about the relationship between natural law and culture provides our paper with an important intra-comparative layer of moral reflection. Considering these two contexts together, we ask whether natural law is a context-independent basis for cross-cultural moral judgment or if it is instead context-dependent. Both historical contexts offer new ways to think about the relationship between the gospel, natural law, and culture, requiring theologians to envision something between natural law and culture. To help us to name this "in between" space, we focus on the ideas of moral memory and moral creativity.

Finally, we offer an argument for the centrality of comparative method for the necessary engagement of Catholic moral theology with other religious traditions based on these two examples of debates about inculturation. In short, our argument runs as follows. As a meditation on the meaning and practical implications of life in Christ, Catholic moral theology is a tradition of the development of human character and vocation—a virtue tradition. But the people whose character is being formed into Christ live between worlds, or we might say in many worlds at once.[2] This was true in limited ways in earlier epochs of the church, and is even more profoundly true of the church today. It has been tempting to see the church's engagement with the modern world through the vocabulary of the natural law. Yet as we demonstrate with our two cases, the church discovers a fuller meaning of the natural law as a methodological resource attentive to historical and cultural contexts only through the painstaking comparative work of getting to know the cultures in which the gospel is proclaimed and received. The natural law provides normative basis for a richer and more effective inculturation of the gospel because it points to the fundamental unity of humankind amidst diverse cultural expressions. It is precisely through those intercultural negotiations that the status of the natural law can become clear, as does the complex nature of virtue understood as life in Christ cultivated in a global church.

---

[2] Methodist theologian William Schweiker describes our age as one in which people live in many worlds at once, and even in between worlds. He writes, "The idea of a 'world' signals that human beings always inhabit some space of meaning and value structured by cultural and social dynamics. Currently, diverse peoples and cultures, diverse 'worlds', are merging into one global reality." See William Schweiker, *Theological Ethics and Global Dynamics: In the Time of Many Worlds* (Oxford: Wiley-Blackwell, 2004), xi.

NATURAL LAW IN THE NEW WORLD: 16ᵀᴴ CENTURY SPANISH DEBATES ABOUT RELIGIOUS COERCION AND EVANGELIZATION

The transatlantic political expansion of Iberian kingdoms in the 15th and 16th centuries provides a clear example of how conflicting views regarding the proper way to evangelize new cultures had a direct impact on the church's relationship with the non-Christian world. Christ gave his apostles the Great Commission to preach the gospel of salvation to all nations. But what should believers do if the gospel is rejected? What if believers are persecuted and attacked in missionary contexts? The answers to these questions in the first half of the 16th century brought into sharper relief two opposing viewpoints among Spanish jurists and theologians regarding the ethics of evangelization: one view that supported force and threats to convert non-Christians and another that condemned the use of force by promoting peace and persuasion as the only legitimate Christian means. As we will show, these opposing perspectives corresponded to two very different conceptions of the natural law and its role in bridging the church with the New World.

The peaceful method of persuasion, first endorsed in the New World by Spanish Dominicans who arrived at the island of Española in 1510, was practiced by fray Pedro de Córdoba and later developed in the scholarly and pastoral life of the "Protector of the Indians," Bartolomé de las Casas. Las Casas's treatise *De unico vocationis modo* (*The Only Way*), composed in the 1530s, provided the biblical, philosophical, Roman legal, patristic, canonistic and scholastic defense of what he called the apostolic method of evangelization.[3]

Although the peaceful method promoted by Las Casas and others had a strong biblical and apostolic basis, the coercive method of evangelization also belonged to the Christian tradition of the Latin West. The free consent of the will in receiving baptism and faith was an undisputed theological doctrine in the Latin West.[4] Yet the practical question of precipitating conversion for the sake of another's salvation remained a challenge for acclaimed bishops and theologians of the church, such as Saint Augustine and Gregory the Great. Their pastoral concerns for heretics and pagans had left open the possibility of using threats and fear to hasten the conversion of pagans or bring heretics back to the fold. Augustine infamously remarked in his letter to a Donatist bishop that although he initially opposed using force to bring people back to the Church of Rome, he eventually changed his mind. His view changed for several reasons. Allegedly, nothing works as effectively as fear and the threat of punishment in

---

[3] The full title of this work is *De unico vocationis modo omnium gentium ad veram religionem* ("The Only Way of Calling All Peoples to the True Religion").
[4] Augustine offered the classic axiom in his *Homilies on the Gospel of John*, 26.2: "Man cannot believe unless he is willing [*credere non potest homo nisi volens*]."

getting someone to renounce their hostile prejudices and examine the truth.[5]

Two centuries later, Pope Gregory the Great would suggest to his bishops on the island of Sardinia that obstinate pagan peasants should be burdened with heavy taxes in order to hasten their conversion.[6] Medieval canon lawyers cited these church authorities to justify the usefulness of religious coercion. As the canonists would aptly put it, "a coerced will is voluntary nonetheless."[7] Accordingly, church authorities and canonists could simultaneously support the Augustinian maxim that one cannot believe unless willingly *and* that the free will is not abolished by indirect (or conditional) coercion in the use of fear and punishment.[8] This idea would be the backbone for certain ecclesiastical policies towards Jews and Muslims in the Middle Ages. In the case of Jews, the more popular examples included the forced listening of sermons or forced public debates with Christians in the 13th century.[9]

Negotiating Christian identity alongside non-Christians not only occurred within Christendom and along its borders, but also outside Christian lands. The crusades and *Reconquistas* of the Middle Ages illustrate the migration of religious coercion into an external missionary context. The religious duty to proclaim the gospel evolved into a political institution defending the armed protection of missionaries and the punishment of sins among non-Christians outside Christendom.[10] It amounted to a policy of missionary warfare. This worldly religious vision grounded in a medieval papalist assertion of the church's fullness of power (*plenitudo potestatis*), in not only spiritual matters, but also temporal ones, provided the ideological armature for extending the boundaries of Christendom during the early modern period.[11] The pope was conceived as nothing less than the

---

[5] Saint Augustine, *Letters*, 5 vols., trans. Sister Wilfrid Parsons (New York: Fathers of the Church, 2008), 2:72-4 (letter 93 to Vincentius).

[6] Pope Gregory the Great, Book IV, Letter 26. Cf. Book XII, Letter 65, trans. James Barmby, in *Nicene and Post-Nicene Fathers of the Christian Church, Second Series*, vol. 12, ed. Philip Schaff and Henry Wace (New York: Christian Literature, 1895).

[7] Mario Condorelli, *I fondamenti giuridici della tolleranza religiosa nell'elaborazione canonistica dei secoli XII-XIV* (Milan: Dott. A. Giuffre, 1960), 100.

[8] Condorelli, *I fondamenti giuridici della tolleranza religiosa*, 94-5.

[9] *Church, State, and Jew in the Middle Ages*, ed. Robert Chazan (West Orange: Behrman House, 1980).

[10] The *opinio communis* among canon lawyers defending this position was presented by Pope Innocent IV's commentary on a crusade letter of Innocent III known as *Quod super hiis* found in his *Apparatus super quinque libros Decretalium*, X.3.34.8. James Muldoon has provided an unparalleled history of the political implications of this papal missionary teaching in the Iberian expansion of the 15th and 16th centuries. *Popes, Lawyers, and Infidels: The Church and the Non-Christian World, 1250-1550* (Philadelphia: University of Pennsylvania, 1979).

[11] Jonathan Boyarin, in *The Unconverted Self: Jews, Indians, and the Identity of Christian Europe* (Chicago: University of Chicago, 2009), recently captured this point in

lord of the whole world (*dominus totius orbis*), and consequently, the Church of Rome possessed an unprecedented claim to universal jurisdiction. The principal justification for this worldwide authority over peoples outside the church resided in the natural lordship of Christ over creation. Intervention in the matters of non-Christians, even religious practices, could therefore be justified on the basis of guarding the natural law when respective authorities failed to do so.[12]

Spanish Conquest and the Secularization of Natural Law

In the context of the 16th century Spanish debates about conquest and evangelization, this medieval, papal monarchical view of natural law emerged with strong theological and juridical support. But whereas the medieval popes possessed a singular authority over the natural law, the early modern Iberian context presented a novel political situation in which the crown could exercise such a spiritual function. This was due to the right of royal patronage (*Patronato Real*). The tradition of royal patronage began in the Middle Ages when the church conferred privileges and rights to temporal rulers defending and propagating the faith through holy war. Beginning with the *Reconquista* Bull of Granada in 1486, however, the Spanish Crown of Ferdinand and Isabel gradually extended this right of patronage into newly conquered lands. In 1508, Pope Julius II's Bull *Universalis ecclesiae regimini* conceded to the Spanish Crown a perpetual right to establish churches and oversight in the appointment of bishops.[13] Historian John H. Elliott has described the political climate of 16th century Spain under royal patronage:

> In the New World... the Crown was absolute master, and exercised virtually papal authority of its own. No cleric would go to the Indies without royal permission; there was no papal legate in the New World, and no direct contact between Rome and the clergy in Mexico or Peru; the Crown exercised a right of veto over the promulga-

---

his provocative account of the relationship between medieval Christian views of Jews and Muslims and the Spanish treatment of Indians in the New World. He writes: "Innocent IV's articulation of the extension of the papal vicariate to every human being was a key moment in the ideological prehistory of early modern European imperialism" (46).

[12] Innocent IV, *Apparatus* X.3.34.8, no. 4. The key passage states: "By this power that the pope has, I believe that if a pagan who has no law except the law of nature acts contrary to natural law, the pope is able to punish him lawfully. Consider Genesis 19, where you see that the Sodomites who sinned against the law of nature were punished by God. Now since the judgments of God provide an example for us, I do not see why the pope, who is the vicar of Christ, cannot do this as well.... And I say the same goes if they worship idols. For it is natural to worship the one and only God, the creator, and not creatures." (Translated by David M. Lantigua.)

[13] W. Eugene Shiels, *King and Church: The Rise and Fall of the Patronato Real* (Chicago: Loyola University, 1961).

tion of papal bulls, and constantly intervened, through its viceroys and officials, in all the minutiae of ecclesiastical life.[14]

The system of royal patronage facilitated a move toward the secularization of natural law. This was already evident by the fact that Pope Alexander VI's papal bulls of donation in 1493, granting Spain the right to convert the natives across the Atlantic, came after Christopher Columbus's first voyage. Alexander VI endorsed the expansion of Spanish Catholicism in the New World *post facto*. The authority to enforce the natural law by punishing violations of it, most notably the sin of idolatry, now belonged entirely to the secular power of imperial Spain under the royal patronage system.[15] This shift in church-state relations was concurrent with the major renewal of thought in Renaissance culture. Retrieval of classical pagan ideas within the Spanish imperial context strengthened the secularization of the natural law whereby the content of revelation served merely as an addendum confirming what could already be known fully through natural reason. No thinker represented this outlook more clearly than the principal opponent of Las Casas at the Valladolid *junta* (council) from 1550 to 1551: the imperial-humanist Juan Ginés de Sepúlveda.[16]

Both a royal chronicler and official translator of Aristotle's works, Sepúlveda defended the Spanish imperial mission with classical Greek arguments justifying a natural hierarchy among cultures. He would write in *On Kingship and the Duty of the King*, which he dedicated to King Philip II in 1571:

> Among all nations there exists great difference: some are more civilized and wise whereas others by their lives and customs depart from reason and the natural law, and are considered barbaric and uncivilized. The condition of the latter is such that on account of their barbarity they should obey the rule of those more civilized and cultured according to natural right so that they may be governed by better

---

[14] John H. Elliott, *Imperial Spain, 1469-1716* (New York: Penguin, 1963), 102.
[15] The legal document known as the Requirement codified in 1513 by the canon lawyer Juan López de Palacios Rubios is perhaps the most notorious expression of Spanish imperial assertions in the New World wrought by the right of royal patronage. This document was read before Amerindians without knowledge of Spanish in the conquests of Mexico, Panama, and Peru. According to Latin Americanist Rolena Adorno, the document stipulated that "the pope, surrogate for God on earth, gave the Indies, possessed by idolaters, to the Castilian king, who likewise could rightfully demand (*requerir*) that the Indians, as idolaters, relinquish their lands to the Christian monarch to whom the pope had assigned it. If the Indians failed to give up the land, the king could take it by force, killing and capturing and granting as slaves those who were prisoners." *The Polemics of Possession in Spanish American Narrative* (New Haven: Yale University, 2007), 265-6.
[16] For a comprehensive overview of this most significant debate at Valladolid, see Lewis Hanke's *All Mankind is One* (DeKalb: Northern Illinois University, 1974).

> laws and institutions. If they refuse to submit to this superior rule that is just and beneficent for them, they can be forced by natural right.[17]

This representative summary of Sepúlveda's view highlights that the natural law provides a permanent benchmark for assessing the irrationality of other cultures and justifying the political superiority of civilized peoples.

In an earlier work, Sepúlveda asserts that what constitutes the natural law in the most basic sense is a timeless list of moral precepts that command or prohibit certain actions, as contained in the eternal Decalogue.[18] The natural law is a divine code emanating directly from the eternal law by which the laws and customs of every society can be judged. The secular humanist move of Sepúlveda is especially evident when he identifies Aristotle, rather than the pope, as "the most excellent interpreter and judge" of natural law.[19] Faith and the gospel do not factor into this secular account of the natural law except as a mere confirmation of reason's judgments. Jesus taught his disciples that it was necessary for them to keep the commandments; for Sepúlveda, this meant that the active secular life devoted to safeguarding the moral law through martial virtues merited eternal life.[20]

Sepúlveda's secularization of the natural law anticipates 17th century Protestant views of Hugo Grotius and John Locke as well as later Enlightenment versions. In the Spanish imperial context, violations of the natural law authorized the crown to punish sins such as idolatry and human sacrifice. Sepúlveda justified the political subjugation of "lesser" peoples to the superiority of Spanish religion and culture on the basis of this natural law argument. With ancient Rome as the model, he concluded that Spain exercised the "supreme right" to rule over Amerindians just as "children are subject to adults, women are to men, or the cruel and vicious are to the continent and temperate."[21] All may be considered human, but not all are rational, civilized or fit to rule. Sepúlveda thus provided a compelling argument to 16th century Spaniards for a natural right to conquer non-Christians with reason rather than revelation as its sole justification. It is reason, after

---

[17] *Del Reino y Los Deberes del Rey*, in *Tratados Politicos de Juan Ginés de Sepúlveda*, trans. Angel Losada (Madrid: Instituto de Estudios Politicos, 1963), 34-5. (Translations from Spanish by Lantigua.)
[18] "Democrates Primero" (*Democrates primus*), in *Tratados Politicos de Juan Ginés de Sepúlveda*, trans. Angel Losada (Madrid: Instituto de Estudios Politicos, 1963).
[19] "Democrates Primero," 199.
[20] "Democrates Primero," 160-1.
[21] *Demócrates segundo, o, De las justas causas de la guerra contra los indios* (Democrates secundus), trans. Angel Losada, (Madrid: Consejo Superior de Investigaciones Científicas, 1984), 33.

all, that compels persons to worship only one God, as the pagan philosophers Plato and Aristotle presumably did.

Religious coercion is at the center of Sepúlveda's defense of the Spanish right of conquest. It provided the instrumentalist rationale that underlies conquest. Sepúlveda claimed: "The barbarians can be reduced to our sovereignty with the same right [*eodem iure*] by which they can be forced to hear the Gospel."[22] Conquest and threat of war, then, served the purpose of making conversion easier for conquered subjects and disciplining them in the moral life.[23] Due to a hierarchy of natural rights established by virtue and cultural superiority, punishment and war are intrinsic to enforcing the natural law in social relations. Conflict is necessary in the attempt to bridge superior Christian culture to depraved, idolatrous ones through the natural law.

Peaceful Evangelization and the Natural Rights of Amerindians

In contrast to Sepúlveda, Las Casas's account of natural law began with an entirely different philosophical premise and would serve a radically different spiritual aim. The main thesis of *The Only Way* was that the attraction of people to God and knowledge of the truth must be accomplished through rational persuasion and enticement of the will. Las Casas appealed to Aristotelian-Thomistic teleology and Ciceronian rhetorical norms to make his argument that nature is inclined to do what is good by gentle means. The best way to induce listeners to seek the good is to persuade them using the force of truth, not coercion by fear of punishment or threats of war and weapons. His conclusion was this: "If violence (or compulsion) is employed so that others may listen, it becomes more evil and makes the objective vain. This method is entirely contrary to the other one that is gentle and natural."[24] The preacher follows the basic norms of the orator or teacher. Grace and revelation build upon the order of natural reason. What holds the continuity between nature and grace, then, is not force and coercion. Rather, it is the opposite: freedom. Every stage of the act of faith, just like the act of knowing, requires freedom of the will. Imposing force on another in the apprehension of truth creates an obstacle to truth that can only lead to anger and sadness for the coerced party.

Immediately following the first draft of *The Only Way*, Las Casas put the nonviolent principles of evangelization into practice on his

---

[22] *Demócrates segundo*, 65.
[23] This was, after all, the principal point of contention of the Valladolid debate between Las Casas and Sepúlveda.
[24] *De unico modo* in *Obras Completas*, eds. Paulino Castañeda Delgado and Antonio García de Moral, vol. 1 (Madrid: Alianza Editorial, 1988-90), 5, no. 4.

mission to Guatemala.²⁵ Accompanied by several other Dominican friars, Las Casas entered a region known as *Tierra de Guerra* ("Land of War"), so-called by Spaniards because of the allegedly hostile inhabitants. The Dominican missionaries were able to make peaceful contact with these Amerindians, however, primarily through music, singing, and the liturgy. The local *cacique* (chieftain) was impressed and encouraged to learn that the Dominicans brought a religious message that fundamentally respected Amerindian freedom from the Spanish institution of forced labor, or the encomienda. The region would later be called Verapaz ("True Peace"), as it is still known today.

The roots of the *encomienda* go back to the Middle Ages when military orders were given land and its profits in exchange for protection.²⁶ In the New World, conquistadors like Hernán Cortés and Francisco Pizarro understood themselves as valiant soldiers for Christ entitled to receive tributes from natives in the lands they conquered. From the very beginning of its use in Española, the *encomienda* presented a problem for the Spanish Crown in that it introduced a hereditary caste with complete control over a powerful economic institution. It represented a kind of transatlantic fiefdom that threatened Queen Isabel's dream of making the Indians her "free vassals." Nevertheless, the *encomienda* was incredibly difficult to overcome in the Spanish American context. The *encomienda* had the advantage of consolidating spiritual, humanitarian, and commercial interests into a single institution that brought Spanish Christians into close proximity with unbelievers. The *encomenderos* were responsible for "civilizing" the natives by training them in good customs and virtue, especially in religious matters.

When the first Dominicans arrived to Santo Domingo in 1510, the Taíno labor population was oppressed and diminished. After a year spent in prayer and fasting, the Dominicans unanimously agreed to address the injustice by boldly proposing during an Advent sermon in 1511, "By what right and with what justice do you so violently enslave these Indians? Are they not human beings? Do they not have rational souls? Are you not obligated to love them as you love yourselves?"²⁷ This reflexive Christian message was accompa-

---

²⁵ Helen Rand Parish, "Introduction," in *Bartolomé de las Casas: The Only Way*, ed. Helen Rand Parish (Mahwah, NJ: Paulist, 1992).
²⁶ Mario Góngora, *Studies in the Colonial History of Spanish America*, trans. Richard Southern (New York: Cambridge University, 1975), 132.
²⁷ The only historical record of this sermon comes from Las Casas's *Historia de las Indias*, ed. Agustín Millares Carlo (México: Fondo de Cultura Economica, 1986), III, c. 4. For two excellent historical accounts of this momentous event with an English translation of the entire sermon in the broader context of the Spanish conquests see Lewis Hanke's classic, *The Spanish Struggle for Justice in the Conquest of America* (Dallas: Southern Methodist University, 2002), and Lawrence Clayton's more recent

nied by a spiritual discipline that rebuked slave holders as mortal sinners who would be denied absolution in the sacrament of penance until they freed their laborers. Las Casas was himself among the *encomendero* class at this time but would experience a conversion in 1514 after reading Scripture in light of his experience and the uncompromising message of the Dominicans.[28] He would dedicate the rest of his life to defending the Amerindians and preaching the message of salvation.

The first Dominicans combined the gospel method of peaceful evangelization with a Spanish legal and scholastic doctrine affirming the natural rights of all persons made equally in the image of God. The Dominican theologians back in Salamanca, Spain, such as Francisco de Vitoria and Domingo de Soto, would expand upon this inculturated faith by formulating some of the earliest defenses of human rights in the West.[29] Las Casas would be among these Dominican defenders of human rights.[30] As the Dominicans saw it, the greatest obstacle to Amerindian conversion were Christians themselves, who not only failed to live in accordance with the gospel but, worse yet, turned it into a violent weapon serving as a pretext for profit and gold.

According to these Dominicans, the principal end and only justification for Spanish presence in the New World was for the salvation of souls.[31] This evangelical commitment defined the spiritual arc of Las Casas's arguments against colonial policies from the beginning of his conversion to the end of his life. It provided the rationale for his critique of the *encomienda*, which he would condemn as an "intrinsi-

---

Bartolomé de las Casas and the Conquest of the Americas (Oxford: Wiley-Blackwell, 2011).

[28] The life-altering passage came from Sirach 34: "Ill-gotten goods offered in sacrifice are blemished. Gifts from the lawless do not win God's favor. The Most High approves not the gifts of the godless, nor for their many sacrifices does he forgive their sins. Like the man who slays a son in his father's presence is he who offers sacrifice from the possessions of the poor. The bread of charity is life itself for the needy; he who withholds it is a man of blood. To take away another's living is to commit murder; to deny a laborer wages is to shed blood." This event was recorded in Las Casas's *Historia de las Indias*, III, c. 79, 92.

[29] The earliest Salmantine treatment of the Amerindian question in public was the *Relectio de Dominio* of Domingo de Soto given at the University of Salamanca in 1535. The better known and translated *Relectio de Indis* of Francisco de Vitoria was given in 1539. Both of these works present an account of natural rights founded on the *imago Dei* doctrine.

[30] Paolo Carozza, "From Conquest to Constitutions: Retrieving a Latin American Tradition of the Idea of Human Rights," *Human Rights Quarterly* 25, no. 2 (2003).

[31] Gustavo Gutiérrez, *En busca de los pobres de Jesucristo: El pensamiento de Bartolomé de las Casas* (Lima: Instituto Bartolomé de Las Casas, 1992), 33.

cally evil" institution.³² Las Casas's argument was quite simple: If the spiritual aim of the *encomienda* was to convert the Indians, then any means disproportionate to the end of faith, which must be received freely through grace, was prohibited as an act of forcible conversion. However, Las Casas and his supporters had to contend with the strong medieval argument for missionary warfare that could justify coercion, in a purportedly "indirect" way, through the use of threats and fear. Undermining this tradition and proposing the peaceful method of evangelization in conformity with natural reason was the lasting significance of *The Only Way*.

The Only Way defended the peaceful method of evangelization modeled on the virtues of Christ and the apostles with a robust account of freedom and natural rights for the Amerindians. All human beings, believer and unbeliever alike, are united together into a single human family by a right of kinship (*ius cognationis*). This kinship, established by God's providential order, has arranged a fundamental equality among all peoples. Peace, rather than conflict, is the norm for social relations between different cultures; this is both natural and in conformity with Scripture as shown by the Lord's precept: "Love one another as I have loved you" (John 13:34). The missionary wars that the Spaniards were waging against the Amerindians shattered this right and violated all other natural rights.³³ These fundamental natural rights include the right to property and self-rule, and freedom not only in political matters but a spiritual freedom described as "time over life."³⁴ The latter is deemed necessary for receiving faith and baptism at one's own pace.

Natural Law and Comparative Idolatry

The natural unity of human beings proposed in *The Only Way* remained a consistent teaching of Las Casas's writings as he explored Amerindian cultures and religious customs more closely. Painfully aware of the great injustices and harms to the Amerindians perpetrated by Spaniards in the name of God, Las Casas exercised a profound level of humility and compassion in trying to understand indigenous practices and beliefs, especially in religious matters. His *Apologética historia sumaria* composed during the last decade of his life was the quintessential expression of this unflinching commitment to the fundamental unity of all peoples—a unity he explicitly grounded in the *imago Dei* doctrine.³⁵ Las Casas writes:

---

³² *Carta al Maestro Fray Bartolomé Carranza de Miranda* (1555): "The *encomienda* is intrinsically evil and can never be justified in any manner or under any circumstance" (*Obras completas*, vol. 13, 290).
³³ *De unico modo* 7, no. 2.
³⁴ *De unico modo* 7, no. 2.
³⁵ The clear influence of the Salmantine theologians on Las Casas's thought with regard to the *imago Dei* teaching is unmistakable. His writings begin to incorporate

> Man, who was created in the image and likeness of God... at the moment of creation was given a natural light of knowledge and understanding, albeit in a confused manner, and an appetite or natural inclination to know there is a God and creator and that he should seek to serve and worship as God and Lord as the principle of being for all creation. That is because all creatures have a natural inclination and desire to unite, as to their end, with the cause of their existence.[36]

According to Las Casas, the natural law is expressed principally through a rational creature's natural knowledge and love of God, however confused. This is the touchstone for all natural rights.

From this theological standpoint, the religious practices of Amerindian cultures could be approached with a respect and sensitivity toward the genuine desire for religious truth informing their way of life. The unity of humankind established by the natural law and the *imago Dei* supplied the principles for the comparative methodology of the *Apologética*. One scholar has rightly noted that this unity permitted Las Casas to dismiss absolute hierarchies among different nations.[37] His three-volume engagement with diverse Amerindian practices alongside classical Greek and Roman religion produced a work that deserves to be considered a *City of God* for the New World. Like Augustine, Las Casas's comparative idolatry was not from a descriptively "neutral" standpoint; it was from a theological one focused on the evangelization of cultures.

The underlying aim of the *Apologética* was to demonstrate the rationality and virtues of Amerindian peoples against their Iberian cultured despisers like Sepúlveda or chroniclers such as Gonzalo Fernández de Oviedo and Francisco López de Gómara. The greatest challenge here was Amerindian religion, which included idolatrous practices and the shockingly violent custom of self-immolation. Las Casas's comparative methodology was primarily informed by a sophisticated appropriation of Thomas Aquinas' theological account of the natural law. With the natural law as a methodological starting point, Las Casas concluded that outside of revelation and grace, the expression of the natural law in religious matters within diverse communities shaped by political prudence takes different forms. Following Aquinas, he identified sacrifice as a dictate of natural reason but recognized that the specific offerings made by non-Christians is

---

the *imago Dei* doctrine as a basis for Amerindian natural rights following his 1552 treatises published in Seville. This would have come after his direct contact with Domingo de Soto during the Valladolid debates.

[36] *Apologética historia sumaria* in *Obras Completas*, vol. 7, II, c. 71, 634.

[37] José Alejandro Cardenas Bunsen, *Escritura y Derecho Canonico en la obra de fray Bartolomé de las Casas* (Madrid: Iberoamericana, 2011), 248.

something determined by human law and customs.[38] Furthermore, these non-Christian religious customs have the purpose of forming citizens in morals and directing them to the common good.[39]

Therefore, religion belongs to a natural order whereby individuals and communities attempt to sacrifice what is best with the aim of advancing the commonweal. Outside of revelation, and because of sin, the political expression of religion will inevitably terminate in some kind of communal devotion to the state as the natural expression of the highest good. But this need not be considered something fundamentally debased. Drawing upon classical sources and the wide array of examples in Amerindian cultures, Las Casas observed that practical reason and justice within a political context orders social life to an end that is greater than the individual. A natural love for the good of the whole is expressed in the desire for permanence or constancy achieved by identification with the life of a city or an everlasting reign.[40] The state and its political order are considered expressions of natural authority, so for the individual to desire the good of the whole community above himself is reasonably just and religious, even for a believer. The Christian difference, however, is that devotion to the city of God remains the final end, since that is the only commonwealth under God that will last forever.

The Amerindian civilization of Peru provided an exemplary pagan case, however, as one scholar has noted: "The gods, particularly the Incan ancestral Sun, ordered everything and were worshipped with unfailing devotion. This devotion, the temples, rituals and sacrifices which made it palpable, were the quintessential expression of Inca statecraft for which Las Casas expressed nothing but admiration."[41] Communal devotion in Peru could therefore be seen as a natural desire to preserve and perpetuate the Inca state as an everlasting reign. This natural law perspective offered a radically different standpoint for engaging the Amerindian practice of human sacrifice. Although this deeply misunderstood aspect of Las Casas's thought has been explored in greater detail elsewhere, we wish to conclude this section by focusing briefly on his comparison of Roman idolatry with Amerindian idolatry.[42]

---

[38] *Summa theologiae*, II-II, q. 81, a. 2, *ad.* 3 and q. 85, a. 1 *ad.* 1; Aristotle, *Nicomachean Ethics* V. 7.
[39] *Summa theologiae*, I-II, q. 99, a. 3.
[40] *Apologética historia sumaria* in *Obras Completas*, vol. 6, I, c. 40. Cf. Thomas Aquinas, *Summa contra gentiles* II, c. 79.
[41] Sabine MacCormack†, "Gods, Demons, and Idols in the Andes," *Journal of the History of Ideas* 67, no. 4 (2006): 634.
[42] Gutiérrez, ch. 6. See also David M. Lantigua, "Idolatry, War, and the Rights of Infidels: The Christian Legal Theory of Religious Toleration in the New World" (Ph.D. diss., University of Notre Dame, 2012), ch. 8.

Like Augustine, Las Casas did not avoid making normative judgments in his comparative assessments of other cultures as well as his own. The main difference with Augustine, however, was that the Christian civilization among the Spaniards was now under theological scrutiny. Furthermore, Las Casas engaged the practice of idolatry on a political level with a robust theological doctrine of the *imago Dei* and natural rights that resisted turning pagan religion into a cause for war. In order to draw normative comparisons, Las Casas turned his attention to the objects of worship among the various nations to examine the relationship between devotion and justice. In Augustinian fashion, Las Casas observes that an evil object of worship can produce such vicious behavior that it makes one's debased desires seem natural. The Dionysian cults of the Hellenistic world made "public and shameless what is secret and shameful."[43] They lacked a taste for modesty and a genuine sense of reverence for the divine. For the Romans, the supreme devotion to Mars, the god of war, had the effect of strengthening and cultivating "the natural inclination that they recognized in themselves to overrun and harass the world with wars and battles."[44] Roman imperial religion worshiping glory and war were therefore comparable to the Spanish wars of religion in pursuit of gold. The temple treasures seized from the Incas following Pizarro's conquest in the 1530s is one of numerous examples of Spanish pillaging in the New World. A society becomes what it worships. Spain was no different than ancient Rome in this regard.

Las Casas wholeheartedly condemned the worship of the gods and its demonic influences as seen in acts of human sacrifice.[45] Still, his comparative method yielded judgments that enabled him to distinguish forms of idolatry aimed at the promotion of the commonweal from vicious forms of idolatry concerned with vain and narcissistic pursuits. Outside of revelation and grace, idolatry is not something self-evidently wrong, especially in hierarchically complex pagan societies that enshrine the perpetuation of the state. But whereas the Romans were sorely lacking in humility and made war the most glorious altar, the diverse Amerindian communities generally took better care of their sacrifices and rituals by engaging in profound acts of public penance, prayer, fasting, and reverence.[46] According to Las Casas, it is precisely these noble virtues that provide the natural bedrock for grace and the evangelization of culture.

---

[43] *Apologética historia sumaria* II, c. 78.
[44] *Apologética historia sumaria* II, c. 148.
[45] Sabine MacCormack†, *Religion in the Andes* (Princeton: Princeton University, 1991), ch. 5.
[46] See David A. Lupher, *Romans in a New World: Classical Models in Sixteenth-Century Spanish America* (Ann Arbor: The University of Michigan, 2006), 255-70.

The remarkable conclusion of the *Apologética* was that Amerindian societies, on the whole, not only demonstrated practical reason by fulfilling Aristotle's criteria in the *Politics*, but even exceeded the Greeks and Romans "beyond comparison in their supreme use of rational judgment."[47] Las Casas had the theological vision to imagine the Amerindian context as an even greater opportunity for inculturation than that of Hellenistic civilization in the early church. The blueprint for inculturation was stated clearly in his *History of the Indies* when he wrote, "Our Christian religion is one and adapts itself to all nations of the world and by all it equally receives. It neither takes their freedom nor their political authority."[48] The Christian faith is undoubtedly enriched by inculturation, but that is only possible if all peoples are deemed equal in their humanity and freedom to accept or refuse the gospel.

Through the respect that Las Casas showed to Amerindian religious life, we have a profound historical example of comparative theological engagement that emerged from the pastoral life of the church. His concern for understanding religious difference emerged neither from political expediency nor from intellectual curiosity. Rather his comparative thinking was prompted by the recognition of the humanity of those he served and the realization that the gospel's encounter with new cultures would, in time, correct certain excesses in those cultures while also respecting those cultures as gifts that prepared their peoples for evangelization, enriching the Christian faith and calling those that preached it to more consistently witness its message.

NATURAL LAW AND INCULTURATION: RECENT DEBATES IN AFRICAN CATHOLIC THEOLOGY

In our time, elements of Las Casas's insight persist in church teaching on religion and culture; but these elements have not been examined sufficiently to determine their impact on Catholic moral theology. Inculturation, as the term is used today, describes a process of inter-cultural negotiation from within a community of belief, pressing those who embrace the gospel to undertake a careful and serious discernment of their own culture's values and practices while at the same time calling Christians to uphold, as John Paul II has said, the "wealth of cultural values and priceless human qualities which [each culture] can offer to the Churches and to humanity as a whole."[49] What marks inculturation as a process distinct from the related notions of "enculturation" (which aims at early socialization into a culture) and "acculturation" (which aims at changing the cul-

---

[47] *Apologética historia sumaria* III, c. 193. See also II, c. 46.
[48] *Historia de las Indias* III, c. 149.
[49] Pope John Paul II, *Ecclesia in Africa* (September 14, 1995), no. 42.

ture one encounters to make it more like the culture one brings), is its focus on the *process of discerning authentic values* within a culture when one finds in one's cultural heritage simultaneously two sources of valuation, both equally "comprehensive, incapable of abandonment, and of central importance."[50] Inculturation emphasizes that when the gospel encounters and transforms culture, its wisdom is revealed in a new way that could not have been seen prior the cultural encounter. The new culture is like a new light cast on the gospel to reveal deeper levels of meaning that have not previously been seen by the church.

Las Casas noted the ancient roots of inculturation in the church's critical assessment of Greek and Roman modes of worship while integrating those cultures' basic categories of thought. Inculturation remains an important topic in Catholic theological discourse today, although it gained particular prominence in Catholic liturgical studies in the years leading up to and immediately following the Second Vatican Council.[51] While the language of "inculturation" was not used in the Conciliar documents, as Aylward Shorter notes, it was used prior to and immediately following the Council.[52] Its deploy-

---

[50] Paul J. Griffiths, *Problems of Religious Diversity* (Oxford: Blackwell, 2001), 7.

[51] Topics bearing on inculturation, if not the specific theme, received significant attention at the Council in part because of its importance in formulating the instruction on the liturgy. In *Sacrosanctum Concilium* (1963), "restoration of the liturgy" was said to involve careful attention to "unchangeable elements divinely instituted" on the one hand, and to those "elements subject to change" (no. 21) on the other. The Council sought a delicate balance between "the true and authentic spirit" of the liturgy and "the temperament and traditions of peoples" which would "respect and foster the qualities and talents of the various races and nations" (no. 37). Such respect extended not only to the use of prayers and readings in the vernacular, but also to sacred music and art, signals that in the Council's view inculturation moves well beyond matters of text and translation (nos. 112-30).

[52] Shorter attributes the first use in published theological exchange to Joseph Masson, S.J. (in a 1962 article in *Nouvelle Revue Théologique*, "L'Église ouverte sur le monde"), but Shorter notes that more frequent use of the term "inculturation" and "inculturated Church" would not come until the first meeting of the Federation of Asian Episcopal Conferences in 1974, the 1974-5 Congregation of the Society of Jesus, and Jesuit Superior General Pedro Arrupe's 1978 "Letter to the Whole Society on Inculturation." See Aylward Shorter, *Toward a Theology of Inculturation* (Eugene: Wipf & Stock, 1999), 10. The Council did consider how the gospel and culture relate in the various local churches around the world. For example, *Ad Gentes* (1965) explained that, in places where the church has not enjoyed a longstanding presence, it would be important for missionaries to encourage that "the young church keep up an intimate communion with the whole Church, whose tradition they should link to their own culture, in order to increase, by a certain mutual exchange of forces, the life of the Mystical Body" (no. 19). An important theme was signaled here, also prominent in later reflection on inculturation, that the exchange between the gospel and culture would develop existing cultural elements in a "mutual exchange," prompted by a love for the gospel which would in turn occasion a loving appreciation and engagement with local cultures.

ment in later documents balanced a concern for the holistic aspects of culture with an acknowledgement that cultures are always changing and evolving, constructed by and constructing the persons inhabiting them.[53] While we cannot examine church teaching on inculturation in any detail here, it is important to note that significant analogies between inculturation and interreligious dialogue, such as those highlighted by Las Casas, have been recognized in official church documents since the Council and have continued to gain prominence in official church discourse as the primary theological means of engaging with culture.[54]

Over the last several years, inculturation has come to hold an increasingly prominent place in international Catholic moral theology and has strongly informed the first two international meetings of Catholic moral theologians, in Padua in 2006 and in Trent in 2010,[55] which examined the challenges of moral theology done in cultural contexts characterized by religious plurality. Yet these events and the publications that followed have not yet offered a compelling account

---

[53] For example, Pope John Paul II, commenting on the Synod of African Bishops in 1995, noted, "Inculturation includes two dimensions: on the one hand, 'the intimate transformation of authentic cultural values through their integration in Christianity' and, on the other, 'the insertion of Christianity in the various human cultures'." Pope John Paul II, *Ecclesia in Africa* (September 14, 1995), no. 59. In a similar way, the Lineamenta for the *Synod of Bishops for the Special Assembly for Asia* (1996) characterizes inculturation and dialogue as two central aspects of the mission of the Church. In an exegesis of John 1:14, the document explains how inculturation exemplifies the gospel teaching that "the Word became flesh and dwelt among us" (nos. 17-18).

[54] Carl F. Starkloff, S.J. has noted the connection between inculturation and interreligious dialogue in his essay, "Inculturation and Cultural Systems (Part 1)," *Theological Studies* 55 (1994): 66-81, and "Inculturation and Cultural Systems (Part 2)," *Theological Studies* 55 (1994): 274-94. Starkloff notes that one of the reasons that theologies of inculturation and interreligious dialogue have not been pursued together is due largely to an unquestioned assumption by early contributors to theology of religions (especially, he notes, Panikkar and Küng) that it was not possible to find a productive way to talk about inculturation apart from a unidirectional movement toward proselytization (67). Starkloff suggests that it would be the study of African traditional religions, considered from both an inculturation and a comparative religion and culture perspective, that would be the most likely to challenge theology of religions to take inculturation more seriously. We see an earlier positive model for this work in the theology of Las Casas.

[55] For proceedings of the conferences, see www.catholicethics.com. Two volumes of papers were published from the first conference. See James F. Keenan, S.J., ed. *Catholic Theological Ethics in the World Church: The Plenary Papers from the First Cross-cultural Conference in Catholic Theological Ethics* (New York: Continuum, 2007) and Linda Hogan, ed. *Applied Ethics in a World Church: The Padua Conference* (Maryknoll: Orbis, 2008). Some of the practical issues discussed at the conference were treated in an earlier collection of essays: James F. Keenan, ed. *Catholic Ethicists on HIV/AIDS Prevention* (New York: Continuum, 2000). See also, Paulinus Odozor, "Classical Catholic Moral Theology and the World Church: Some Suggestions on How to Move Forward," *Louvain Studies* 30 (2005): 276-298.

of how inculturation is related to the comparative theological study of religion. In this section, we would like to offer an initial formulation of this problem by tracing certain similarities and differences between our account of Las Casas and some of the arguments advanced recently for a fully inculturated moral theology. Although there are many places where one could begin, we examine the particularly rich discussions among African theologians because the themes of community discernment, freedom and respect for traditional religion, and natural law have been prominent, although in different ways.[56]

Over the past fifty years, the varieties of African Christian theology have developed, as Justin Ukpong has argued, in reference to three central concerns in the African Christian churches: the coherence within diversity of African cultures, the meaning of color and the question of race in society, and the challenges of poverty to meaningful accounts of liberation.[57] In Catholic theological circles, these three topics have come to more particular expression in debates about the meaning of inculturation and the extent to which the first of these three topics (cultural coherence and diversity) ought to mediate judgments about how to pursue racial justice and combat the reality of poverty. While we cannot fully honor the complexity of these discussions in our short essay, we can nonetheless discern two main paths for examining how inculturation relates to moral theology thereby illustrating continuities with the concerns exhibited by Las Casas in his context.[58]

The first path, which we might label the path of *memory*, considers inculturation as a necessary movement to meet the pastoral needs of the church in its attempts to address the great moral issues of our time in their culturally distinct expressions. The dialogue between the gospel and culture has the capacity to seek out, recover, and apply regions of untapped wisdom in the Catholic tradition so that the church will find new ways to speak to the problems of the day. For thinkers along this path, inculturation illustrates how the church remembers its own history, where encounters of the gospel with cul-

---

[56] On the place of the religious imagination formed by African Traditional Religions and Christian faith, and the effects of this unity on the renewal of Christian faith, see Kwame Bediako, *Christianity in Africa: The Renewal of a Non-Western Religion* (Maryknoll: Orbis, 1995), 91-108.
[57] Justin K. Ukpong, "The Emergence of African Theologies," *Theological Studies* 45 (1984): 501-36.
[58] The literature on African theology is wide and complex, and no account of inculturation theology in Africa is complete without it. For an historical review focusing on the relationship between Christian theology and African Traditional Religions, see Kwame Bediako, "The Roots of African Theology," *International Bulletin of Missionary Research* 13, no. 2 (1989): 58-65. For a review of these theologies' implications for moral theology, see William R. O'Neil, S.J., "African Moral Theology," *Theological Studies* 62 (2001): 122-139.

ture in new places today call the church back to analogous encounters in earlier times. Each distinct region of the church, in each phase of its history, draws from the wellspring of Christian wisdom in its own way. Inculturation theologians on this path share with official teaching of the Catholic Church the understanding that the gospel is never fully proclaimed until it undertakes a journey into every culture. They further recognize that the church itself stands to learn much about how to live as a community of faith when these different wisdoms of inculturation are brought back to nourish the life of the wider church. The comparative impulse, in other words, is expressed as an exercise in the wide memory of tradition meant to serve the needs of an equally wide family of belief. Moreover, this theological path most closely mirrors the bishops' understanding of their own theological role—as the custodians of the church's memory of its way of life.[59]

The second path might be labeled the *creation* path. Here, inculturation has a more constructive role to play as the church reformulates and develops its teaching through simultaneous consideration of its existing moral priorities and new challenges that each culture poses to the universal wisdom of the gospel. Along this path, the dialogue between the gospel and culture articulates new and legitimate forms of Christian wisdom drawn from recent experience. Although similar to the memory path in its recollection of the church's history, theologians who emphasize the more creative path insist that the church's ancient wisdom does not speak fully to the questions and needs of the world church today. Like many Catholic comparative theologians who are involved in interreligious conversation, these inculturation theologians see the comparative impulse as theologically central. The wisdom of local cultures, especially their religious heritage, must be taken seriously in addressing the complex moral problems of the day. Let us now examine some examples from each path, keeping in mind how the comparative impulse is expressed differently within each one and how they suggest similarities and differences with Las Casas's theology of law and culture.

Moral theologians interested in inculturation who work along the memory path have tended to focus on axiological concerns, asking what constitutes a true "Gospel value" and how these values relate to other values arising in culture. The moral priorities of any culture, including the operative cultures of official church teaching and of each local church at any time, reflect its basic values, so the dialogue between the gospel and culture has the capacity to highlight both the good and the disordered in any culture. For example, biblical theolo-

---

[59] See Joseph Ratzinger, "Bishops, Theologians and Morality," in *On Conscience* (Philadelphia: National Catholic Bioethics Center/San Francisco: Ignatius, 2007), 43-75.

gian Joseph Osei-Bonsu of Ghana has isolated several topics that were central to what he views as New Testament and early church instances of inculturation. The church community sorted out the authentic values of the surrounding culture in conversation with the gospel on topics such as divorce prohibitions, circumcision, meat sacrificed to idols, and sacramental practices.[60] For Osei-Bonsu, inculturation prompts an exercise in looking backward, of remembering in order to compare the early Christian community's values with those of its surrounding community and with those of other premodern cultures.

Since cultures are both creators and carriers of values, the values arising in particular cultures may be judged complementary or in conflict with the values to which a theological tradition is committed; time is then required to see how historically constituted values are expressed in the behaviors of different communities. For this reason, moral theologians such as Paulinus Odozor of Nigeria have suggested that inculturation is best described as an "attempt to preach the gospel of Jesus Christ in any human situation," emphasizing that it should be understood as an ongoing negotiation for Christians of the "older" and "younger" churches alike.[61] Inculturation is grounded in the historical memory of the church about the meaning of its own moral witness, even as it is open to—indeed requires—growth in light of each new context.

Whereas Odozor emphasizes how inculturation in the younger churches must be guided by the memory of the older churches, Tanzanian theologian Laurenti Magesa signals the important place that law and regional custom play in guiding inculturation's remembering. As the church undertakes the discernment of authentic cultural values, it must remain sensitive to the local culture's own memory of what allowed its communities to thrive in the face of internal and external challenges to its way of life: "custom, taboos, divination, mediumship, ordeals, and the [social] expectation of sharing, harmony, play and good company in general."[62] For Magesa, these practices express a legal dimension of the community's life in the sense that they set the parameters through which the community can rightly express its openness to, and celebration of, the abundance of life in its many expressions, and in the affirmation of a responsibility to maintain balance and order in the cosmos.[63] In a similar way, these practices are the means through which inculturaiton is a critical un-

---

[60] Joseph Osei-Bonsu, *The Inculturation of Christianity in Africa* (Frankfurt: Peter Lang, 2005).
[61] Paulinus Ikechukwu Odozor, "An African Moral Theology of Inculturation: Methodological Considerations," *Theological Studies* 69 (2008): 584.
[62] Laurenti Magesa, *African Religion: The Moral Traditions of Abundant Life* (Maryknoll: Orbis, 1997), 269.
[63] Magesa, *African Religion*, 73.

dertaking for the church: "Inculturation can never become the uncritical acceptance of a culture, any more than it can become the cosmetic adaptation of foreign forms of worship and spirituality. It must, however, be to some degree a 'revelation' of a hitherto unknown or unimagined part of Christ."[64]

On the path of memory, the traditional concerns of natural law thinking are expressed in terms of longstanding social practices that can be cross-culturally affirmed. As Laruenti Magesa suggests of African traditional religions, the "living fabric of nature—including people and other creatures—is sacred. Its sanctity does not mean that nature should be worshiped, but does mean that it ought to be treated with respect."[65] This respectful treatment includes honoring sacred rituals, such as initiation and marriage, that ensure the continuation of the community in harmonious relation to the cosmos. When the community debates certain cultural forms, such as polygamous marriage, they ought to consider whether the practices advance or frustrate the centrality of marriage and procreation to the healthy life of the community.[66] It is necessary, for example, for those considering polygamous unions to discern whether one can care for the larger family that such a union would entail and what burden this would place on the wider community.

For moral theologians working along the path of *creation*, we find a different set of orienting concerns more directly focused on how the community's new experience might challenge and perhaps even require the revision of the inherited tradition and the means by which it undertakes moral discernment. Although building on the church's own memory of cultural scrutiny, these theologians are more deliberately self-critical and forward-looking in their views about inculturation. Nathanaël Yaovi Soédé of Benin suggests that an inculturated moral theology means not only listening to the new moral questions arising in local Christian communities throughout the world but also embracing inculturation as an "obligation" arising out of love.[67] Echoing aspects of church teaching on the nature of dialogue, Soédé states, "Inculturation and love: this is what must provide structure and inspiration to our understanding of the faith," which, he claims, requires an investment in our fellow Christians' struggles to live a gospel that has travelled to them from a different land while also being truly the good news to all people.[68] This will

---

[64] Laurenti Magesa, *Anatomy of Inculturation: Transforming the Church in Africa* (Maryknoll: Orbis, 2004), 176.
[65] Magesa, *Anatomy of Inculturation*, 73.
[66] Magesa, *Anatomy of Inculturation*, 124-42.
[67] Nathanaël Yaovi Soédé, "The *Sensus Fidelium* and Moral Discernment: The Principle of Inculturation and of Love," in James F. Keenan, S.J., ed., *Catholic Theological Ethics in the World Church* (New York: Continuum, 2007), 200.
[68] Soédé, "The *Sensus Fidelium* and Moral Discernment," 200.

involve a commitment by all Christians to intercultural conversation with their fellow Christians, which ought to be understood primarily as an expression of solidarity. Often this commitment will invest people in the moral and intellectual struggles of others in the church, many of whom are working through their discernments with a complex set of cultural resources unfamiliar to those inhabiting different regions of the church. The proper end for this solidarity is not only a patient forbearance with cultural diversity in a global church, but a commitment-forming investment in the struggles of the Body's other members.

Congolese theologian Bénézet Bujo argues a similar point about the effect that deep cultural engagement has on moral sensitivity. Expressing a concern that traditional Catholic moral teaching, especially as presented in the revised *Code of Canon Law*, the *Catechism of the Catholic Church*, and John Paul II's *Veritatis Splendor*, "simply failed to take heed of the concerns of the non-European churches." Bujo charges that "[n]ot only its juridical thinking, but its entire theological and ethical categories remain wholly Western."[69] Yet Bujo acknowledges that African ecclesial communities, like official church teaching, seek a balance between the universal and the communal. For example, Bujo has proposed that a version of the traditional African palaver ceremony, the back-and-forth exchange of a community's practical deliberations, should serve as a model for Catholic discernment regarding inculturation. According to Bujo, the central element in the palaver is the concept of listening to the words of the elders, but the elders (especially the tribal chief) also maintain special relations to the divine and to deceased elders of the tribe. A true palaver does not exist if significant segments of the community (past and present) are not given a chance to speak and if the ears of the elders are not open to what they say.[70] In a similar way, "The task of the magisterium is to permit all cultures and people to hold a palaver, in order to discern their own understanding of Christ and his message, without, however, reducing the basis of the faith that is common to all. This presupposes that the magisterium first *listens* and develops large, broad ears."[71] For Bujo, a responsible inculturation of natural law thinking will focus not only on the cross-culturally and historically tested moral norms; it will also focus on

---

[69] Bénézet Bujo, *Foundations of an African Ethic: Beyond the Universal Claims of Western Morality*, Brian McNeil, trans. (New York: Crossroad, 2001), 73. On the significance of the Bujo-Odozor debate for comparative religious ethics, see David A. Clairmont, "Cultures of Comparison and Traditions of Scholarship: Holism and Inculturation in Religious Ethics," in Elizabeth M. Bucar and Aaron Stalnaker, eds. *Religious Ethics in a Time of Globalism: Shaping a Third Wave of Comparative Analysis* (New York: Palgrave Macmillan, 2012), 81-112.
[70] Bujo, *Foundations of an African Ethic*, 150-4.
[71] Bujo, *Foundations of an African Ethic*, 157.

the process by which such norms are identified and introduced into the community's moral life. The palaver represents an inculturation of natural law thinking that is universal in scope but inductive in the determination of values and norms.[72]

Anglican philosopher John Mbiti of Kenya notes the importance of the fully participatory discernment by the community as a guarantor of the community's connection to the divine order. Offenses against an individual (such as theft) are understood as offenses against the community, and right relation must be restored for the good of each.[73] This community includes both those present and those who have gone before (ancestors) whose guidance was crucial for the community's stability and prosperity today. For this reason, Mbiti notes, violations of justice impacting the present community are also violations against the ancestors and must be made right.

This intergenerational structure of moral discernment illustrates well what is at stake in describing the distinctive paths of memory and creation in recent inculturation theology. On the one hand, the church must look to the history of its own community and the faithful in the many cultures of its past for guidance in how to live the gospel in a new cultural context. We have seen that some African theologians observe a similar dynamic in traditional African cultures as well, a dynamic that tests the present community's needs and its practical moral thinking against the wisdom of the ancestors. On the other hand, the church is faced with new problems which require discernment by the full community of faithful witnesses today. This means that other theologians advocate a parallel discernment in the church to what takes place in the communities where the church is a relative newcomer. Reference to universal values and norms, while not foreign to the church's new cultural contexts such as those in Africa, tends to be articulated differently and revealed through the breadth of the community's needs and the links between its future and past.

To be sure, neither the memory nor the creation paths are trod by only one group of theologians. Moreover, along each path the legacy of colonialism has left an enormous impact, even though it has marked the church in post-colonial Africa in different ways from those present in early Spanish encounters with the Amerindians. Kenyan theologian Teresia Hinga claims that the connection between "colonialism and inculturation" might make it impossible for certain classic Christian theological concepts to provide all the resources necessary for the church to speak credibly to the full range of moral, social and political challenges arising in the churches of the global

---

[72] Bujo, *Foundations of an African Ethic*, 11-24.
[73] John S. Mbiti, *African Religions and Philosophy* (Garden City: Doubleday, 1970), 270-4.

South.[74] Moreover, even though many of these texts have even been used to support the most violent colonialist projects, these same texts have, in words of Musa Dube, retained the capacity to form Christian communities in justice and encouraged theologians toward a "prophetically healing scholarship."[75]

Agbonkhianmeghe Orobator of Nigeria has called this aspect of inculturation theology its "incarnational pedagogy," which expresses the deep connection between the work of inculturation and its implied ecclesiology.[76] We see an example of this pedagogy in the work of the Circle of Concerned African Women Theologians, formed in 1989 by roughly 70 theologians from across the continent, focused on the distinctive theological concerns and moral problems facing women in this region.[77] The Circle's membership, which has now grown to over 500 scholars from Africa and beyond, discerned that the social and cultural context of their work required thinking about inculturation as an inter-religious and ecumenical opportunity as well. As Hinga describes the Circle's concerns:

> To speak of religion and culture in Africa is to speak of at least three major heritages, namely, indigenous African religion, Christianity, and Islam.... In analyzing the impact of culture and religion on their lives, African women have had to reckon with the diversity of concepts and interpretations of womanhood that are implicit in these traditions. It is this cultural pluralism which made it methodologically imperative for the women to adopt what they called a dialogical approach.[78]

Yet it is precisely through these layers of religious and cultural difference that the full comparative force of the inculturation becomes clear. The dialogical approach emerges from "the call to develop

---

[74] See Teresia Hinga, "Between Colonialism and Inculturation: Feminist Theologies in Africa," in Elisabeth Schüssler Fiorenza and M. Shawn Copeland, eds. *Feminism in Different Contexts* (Maryknoll: Orbis, 1996), 26-34.
[75] Musa Wenkosi Dube, *The HIV & AIDS Bible: Selected Essays* (Scranton: University of Scranton, 2008), 13.
[76] Agbonkhianmeghe E. Orobator, S.J., *From Crisis to Kairos: The Mission of the Church in the Time of HIV/AIDS, Refugees and Poverty* (Nairobi: Paulines Publications Africa, 2005), 238-42.
[77] For more information on the Circle, see www.thecirclecawt.org/index.html. The group's concern with inculturation as an interreligious dialogical exercise is clearly articulated in its mission statement: "The Circle members are women who are rooted in Islam, Christianity, Judaism and African Indigenous Religions. They are indigenous African women and also African women of Asiatic and European origins. These concerned women are engaged in theological dialogue of the cultures, religions, sacred writings and oral stories that shape the African context and define the women of this continent. The Circle members attempt to reflect together on justice across boundaries of gender, faith and belief."
[78] Hinga, "Between Colonialism and Inculturation," 29-30.

strategies for self- and social transformation from the local context is born out of the realization that Africa itself is tremendously diverse."[79]

BETWEEN INCULTURATION AND NATURAL LAW: A VIRTUE ETHICS OF MEMORY AND CREATION

We have examined two examples of inculturation in Catholic moral theology, and in the process, we have attempted to demonstrate that the dialogue between the gospel and culture has been and continues to be a central aspect of Catholic moral thinking. In that dialogue, natural law remains an important reference point because it offers a meeting point between the gospel and culture, against which the originality of the gospel might be measured and in reference to which the gifts of human cultures and their occasional deformation come into clearer relief. This comparative emphasis in recent moral theology is noteworthy, especially given that the nearest approximation to this sort of comparative impulse among moral theologians in the United States and Europe has previously been limited to the "distinctiveness of Christian ethics" debates of the 1970s and 80s.[80] While thinkers such as Jean Porter have acknowledged strong affinities between Catholic virtue ethics and theologies of natural law and some recent proposals in comparative religious ethics, there remains relatively little interest in comparative issues among moral theologians.[81]

---

[79] Teresia Hinga, "African Feminist Theologies, the Global Village, and the Imperative of Solidarity Across Borders: The Case of the Circle of Concerned African Women Theologians," *Journal of Feminist Studies in Religion* 18, no. 1 (2002): 83.

[80] For an older but helpful introduction to this discussion about the similarities and difference between Christian morality and other approaches to ethics, especially in dialogue contemporary philosophy, see Charles E. Curran and Richard A. McCormick, *The Distinctiveness of Christian Ethics*, Readings in Moral Theology No. 2 (Mahwah: Paulist, 1980). This North transatlantic debate between the *Glaubensethik* and autonomous schools tended to reduce dialogue to conversation with secular humanism and overlooked the distinctive dialogue to be had with interreligious partners. For example, we are thinking here of Josef Fuchs, who has been associated with the autonomous school, when he wrote: "we must also ask how Christian morality relates to the morality of non-Christians. We shall speak only of the 'humanists'" ("Is There a Christian Morality?" in *Readings in Moral Theology*, vol. 2, ed. Charles Curran and Richard McCormick (Mahwah, NJ: Paulist Press), 16).

[81] See Jean Porter, *Nature as Reason: A Thomistic Theory of the Natural Law* (Grand Rapids: Eerdmans, 2004), esp. 132-3, 378-398 where Porter examines the work of Lee Yearley on virtue ethics. Indications of comparative interest are also expressed by Alasdair MacIntyre and others in Lawrence S. Cunningham, ed. *Intractable Disputes about the Natural Law: Alasdair MacIntyre and Critics* (Notre Dame: University of Notre Dame, 2009). Official church teaching has just begun to take up the issue again at the urging of Pope Benedict XVI, with its recent reexamination of the comparative possibilities in natural law thinking; see the recent work by the International Theological Commission, "In Search of a Universal Ethic: A New Look at the Natural Law" (2009).

Our examination of two contexts for inculturation was intended to show how comparative method has in fact been a fundamental part of Catholic moral thought for a long time, even as it is now recovering an approach articulated several hundred years ago and seeing its reemergence in a different part of the globe. The early case of Las Casas showed that natural law could be brought into helpful dialogue with culture in a way that preserved the distinctiveness of the Christian faith and its moral teaching while also acknowledging the moral status of new cultures. Indeed, the encounter with culture forced the missionaries to define freedom in religious matters as a necessary space for this negotiation to happen. It offered a space between the gospel and natural law as a place where moral exchange could happen in the context of culture, rather than in the shadow of its denial or destruction. The burden of evangelization rested first and foremost on preachers living in accordance with gospel virtues rather than those hearing the word and receiving it freely.

In the more recent case of African moral theologies of inculturation, we saw that moral debate developed along two trajectories—memory and creation—which represented dynamics of comparative engagement. Along the path of memory, inculturating Catholic moral teaching meant moving into the particularities of global cultures in order to recall elements of the Christian way of life that had not been fully articulated or had lost the importance they once had for the tradition. A somewhat analogous move happened in the case of Las Casas, where the resources of natural law thinking were brought forth from the cultural matrix in a way that they could not have been developed without this cultural encounter. This was also evident in his deep pastoral concern to preserve the memory of Amerindian customs and religion through the *Apologética historia*.

Along the path of creation, we observed different ways that the tradition was being pulled toward development, even reformed, in light of the pastoral needs of the church today. The impetus toward the creative path was the presence of new and complex moral realities that the traditional categories of moral thinking had not foreseen, described, or offered a response. The Spanish articulation of the gospel as a basis for freedom and natural rights in the Latin American context may be seen as one expression of this creative path. The inseparability of both has prompted some modern Catholic thinkers to conclude that the Christian belief in God makes "freedom the structural form of all being" thus creating new freedoms that can better express the gospel message of universal concrete love in new social and political contexts.[82] The life and writings of Las Casas attest to

---

[82] For two distinctively modern Catholic defenses of this view, see Joseph Cardinal Ratzinger, *Introduction to Christianity*, trans. J.R. Foster (San Francisco: Ignatius,

this Christian commitment and anticipate these modern theological sensibilities. While the modern African context also emphasizes its movement along the creative path, its concerns with the norms of traditional community as an operative law, the close connection between theological memory in the church, and the cultural memory of local traditions show strong movement along the memory path as well. In this case, as in the Latin American case, we see a complex dynamic, a push and pull between memory and creativity that happens between the boundaries of comparative moral theology: inculturation and natural law.

Finally, we return then to the question offered at the outset of our essay: *Is natural law a context-independent basis for cross-cultural moral judgment or is it rather context-dependent, and if so to what degree?* The cases examined above reveal that this peculiarly modern question should be answered in terms of a both/and approach rather than an either/or one. That is to say, to defend one view at the expense of the other is to deform Catholic moral theology in a certain sense. As we saw in the Spanish colonial arguments of Sepúlveda, appealing to the natural law strictly as a context-independent source for moral judgment tends to degenerate into a universalizing secular project of resolving moral conflicts by means of a superior culture and political power. On this view, the meeting between cultures occurs through universal homogeneity rather than the inculturation of the gospel. In the latter case, the encounter enriches the uniqueness of both cultures, and natural law inquiry is carried out in a context-sensitive form attentive to the fundamental unity of all peoples and their respective natural rights.

From the historical contexts of the global South considered in this essay, natural law inquiry is grounded in a philosophical and scriptural framework for making sense of other communities and practices in the effort to get the gospel to take root among respective non-Christian cultures. Natural law inquiry begins with a firm commitment to the belief that non-Christian communities are inhabited by rational persons made in God's image and capable of receiving the Christian faith. We might think of the natural law today as a comparative resource for articulating the diversely rich expressions of our common humanity rather than a strategy for eliminating moral conflicts and pacifying the world. Only Christ and his gospel message of self-emptying love and freedom from sin and death can bring about true conversion and lasting peace. Natural law inquiry in a comparative mode provides a basis for a theology of inculturation that respects the genuine "dialogue" of cultures in which Christian identity

---

2004), 157-8 and Charles Taylor, *A Catholic Modernity?* (New York: Oxford University, 1999).

is negotiated and transformed, but also inspires others through the virtues of humility, patience, and charity. M

Syncretism: Why Latin American and Caribbean Theologians Want to Replace a "Fighting Word" in Theology

Ramón Luzárraga

SURINAME, A COUNTRY on the northeast Atlantic coast of South America bracketed between Guyana, Brazil, and French Guiana, boasts a well-established local Roman Catholic Church community. Since the 18th century, the church has been a continuous and major presence in that country.[1] Out of a total population of slightly more than half a million persons, Catholics form a quarter of Suriname's population. The Surinamese are overwhelmingly Creole, which they define as any person who is part of any long-established group in their country.[2] This broad understanding of the term is unsurprising because like their Caribbean and Latin neighbors, the Surinamese possess heterogeneous roots drawn from Africa, Asia, Europe, and the people indigenous to the Guianas region. There continue to be indigenous tribal communities scattered across the rain-forested interior of Suriname, descended from the people the British and Dutch explorers and settlers first encountered,[3] and the Maroons, descendants of African slaves who escaped

---

[1] Mission efforts in the Guianas region stretch back to the 1650s. See John Bridges, S.J., *The Good News on the Wild Coast: Highlights of the Early Efforts of the Catholic Church in Guiana 1650's to 1850's* (Arima, Trinidad: St. Dominic, n.d.), 9-11.

[2] See Margarite Fernández Olmos and Lizabeth Paravisini-Gebert, *Creole Religions of the Caribbean: An Introduction from Vodou and Santería to Obeah and Espiritismo*, 2nd ed. (New York: New York University, 2011), 5. Notice how the Surinamese definition of a Creole is a departure from its original definition: white Europeans born in the New World. It is one of a myriad of contemporary definitions of a Creole as an ethnic hybrid; and these definitions are a product of much debate in Suriname's Caribbean neighbors. See Anna L. Peterson and Manuel A. Vásquez, *Latin American Religions: Histories and Documents in Context* (New York: New York University, 2008), 15; and Percy Hintzen, "The Caribbean: Race and Creole Ethnicity," in *Cultural Identity and Creolization in National Unity: The Multiethnic Caribbean*, ed. Prem Misir (Lanham: University Press of America, 2006), 9-31.

[3] Duncan Wielzen, "Popular Religiosity as an Internal Dynamic for the Local Church: The Case of Suriname," *Exchange* 34:1 (2005): 2.

the plantations on the coast and organized themselves into clans clustered in riverine settlements also in the interior.[4]

These heterogeneous roots conspired to bring about a blending of Roman Catholic worship with other forms of religious worship unique to Latin America and the Caribbean. In Suriname, Catholic worship was melded with Winti, an Afro-Surinamese religion which itself is a product of the syncretism of western African religions brought over by slaves whose descendants incorporated Amerindian and European influences.[5] Catholic worship was blended in Suriname and Jamaica with Maroon religion too, another blend of African religious worldviews and practices.[6] Rejecting the European form of Roman Catholic faith, many Surinamese practice what the sociologist Harold Jap-A-Joe identifies as a "creolized" form of it.[7] This blending of religious traditions finds expression in popular religious practices, particularly those rituals marking the stages of human life where plainly Catholic liturgical elements freely commingle with Winti[8] or Maroon[9] cosmology. In both cases, much of the worship is

---

[4] See Gad Heuman, *The Caribbean* (London: Hodder Arnold, 2006), 63-4.
[5] Harold Jap-A-Joe, "Afro-Surinamese Renaissance and the Rise of Pentecostal-ism," *Exchange* 34:2 (2005): 137-8.
[6] Joop Vernooij, "Mapping Religious Suriname," *Exchange* 31:3 (2002): 232.
[7] Wielzen, "Popular Religiosity," 8.
[8] A prominent example of popular religion blending Catholic with Winti or Maroon elements is found with the rituals surrounding the burial and mourning of the dead. A Catholic funeral with Winti elements begins with the *dede oso* liturgy, a wake. Before the *dede oso* begins, food and drink are put aside for the deceased because the Winti religion treats the dead as family members whose status is not compromised by death. This is followed by the wake itself, the first part of which begins with prayers, Bible reading, ands songs of mourning, and concludes with another round of prayers. After a break where family members serve food and drink to guests, the second part of the wake begins following the same sequence of events as the first, with one difference: the songs are joyful. The belief here is that the soul of the deceased is about to go to heaven, and the songs are meant to accompany the person on the journey. Close to midnight the lights are turned off, and people sing the song *'t Is middernacht* (It is midnight) while the *kabra* (the ancestral spirits of the baptized dead) come to take the soul of the deceased to Heaven. Winti religion calls Heaven the *kowru kondre*: the cold country. This part is concluded with the praying of the Lord's Prayer, the singing of the final verses of "It is midnight," the turning on of the lights and more eating and drinking. The final part of the *dede oso* is marked by storytelling featuring anecdotes about the deceased and remembering other family members who had passed and the telling of jokes and riddles, some of which carry a moral lesson. The wake breaks up without any formal closing rite. The food and drink set aside for the deceased at the beginning of the *dede oso* gets buried in the yard of the family home. This funeral rite is followed by the *ayti dey* (celebrated the eighth day following the funeral) and the *siksi wiki* (celebrated six weeks following the funeral). See Wielzen, 6-7.
[9] Maroons venerate the dead with the *puru blaka,* but this honor is something the deceased person must earn while alive. Only a person who lived an exemplary moral life supporting the community may receive veneration. This is because the Maroons believe such persons become something akin to Catholic saints; they can intercede

led by a layperson, either male or female, and the participants are not all Catholic.[10]

In the past, the Roman Catholic Church officially condemned these practices as pagan, which forced these Winti and Maroon practices underground.[11] Today, the Catholic Church in Suriname takes no official stance at all, while the Catholic clergy and hierarchy in their day-to-day work allow these creole inculturations of the faith. So, on the one hand, these blended forms of worship do not have any official ecclesial status, but on the other hand, the lack of church approval "does not automatically imply that it lacks ecclesial justification."[12] It is common to find clergy or lay catechists taking a leadership role for part of these rituals,[13] which suggests that the leadership of the church in Suriname offers more than a simple toleration of the incorporation of Winti and Maroon religion into Catholic worship.

Other examples similar to Suriname's inculturated Catholic popular worship, which attract neither condemnation nor endorsement of the church but are often tolerated by the local bishop[14] and clergy, can be found throughout Latin America and the Caribbean.[15] These examples of Catholic popular worship are described by some theologians as the product of poorly catechized peoples ignorant of orthodoxy, and they are caricatured by some social scientists who

---

on behalf of the community before God because a morally upright person would be close to God, making his or her prayer more efficacious. The *puru blaka* itself begins with the family of the deceased clad in black clothes and the assembly saying prayers and singing hymns. The mourning period is concluded with the family of the deceased taking a ritual bath in a local river, followed by a common meal. All of this is to celebrate the passing of the deceased into *Gado kondre* (God's kingdom). Like Winti funeral rites, food is set aside for the deceased person. See Wielzen, 10.

[10] Wielzen, *"Popular Religiosity,"* 7.

[11] Harold Jap-A-Joe, Peter Sjak Shie and Joop Vernooij, "The Quest for Respect: Religion and Emancipation in Twentieth-Century Suriname," in *Twentieth Century Suriname: Continuities and Discontinuities in a New World Society,* ed. Rosemarijn Hoefte and Peter Meel (Kingston: Ian Randle, 2001), 200.

[12] Wielzen, "Popular Religiosity," 8-9.

[13] Wielzen, "Popular Religiosity," 7.

[14] Having said that, the general tendency of the bishops has been to lean toward those popular practices they judge to be orthodox, which would correspond to what they view to be the Church's institutional interests in relation to the people. See, Jorge Ramírez Calzadilla, "La Religiosidad Popular en La Identidad Cultural Latinoamericana y Caribeña," in *Religiosidad Popular México, Cuba,* editado por Noemi Quezada (México City: Universidad Nacional Autónoma de México, 2004): 43.

[15] Another prominent example is *candomblé,* the Afro-Brazilian religion practiced in Bahia, whose adherents insist they are good Catholics and practice its rituals side-by-side with Catholic liturgical practices. The only hint of resistance is found with local priests who carefully differentiate between Catholic and *candomblé* beliefs, differences which most Afro-Brazilian practitioners of both faiths see as non-existent. See Roger Bastide, *The African Religions of Brazil: Towards a Sociology of the Interpenetration of Civilizations,* trans. Helen Sebba (Baltimore: Johns Hopkins University, 1978), 260-1 and 271.

think that they are simply a product of racial and class resistance to organized religion.[16] On the contrary, the ambivalence of the church toward popular religion is due to its struggle with the difficult task of understanding the complex relationship between official Catholic faith and practice on the one hand and popular manifestations of the faith which can defy easy categorization on the other.[17]

In response to this ambivalence, Latin American and Caribbean theologians and persons active in ministry in those regions are working to redefine what constitutes appropriate forms of syncretism—how the Christian faith inculturates itself with popular religious practices in Latin America and the Caribbean. They are doing so through their critique of the use of the word "syncretism" and its definition, often to the point of replacing it with the inoffensive word "inculturation." These theologians think that the word "syncretism" has been used by people outside Latin America and the Caribbean to accuse their local churches of attempting to inculturate the celebration of worship and sacraments in ways detrimental to Christianity. Latin American and Caribbean Christians claim that their work of inculturating worship and sacraments on a popular level is theologically sound overall, but some Christians outside these regions criticize it as syncretism because the worship customs and practices look and sound odd. Latin American and Caribbean theologians tend to give local incarnations of worship the benefit of the doubt without going so far as to accept the naive generalization that inappropriate forms of syncretism do not exist. Latin and Caribbean theologians, clergy and lay ministers all agree that unacceptable forms of syncretism exist in their respective regions, and their writings show an abiding but not obsessive concern with the issue. These theologians instead seek to redefine how the church distinguishes between what is acceptable syncretism and what is unacceptable in order to better inculturate worship and sacraments in Latin America and the Caribbean.

In the Caribbean, the overall goal behind this redefinition of acceptable syncretism is the acceptance and purposeful incorporation of African and Indian (as in Carib and Arawak) cultural elements into the worship life of the church. This "creolization" of religion is

---

[16] Anthony M. Stevens-Arroyo, "The Contribution of Catholic Orthodoxy to Caribbean Syncretism: The Case of la Virgen de la Caridad del Cobre in Cuba," *Archives de sciences sociales des religions* 47:117 (2002): 37.

[17] A representative example of how popular devotions in Latin American and the Caribbean defy easy categorization are the popular devotions of Cuba toward San Lázaro, la Virgin de la Caridad, la Virgen de Regla, la Virgen de la Merced, and Santa Bárbara. Jorge Ramírez Calzadilla describes these devotions as "not properly Catholic, nor Santeria, nor Spiritist." Those who practice these devotions "declare a dependency on their object of worship, but fail to explain, let alone situate it within a religious system." Calzadilla, 40 [Translation mine].

not solely to satisfy an ecclesiological concern to fully incorporate Caribbean people into church life, but basic to the project of Caribbean cultural liberation.[18] Given the ubiquity and influence of Christianity in the Caribbean, it is natural for theologians and ministers there to have Christian faith and practice play a decisive, animating role in forging a unique Caribbean identity. Caribbean people themselves would meld the disparate European, African, Indigenous, and sometimes Asian elements into a Caribbean identity they can call their own, liberating themselves from being culturally defined by former colonial and prevailing metropolitan or hegemonic powers in that region.[19]

In Latin America, the general motivation for moving the line distinguishing acceptable from unacceptable syncretism is tied with the efforts of theologians in that region to promote the integral liberation of their people.[20] Key to this liberation is the critical acceptance and incorporation of indigenous views of the spiritual and their practices of worshipping God alongside the Spanish, Portuguese and other European elements that shaped the church there for centuries. The church in Brazil shares concerns similar to the church in the Caribbean with the incorporation of African elements into church wor-

---

[18] See Joop Vernooij, "Religion in the Caribbean: Creation by Creolization," in *Global Christianity: Contested Claims,* ed. Frans Wijsen and Robert Schreiter (Amsterdam: Editions Rodopi, B.V., 2007): 153-4.

[19] There is also a question faced by the Catholic Church in parts of the Caribbean concerning relations with non-Christian religions. In Trinidad, Guyana, and Suriname there exists a significant Hindu population who use Christian worship practices and symbols for their own spiritual edification. A famous example is on the island of Trinidad, where Hindus honor Our Lady of the Good Shepherd as a manifestation of the goddess Kali. There follows a related question concerning Hindu converts to Christianity, and which Hindu religious practices the Church would deem acceptable for their new congregants to continue using as Christians. See Freek L. Bakker, "The Mirror Image: How Hindus Adapt to the Creole Christian World of the Caribbean," *Studies in Interreligious Dialogue* 13:2 (2003): 180-1. Holy Thursday is a time of special devotion to Mary by both Christians and Hindus, who share the same veneration but do so with different motives and understandings of whom is being venerated. The pastor of the parish, Father Martin Sirju, has the image moved to the parish hall to accommodate the throngs of Hindu worshippers (and avoid accusations of syncretism by some Christians on the island) while Catholic Mass is celebrated next door in church. This is an event I had the privilege of witnessing firsthand three years ago. See also Gerald Boodoo, "The Faith of the People: The *Divina Pastora* Traditions of Trinidad," in *Religion, Culture, and Tradition in the Caribbean,* ed. Hemchand Gossai and Nathaniel Samuel Murrel (New York: St. Martin's, 2000): 65-72.

[20] See Julio de Santa Ana, "Popular Religion and Liberation in Latin America: Between Common Sense and Good Sense," in, *Popular Religion, Liberation and Contextual Theology,* ed. Jacques Van Nieuwenhove and Berma Klein Goldewijk (Kampen: Uitgeversmaatschappij J.H. Kok, 1991), 106.

ship, a concern that has spilled over into neighboring Argentina and Uruguay.[21]

This ambiguous status of popular religious practices in the Catholic Church in Latin America and the Caribbean (practices not officially recognized as part of church worship or devotional traditions) is an important ecclesiastical and ethical question that requires a sustained, long-term commitment by theologians and people in ministry toward achieving a resolution. A lack of formal recognition of the legitimacy of a local church's worship and devotion can affect the self-image of the people within that church, casting doubt as to their status as fully constituent members of the universal church.[22] People and those who minister to them may think themselves marginalized because their worship of God may not be recognized as legitimate worship. It is a question of justice because the people of a Latin American or Caribbean local church are left doubting the legitimacy of their place in the universal church. Short of an official recognition of popular worship practices, the unofficial tolerance practiced by the church today concerning popular religious practice can be revoked at any time by church authority and by believers outside the region in general. Latin American and Caribbean theologians at their most blunt label this a form of neo-colonialism.

More importantly, the lack of official recognition of popular worship impacts the ability of Latin American and Caribbean peoples to commit to living the Christian life by incorporating it fully into how they lead their lives. This statement may seem puzzling, considering that Latin America and the Caribbean as we know it are cultures that have been defined by Christianity, especially by the Catholic Church, since the Age of Exploration and the Conquest of the Americas. At issue here is how the people themselves need to have a voice in how they understand and practice their faith instead of being defined exclusively by an outside authority that rejects popular religion out of hand and who alone defines how their Christianity ought to be lived out. Ben Knighton observes that Christian faith "becomes enfleshed in the lives, not so much of those who passively receive it, but of those who actively accept and, in doing so, remould it."[23] In other words, the people of Latin America and the Caribbean who are committed to practicing the Christian faith need to incarnate the faith themselves, in particular how the gospel is proclaimed, the prac-

---

[21] See Edward L. Cleary, O.P., *How Latin America Saved the Soul of the Catholic Church* (Mahwah: Paulist, 2009), 83-8.

[22] Here again, I am speaking of those who belong to the local Roman Catholic Church in Latin America and the Caribbean whose practice of the faith is neither recognized nor condemned by Church authority.

[23] Knighton, "Christian Enculturation," 52.

tice of liturgy and worship, and the development of local theology,[24] and not simply to repeat what was given to them by generations of Latin American and Caribbean elites and missionaries. Robert Schreiter describes this as a process of incarnation whereby "the presentation of the gospel [by those who brought it in the first place] is gradually disengaged from its previous cultural embeddedness and is allowed to take on new forms consonant with the new cultural setting."[25] Of course, the people of the church in Latin America and the Caribbean are assumed to be the agents of this change.

The engagement of Latin American and Caribbean theologians with the question of determining the line between acceptable and unacceptable inculturation begins with the use of the word "syncretism." This word, for Latin American and Caribbean theologians and ministers, is a fighting word whose definition is far from settled. As a purely descriptive term, it means the intermingling of religions. The problem arises when the description includes "an evaluation of such intermingling from the point of view of one of the religions involved" where "as a rule, the mixing of religions is condemned in this evaluation as violating the essence of the belief system."[26] Christianity throughout its history, in its doctrine, theology, and church polity more than in actual religious practice, has kept up its guard in its encounter with cultures whose converts sought to incarnate their newly received faith with practices other than those familiar to European and North American cultures. The fear is that attempts at inculturation involved compromising the essentials of Christian faith. This guardedness comes from the Jewish roots of Christianity, with its abiding concern to not adopt pagan beliefs or practices that would violate the first three commandments of the Decalogue.

Christianity's guardedness concerning syncretism is complex in theory as well as in actual practice. Peter Schineller identifies three basic approaches toward defining syncretism: an outright negative approach, a nuanced critical approach, and an outright positive approach. The outright negative approach understands syncretism as the loss of essential elements of the gospel message in the process of inculturation that are replaced by elements of the culture being evangelized. It assumes that there will always be elements in the gospel that are incompatible with the receiving culture and in such cases the

---

[24] See Mariasusai Dhavamony, S.J., *Christian Theology of Inculturation,* Documenta Missionalia 24 (Roma: Editrice Pontificia Università Gregoriana, 1997): 91.
[25] Robert Schreiter, "Inculturation of Faith or Identification with Culture," in *Christianity and Cultures: A Mutual Enrichment,* ed. Norbert Greinacher and Norbert Mette. *Concilium* 2 (1994): 16.
[26] André Droogers, "Syncretism: The Problem of Definition, the Definition of the Problem," in *Dialogue and Syncretism: An Interdisciplinary Approach,* ed. Jerald Gort, Hendrik Vroom, Rein Fernhout, and Anton Wessels, (Grand Rapids: Eerdmans, 1989): 7.

culture must change and conform by allowing those contradictory elements to die. Here, syncretism amounts to rejecting Christ.[27] Theologians who opt for the nuanced critical approach want to rescue the word syncretism so that it means "the necessary, ongoing process of the development of Christian life, practice, and doctrine."[28] For them, syncretism describes the critical practice of deciding on a case-by-case basis whether a particular attempt to inculturate the gospel is authentic to its message.[29] Then there are those theologians who do not see syncretism as a bad word at all but rather as a wholly positive concept in the theological nomenclature of Christianity. Leonardo Boff argues that considering how the incarnation of God is a central tenet of Christianity, it stands to reason that this faith, by necessity, must be among the most syncretistic of religions. If Christianity is to evangelize the cultures it encounters, it must be "exposed to different religious expressions and then assimilate them, interpret them, and recast them according to its own identity."[30] Boff admits that this process does often lead to "periods of crisis and uncertainty as to whether the religion's true identity is being preserved or diluted" and the process can generate error.[31] Despite these hazards, syncretism is necessary for Christianity to "preserve and enrich its universality" and for the Christian message of God's salvation to avoid being trapped as an abstraction.[32]

Despite attempts by many theologians to defend the word "syncretism," this article will use the word "inculturation" instead to proceed with its argument. The motive is a practical one: to keep the audience of this article together. The word "syncretism" is a distraction from the real issue: "the criteria for distinguishing adequate and inadequate inculturation."[33] Syncretism, precisely because it is seen by too many Latin American and Caribbean theologians as a fighting word, serves the negative function of a debate killer designed to block what one considers unacceptable forms of inculturation.[34] In other words, it is a habit among Christians to approve of how Christian faith incarnates itself in a culture as inculturation. When Christians don't approve, it is called syncretism.

---

[27] Peter Schineller, S.J., "Inculturation and the Issue of Syncretism: What is the Real Issue?" in, *Evangelization in Africa in the Third Millenium: Challenges and Prospects*, ed. Justin S. Ukpong, Teresa Okure, John E. Anyanwu, Godwin C. Okeke, and Anacletus N. Odoemene (Port Harcourt: Catholic Institute of West Africa, 1992), 52-3.
[28] Schineller, "Inculturation and the Issue of Syncretism," 53.
[29] Schineller, "Inculturation and the Issue of Syncretism," 53.
[30] Leonardo Boff, *Church: Charism and Power, Liberation Theology and the Institutional Church,* trans. John W. Diercksmeier (Maryknoll: Orbis Books, 1985), 91.
[31] Boff, *Church*, 91.
[32] Boff, *Church*, 93.
[33] Schineller, "Inculturation and the Issue of Syncretism," 56.
[34] Schineller, "Inculturation and the Issue of Syncretism," 56.

Sacraments in particular and worship in general regularly serve as loci for controversies about inculturation. Sacraments, generally understood by Catholics and other Christians who incorporate them in their worship life, are the visible signs of the spiritual reality made manifest by the sign itself[35] and symbolic actions that mediate the presence of God.[36] Sacraments, by virtue of their being dispensed as concrete signs and actions, are among the things found in Christian life and practice most exposed to cultural influence in their presentation and dispensation. The inculturation of sacraments, liturgy, and other forms of worship has been a consistent historical challenge for the church, one that has brought about recurring problems that, at times, hampered its ability to carry out its evangelical mission.

One major example is the 17th century Chinese Rites controversy, the product of the first serious attempt by the church to use symbols, languages and indigenous customs in its worship and liturgy different from those found in cultures shaped by Christianity.[37] The Jesuits had no problem with Chinese converts participating in liturgy and receiving the sacraments alongside their continuing practice of rites honoring the deceased and celebrations honoring Confucius. The latter two events were judged by the Jesuits to be a secular practice, an observation that the reigning sovereign of the time, the Emperor Kangxi, confirmed as true. Pope Clement IX thought the emperor's intervention in church affairs akin to one done by a European monarch, and therefore offensive. Dominicans and Franciscans, along with much of the church authority of the time, thought that these Chinese Christian practices were idolatrous. None of them, however, possessed the command of Chinese culture, language and on-the-ground experience of the Jesuits. The controversy ended with a botched audience between the papal legate sent to adjudicate the problem and Emperor Kangxi. This encounter featured the poor choice of an interpreter who could not help the legate identify some of the Chinese characters the emperor presented, including Matteo Ricci's name in Chinese "Li Madou." The interpreter demonstrated an ignorance of the catechism Ricci wrote for Chinese people, *On Christian Doctrine*, which meant the papal delegation offended the emperor who knew all these facts. Emperor Kangxi banished the delegation from his presence. The event also ended official tolerance of the Christian religion which in turn spelled the end of the intense cultural exchange between China and the West launched by Matteo

---

[35] Augustine, *Letter 55 to Januarius on Baptism*.
[36] Herbert Vorgrimler, *Sacramental Theology*, trans. Linda M. Maloney (Collegeville: The Liturgical, 1992), 72.
[37] Mario Aguilar, *The History and Politics of Latin American Theology*, Vol. 1 (London: SCM, 2007), 157.

Ricci and the Jesuit mission he founded.[38] This dramatic and unfortunate history underscores how inculturation is an old challenge for the church that reasserts its presence every time a culture is evangelized by it.

Two contemporary examples of the challenge of distinguishing between acceptable and unacceptable forms of inculturation in Latin America and the Caribbean can be found with their reception of the instruction by the Congregation for Divine Worship, *Redemptionis Sacramentum*. When the instruction turns to the issue of where Eucharist can be celebrated, it begins by saying that it must be "carried out in a sacred place, unless in a particular case necessity requires otherwise. In this case the celebration must be in a decent place."[39] The local bishop is left to judge what places are to be considered sacred or decent, but only up to a point. The instruction proceeds to add, "It is never lawful for a Priest to celebrate in a temple or sacred place of any non-Christian religion."[40] This aspect of the instruction is an example of demarcating an unacceptable form of inculturation that Caribbean or Latin American Catholics would accept as a matter of course. On the other hand, that same document's instruction "that each one give the sign of peace only to those who are nearest and in a sober manner" and that "the Priest may give the sign of peace to the ministers but always remains within the sanctuary, so as not to disturb the celebration" is potentially problematic. That instruction "completely overrules local customs and practices of some particular churches, particularly those in Africa and Latin America, where cultural expressions are normally spontaneous and far from sober."[41] This concern would be raised by a variety of cultures across the entire Caribbean region. The document only gives the priest latitude "for a just reason he wishes to extend the sign of peace to some few of the faithful" and the local bishops' conference latitude to pick the manner by which the sign of peace is to be exchanged.[42] By setting boundaries alien to the worshipping community at large, especially one whose laity are well-catechized, enjoy increasing levels of theological education beyond catechesis, and a strong charismatic sense of vocation, this could risk "a danger of estrangement from the peo-

---

[38] Michela Fontana, *Matteo Ricci: A Jesuit in the Ming Court*, trans. Paul Metcalfe (Lanham: Rowman and Littlefield, 2011), 291-2.
[39] Congregation for Divine Worship and the Discipline of the Sacrament, *Redemptionis Sacramentum: On certain matters to be observed or to be avoided regarding the Most Holy Eucharist* (Libreria Editrice Vaticana, 2004), no. 108, www.vatican.va/roman_curia/congregations/ccdds/documents/rc_con_ccdds_doc_20040423_redemptionis-sacramentum_en.html.
[40] *Redemptionis Sacramentum*, no. 109.
[41] Duncan Wielzen, "Popular Religiosity as an Internal Dynamic for the Local Church: The Case of Suriname," *Exchange* 34:1 (2005): 2.
[42] *Redemptionis Sacramentum*, no. 72.

ple, and the church will have a hard time localizing [itself]."[43] From the word "go," the culturally informed worship habits of the congregation would lead to *Redemptionis Sacramentum* being ignored in practice. The universal church and the church in Latin America and the Caribbean would be left speaking past each other instead of having a dialogue to resolve issues of inculturation.

Specific motives behind why Latin American and Caribbean theologians want to change how the church distinguishes between acceptable inculturation and unacceptable inculturation focus on the following realities. In Latin America, many national elites and others in the higher echelons of society and the academy think that "the people's religious culture must be purified, on the assumption that it is dehumanized by magic and myth."[44] In the Caribbean, accusations of syncretism have been used by what people in that region call missionary Christianity to tamp down emergent indigenous forms of Christian worship that are presented by Latin American and Caribbean theologians and ministers as authentically Christian. This is based on the historic attitude of missionary Christians towards the majority of Caribbean people as practicing evil, primitive, and demonic religious practices.[45] According to Monsignor Patrick Anthony, a Catholic priest and theologian from St. Lucia, taking the point of view of those who were evangelized by missionaries, the churches saw their mission to "baptize the pagans, exorcise their customs, and in the case of more sympathetic missionaries, if possible, Christianize some of the customs."[46] It is unsurprising that attempts by the Afro Caribbean population[47] to incorporate what Anthony identifies as folk culture into the practice of the Christian life historically speaking has been met with condescension or outright bans by church authorities.[48]

Now, it would be a mistake to caricature this conflict as a purely Manichean contest between enlightened Christian missionaries and the people they evangelized, the former exercising a Victorian *noblesse oblige* motoring up the Orinoco River or hiking the Blue Mountains of Jamaica to rescue their charges from a Latin or antipo-

---

[43] Wielzen, "Popular Religiosity," 2.
[44] Diego Irarrázaval, *Inculturation: New Dawn of the Church in Latin America* (Maryknoll: Orbis Books, 2000), 82.
[45] See Carlos F. Cardoza Orlandi, "Conspiracy Among Idols: A Critique of Deconstruction from the Afro-Caribbean Religions," *Koinonia* 4:1 (1992): 27.
[46] Patrick A.B. Anthony, "A Case Study in Indigenization," in *Out of the Depths,* ed. Idris Hamid (Trinidad: Idris Hamid, 1977), 191.
[47] Anthony, "A Case Study in Indigenization," 188. Anthony follows Edward Braithwaite's description of the fragmented nature of Caribbean society. There exists a Euro-centered elite, a Euro-oriented creole upper class, a small creole intellectual elite, and an Afro-Caribbean (black) population.
[48] Anthony, "A Case Study in Indigenization," 191.

dean heart of darkness. Edward Cleary points out that missionary groups "deliberately sought out and lived with indigenous groups, mastered the peoples' language and their conceptions of God and Jesus' death and resurrection, developed sensitivity to local cultures, and influenced the church and theological movements – in particular Liberation Theology – to take seriously, though not uncritically, indigenous conceptions of the Christian faith as "expressing the face of God in imperfect but important ways."[49] Missionaries, who can and should be accused of viewing attempts by the people to inculturate Christian faith with mistrust if not hostility, can also be credited for encouraging and enabling effective inculturation of the faith.

With this caution in mind, the motivation to redefine the distinction between acceptable and unacceptable forms of inculturation involves the church granting popular religion the space to serve Christianity. Theologians believe it can do so by recognizing popular religion as an original means by which the people practice and communicate the faith in the church both inside and outside official worship and sacramental celebrations. Of course, to do so would mean a degree of accepting "the indigenous populations' view of the world" and that, in turn, means accepting "new ways of being church while keeping the continuity of communion with centuries of history."[50] This is the flashpoint where Christianity, historically, puts up its guard.

Yet, inculturation must be done, lest one is ignored by the people and perhaps eventually loses them, or perhaps worse, does not gain their interest in the first place. In Latin America, Diego Irarrázaval points out that the church in Latin America too often either wholly excluded popular culture or reduced it to discrete novel elements that can be safely incorporated into existing liturgical celebrations.[51] Theological movements that consciously dedicated themselves to the popular classes were not immune to this thinking. Juan Luis Segundo wrote that Liberation Theology, in its opening stages of development, was well received among the middle class of Latin America, in particular among university students.[52] Unfortunately, the common people, the very group Liberation Theology wanted to serve, "neither understood nor welcomed anything from the first theology of liberation."[53] Segundo blamed his own theological movement for making a critical error when they "raised all over Latin America a wave of doubt and strong criticism of *popular religion* [otherwise and more

---

[49] Cleary, *How Latin America Saved the Soul*, 82.
[50] Aguilar, *The History and Politics of Latin American Theology*, 168.
[51] Irarrázaval, *Inculturation*, 17.
[52] Juan Luis Segundo, "The Shift within Latin American Theology," *Journal of Theology for Southern Africa* 52 (Sept. 1985): 21.
[53] Segundo, "The Shift within Latin American Theology," 23.

aptly called 'popular Catholicism'] as being oppressive and, all-in-all, non-Christian."[54] Influenced by Marxism, popular religion was denounced by liberation theologians as an opiate numbing the poor to their own oppression. The consequence was that the common people "reacted against [Liberation Theology's] criticism of the supposed oppressive elements of popular religion"[55] by ignoring the movement, and instead, in many cases, turned to charismatic Catholic or Protestant Pentecostal movements.

The Caribbean, with the rise of national independence movements and identity movements like the Black Power movement which had the purpose of trying to forge a unique Caribbean identity in place of the identity imposed by colonial powers, found the church there increasingly out of touch with its members. The reason for this, according to Knolly Clark, was that "the European missionaries never really made any attempt to indigenize the theology of the church, even more so, its liturgical life."[56] Clark proceeded to ask, "Are the Church Services of today relevant? Do they meet the spiritual and emotional needs of our people? Is their language, the language spoken and understood by our people today? Do the hymns and music reflect the life and experience of the average West Indian or Jamaican?"[57] Theologians of the region would say, "In the past, no," and today inculturation is a promising work still in progress with a positive outcome far from guaranteed.

A good and successful inculturation, Knighton argues, is essential to "foster the confidence and morale of the Two-Thirds World churches to work out their own salvation." Otherwise, Latin American and Caribbean Christians would be "powerless to transform it, except superficially or destructively"[58] because the Christian faith, in its full Incarnational and Trinitarian integrity would be incorporated piecemeal and thwarted in its ability engage, transform, and redeem culture.[59] Another, more temporal reason why a successful inculturation of Christianity is important for the people is that recognition in the church historically has served as a necessary step toward achieving political recognition in society at large, particularly for the lower classes in the Caribbean[60] and Latin America.[61]

---

[54] Segundo, "The Shift within Latin American Theology," 25.
[55] Segundo, "The Shift within Latin American Theology," 23.
[56] Knolly Clark, "Liturgy and Culture in the Caribbean: What is to be Done?" in *Troubling of the Waters*, ed. Idris Hamid (Trinidad: Idris Hamid, 1973), 142.
[57] Clark, "Liturgy and Culture in the Caribbean," 142.
[58] Ben Knighton, "Christian Enculturation in the Two-Thirds World," in *Global Christianity: Contested Claims,* ed. Frans Wijsen and Robert Schreiter (Amsterdam: Editions Rodopi, 2007), 63.
[59] See Knighton, "Christian Enculturation in the Two-Thirds World," 63.
[60] This was the experience of Suriname, though observers of that country argue that political parties have supplanted the church as an agent of social change. See Jap-A-

Which specific proposals do Latin American and Caribbean theologians offer to redefine the church's distinguishing between acceptable and unacceptable forms of inculturation of the faith, and help give voice to the people in those regions to practice the faith? The church in Latin America has undergone a shift from concerns for military governments and ruling oligarchies (a concern which ended with the advent of durable democratic governments in the 1980s), to concerns for indigenous rights, the tribal possession of land, and the retention of indigenous and African cultures. The Latin American and Caribbean bishops in their regional meeting in Santo Domingo turned their attention to what indigenous and Afro-Latin cultures could offer to better inculturate Christianity in that region for purposes of evangelization.[62] Latin American theologians point to that meeting as a warrant to redefine how the church distinguishes between acceptable and unacceptable inculturation, and add that it should do this for purposes of liberation, too. Liberation is where a people in Latin America, oppressed in the past by colonialism and, according to some theologians, oppressed by modernity today,[63] can understand and communicate the universal Christian faith in their own unique voice in the church and to the world. These same theologians would add further that the popular church redefined what is acceptable inculturation of the faith long ago, and the rest of the church needs to recognize that. "Popular groups are deeply spiritual," Irarrázaval insists, "even though they are continually repressed and

---

Joe, Shie and Vernooij, "The Quest for Respect," 199. However, this remains the case in much of the Caribbean, where liberation begins with the recognition that God sees the people there as not inferior to their former colonial or post-colonial masters, but as human beings, and that carries socio-political import for liberation. Lewin L. Williams, *Caribbean Theology* (New York: Peter Lang, 2002), 200, 211.

[61] For example, in Brazil, liberation theology has achieved a level of influence where during presidential elections, "the religious language which gives pride of place to the poor became important for the candidates. This means that religious symbols and images are very much present in the awareness of the Brazilian masses" (Santa Ana, "Popular Religion and Liberation in Latin America," 101). This use of language is not entirely cynical. Thanks to the policies of Brazil's governments over the past two decades, the poverty rate has been halved. See "Focus: Brazil," *The Economist* online (November 1, 2011), www.economist.com/blogs/dailychart/-2011/11/focus.

[62] The Latin American bishops concluded at that conference, "The New Evangelization needs to inculturate itself more into our cultures' way of life and being, taking into account the particularities of diverse cultures, especially the Indigenous and Afroamericans. (We urge learning to speak according to the mentality and culture of those who listen according to the forms and mediums of communication that are in use.) Thus, the New Evangelization continues in line with the incarnation of the Word." Consejo Episcopal Latinoamericano, *Santo Domingo Concluciones: IV Conferencia General del Episcopado Latinoamericano* (Bogota: CELAM, 1993), no. 30 [Translation mine]. See also Aguilar, *The History and Politics of Latin American Theology*, 158.

[63] Irarrázaval, *Inculturation*, 29.

discriminated against by the powerful and well educated."[64] What is needed, instead, is a critical engagement by the entire church in Latin America with the already-inculturated spiritual practices of the majority of their people, including how they approach worship and the sacraments.

Irarrázaval identified at least three types of inculturated spirituality to be engaged by theologians and those who minister to the people for a critical inclusion in the sacramental and worship life of the church. The first type is the devotional alliance: the practice of direct and ongoing contact through prayer and celebration between a person and a male or female saint. "It may be the patron saint of a town, the object of an association of devotees, or a mass shrine."[65] It can also be direct and ongoing contact with a popular devotion such as *Nuestra Señora de Guadalupe* (Mexico), Divina Pastora-Our Lady of the Good Shepherd (Trinidad), El Cobre (Cuba), the Sacred Heart, a devotion promoted by a religious congregation, etc. All share an understanding that the relationship is between believers and a protector. "It is a mystical interaction with concrete implications in health, solving family and economic problems, and many more things."[66] The second type is the militant spirituality of groups that choose their particular modes of religious expression that are carried out through particular customs. Social action, Bible reading for the purpose of spiritual edification and catechesis, and groups focused on worship and sacraments are its most common manifestations.[67] The third type is occasional spirituality, where Catholics "participate sporadically and selectively in church activity and in modalities of popular worship, for example, prayer at grave sites and memorials to the dead, attachment to amulets, rituals for protecting oneself against evil and bad luck, ceremonies in emergency situations."[68] Such persons freely blend Christianity with other religions and use these spiritual practices as a tool to try to conjure into reality personal success and fortune, as a divine fire extinguisher to squelch instances of misfortune, or divine armor against evil. Not all of these beliefs and practices would receive acceptance, nor should they, but the people engaging in these beliefs and practices would be dialogued with and have a voice in what theologians and the church would decide to accept officially.

In the Caribbean, Carlos Guillermo Wilson aptly described the development of religion in that region as "a marvelous cradle-

---

[64] Irarrázaval, *Inculturation*, 82.
[65] Irarrázaval, *Inculturation*, 83.
[66] Irarrázaval, *Inculturation*, 83.
[67] Irarrázaval, *Inculturation*, 83.
[68] Irarrázaval, *Inculturation*, 83.

hammock and painful cornucopia."[69] On the one hand, the region is rich with culture, including religious traditions that embrace popular and official church celebrations. On the other hand, the incorporation of the former into the latter has been a fraught process, bound up in the project of Caribbean liberation. This cultural liberation has been described by Joop Vernooij as a "creolization" of the Christian faith. Avoiding the traditional hegemony of European (and one could add North American) Christianity, Christianity gains an understanding of the Caribbean people[70] who wish to define themselves and their faith from within, instead of being exclusively defined by colonial and neo-colonial ideas from without. Idris Hamid, the father of Caribbean theology, argues, "If we examine carefully the folk-wisdom that has arisen among the people we shall find in those practical wisdom-saying elements of a theology or philosophy of life that reflects our historical experience. Thus any attempt at theology must examine many of the ways in which the reality of God was communicated, experienced and expressed among the people."[71] Caribbean theologians do not seek to eliminate the Christianity brought by the missionaries. European liturgical traditions, as Pedrito Maynard-Reid points out, "are also part and parcel of the Caribbean culture" but "in many cases [that] worship scratches where people are not itching."[72] This is why Caribbean theologians want to move the wisdom and expressions of faith of their people to the fore by moving the line between correct and incorrect inculturation to include "our wisdom sayings, our songs and literature, and the oral tradition" as well as the region's song and dance.[73] Recognized by the church both on an official and popular level as an original and authentic means of God's revelation,[74] it would incorporate all that to achieve a "liturgical revolution... that the whole theology of worship in relation to culture... be re-examined and therefore redefined in a radical way."[75] Monsignor Anthony offers several examples of this from his home island of St. Lucia, where each official practice of the sacraments in the Roman Catholic Church is paired with popular Catholic rituals.[76]

---

[69] Carlos Guillermo Wilson, "The Caribbean: Marvelous Cradle-Hammock and Painful Cornucopia," trans. Elba D. Birmingham-Pokorny and Luis A. Jiménez, in *Syncretism in Religion: A Reader,* ed. Anita Maria Leopold and Jeppe Sinding Jensen (New York: Routledge, 2004), 185.
[70] Vernooij, *Mapping Religious Suriname,* 153-4.
[71] Idris Hamid, "Theology and Caribbean Development," *With Eyes Wide Open* (Barbados: CADEC, 1973), 123; Anthony, "A Case Study in Indigenization," 192.
[72] Pedrito Maynard-Reid, *Diverse Worship: African-American, Caribbean and Hispanic Perspectives* (Downers Grove: InterVarsity, 2000), 148.
[73] Clark, "Liturgy and Culture in the Caribbean," 146.
[74] Anthony, "A Case Study in Indigenization," 192.
[75] Clark, "Liturgy and Culture in the Caribbean," 146.
[76] One example Anthony introduces is the use of Holy Water. Aside from its use in baptism, it is used to bless homes and businesses for protection against evil; it is

Again, what these theologians propose is not an uncritical appropriation of indigenous, popular understandings of Christianity. These same people who advocate for the incorporation of indigenous practices in worship and sacraments understand that these sources "have to be subjected to theological inquiry and scrutiny."[77] This task must be done because the distinction between acceptable and unacceptable forms of inculturation is already being moved in the Caribbean by the people themselves both for good and for ill. Theologians, clergy, and lay ministers who acknowledge and work with this reality will be in a position to help the church constructively engage and keep in the church those who practice these forms of belief and worship.

Juan Luis Segundo would argue that all Christian theologians, and not just those who reside in Latin America and the Caribbean, adopt a stance of critical trust. He describes this trust as allowing the people to "evangelize the theologian," in other words, to study and experience how these faithful in their practice of faith (often in the face of suffering) introduce God to the world.[78] Theologians by no means would set aside their formal education. (It is safe to assume those in pastoral ministry are extended the same compliment.) Segundo continues, "As intense as the theologian's conversion to ordinary people might be, this intellectual cannot totally renounce the exercise of a certain criticism."[79] The theologian will recognize in the culture of common people "negative elements" and "magnificent liberating aspects" at the same time. "It is a question, then, of distinguishing one from the other and, to the extent possible, of promoting some while restraining or repressing others."[80] Julio de Santa Ana steps in to argue that theologians then should help people move from what the Marxist Italian theorist Antonio Gramsci identified as their common sense, into developing what he called a "good sense" with their practice of the faith. (The presence of Gramsci should not surprise, since he is among the more influential Marxists amongst Latin American Theologians.[81]) Common sense is a people's uncritical conception of

---

drunk or poured on the body for protection against or healing from illness. He observes too that "bathing with water containing 'holy water' is a common remedy for *lanmaway* (the belief that someone's life has been malignantly 'tied up,' so that the person can make no progress or see any light [and/or] clear direction in their life)." Patrick A.B. Anthony, "St. Lucia, West Indies: Garden of Eden?" in *Popular Catholicism in a World Church*, ed. Thomas Bamat and Jean-Paul Wiest (Maryknoll: Orbis Books, 1999), 99.

[77] Anthony, "A Case Study in Indigenization," 193.
[78] Segundo, "The Shift within Latin American Theology," 24.
[79] Segundo, "The Shift within Latin American Theology," 27.
[80] Segundo, "The Shift within Latin American Theology," 27.
[81] See Enrique D. Dussel, "Theology of Liberation and Marxism," trans. Robert R. Barr, in *Mysterium Liberationis: Fundamental Concepts of Liberation Theology*, ed. Ignacio Ellacuría, S.J. and Jon Sobrino, S.J. (Maryknoll: Orbis Books, 1993), 87-8.

the world as they receive it.[82] For example, the fatalism that accompanied many popular expressions of faith in Latin America and the Caribbean was one major reason why theologians made the initial, erroneous, undifferentiated rejection of its practice. The "good sense" Santa Ana speaks of requires theologians, pastoral ministers, and the people they work with to transform their incultrated understandings and expressions of faith into aspirations for integral liberation of the human person and their communities, confrontation with those who deny them the achievement of these aspirations, and action for liberation as they see fit.[83]

One example from personal experience: I have described how Caribbean theology sees itself as a project of liberation through culture. When I taught my first course for Trinidadians and introduced the people there to theology done by Caribbean theologians using an extensive range of articles covering all topics, I did so out of a sense of giving the course intellectual credibility in the eyes of my students. But one student, a long-serving, high-ranking lay minister in the Archdiocese of Port-of-Spain told me how learning about an intellectual tradition found on his very doorstep affirmed his identity as a Caribbean man. He can inherit and build upon an indigenous Caribbean intellectual tradition that is part of the Catholic theological tradition that helps eliminate the stereotype of that region, held by too many outsiders, as a collection of vacation resorts. More importantly, it is a concrete demonstration that the church sees his practice of the faith as truthful and therefore a source for its theological work.

What concrete steps can theologians employ with Latin American and Caribbean people and the rest of the church, in redefining or, at times, keeping in place, the distinction between acceptable and unacceptable inculturation? Schineller argues that this effort begins with the right disposition toward inculturation. This includes a willingness to risk error, without which one cannot find success, an attitude of freedom in allowing the cultural practices of a group of people to be incorporated into worship and sacraments, a trust that allowing inculturation grants the church a better sense of what the reign of God is, patience with the whole process to the point of it being taxed, a charismatic dimension shown in a confidence that God is at work among the people, including their *sensus fidelium*, and yet this spirit of openness remains a critical one.[84] Beyond the right disposition, the concrete steps for acceptable inculturation include asking the following.[85]

---

[82] Santa Ana, "Popular Religion and Liberation in Latin America," 102.
[83] Santa Ana, "Popular Religion and Liberation in Latin America," 105-7.
[84] Schineller, "Inculturation and the Issue of Syncretism," 57-8.
[85] See Schineller, "Inculturation and the Issue of Syncretism," 56-7.

First, is it faithful to the Christian message? Is the incorporation of cultural customs into the worship and sacramental life of the church able to better communicate the message of the gospel without contradicting its content? Can it do the same with tradition, such as the creeds and councils of the church, the work of theologians, and devotional practices shared by most Christians elsewhere such as Mary and the saints? A small example: Both Yoruba[86] (an African religion which is a major influence on religion in the Caribbean and Brazil) and Judeo-Christian religions share an affinity for hilltops as places to encounter the divine. Affinities like this between Christianity and the customs and religious practices it encounters can be fruitful for inculturation.

Second, does the inculturation of church worship and liturgy build upon the culture of the people? For example, a belief in the all-pervasive presence of God—in which sacraments and sacramentals may enjoy a preeminent unique place, but nonetheless are accompanied by other customs or points of contact with the divine understood along Christian lines—may be acceptable. An unacceptable practice would be the belief that the practice of the sacraments and sacramentals can be employed to harm human beings. During a visit to Barbados, I encountered the belief that the sacraments can be viewed as magic tricks to manipulate the divine to do one's bidding, including casting bad spells on one's neighbor. I brought this up with my Caribbean students on Trinidad, who told me to a person how this belief was common to the region, and well-catechized Christians who embrace the popular worship practices of their region generally would nonetheless judge that specific popular belief as unacceptable.

Third, is the guidance and leadership in official church structures, working in tandem with clergy and lay leaders who minister among the people, tapping into their practice of the faith as a good source for theology? A powerful example of what Schineller speaks of here can be had on Trinidad with the excellent working relationships I found between the clergy and laity on that island. The charismatic nature of the practice of the faith there gives all a powerful sense of vocation. No one was left asking why one lacked a vocation, while the other had one. Energy was devoted to a trusting, yet critical culture of mutual support, with light church oversight, to develop and see through one's vocation in service to the church and people of Trinidad.[87]

---

[86] Peter Clarke, "The Dilemmas of a Popular Religion: The Case of Candomblé," in *The Popular Use of Popular Religion in Latin America,* ed. Susanna Rostas and André Droogers (Amsterdam: Centrum voor Studie en Documentatie van Latijns Amerika, 1993), 101.

[87] The Archbishop of Port-of-Spain, Joseph Harris, has written how the Church in the Caribbean, if it is to be truly the people of God, responsible for each other and for the Church's evangelical mission and social ministry, must understand ecclesiol-

The redefintion of inculturation, distinguishing between acceptable and unacceptable inculturation, is happening now in Latin America and the Caribbean. Theologians from those regions are working alongside pastoral ministers to bring about a just resolution that dispels the stereotype that the people whom they serve engage in peculiar worship practices of dubious pedigree.[88] Instead, the hope is the people of the local church in Latin America and the Caribbean are left with little doubt as to their inclusion and acceptance in the universal church. It is an issue where the resolution will be developed through practice, followed by the theology that will arise and respond to articulate it. Meanwhile, perhaps one can hope that popular religious practitioners, theologians, those in ministry, and church authority continue to relate to each other as friendly though occasionally argumentative and bickering members of the same Catholic family. M

---

ogy as a situation where "Christ's power resides not only in certain members but in the totality of the people of God." Therefore all share in the responsibility of Church ministry. Harris, a Trinidadian who spent years serving as a priest in Paraguay, is representative of theologians and ministers in the Caribbean and Latin America who seek to redefine Church hierarchy as leadership of a people who minister and are ministered to collaboratively. See Joseph E. Harris, "From Dominance to Partnership: The Christian Community as Locus and Agent of Ministerial Formation," *Theology in the Caribbean Today 1: Perspectives,* Patrick A.B. Anthony, ed. (Castries: Archdiocesan Pastoral Center, 1995), 48.

[88] Catholic theologians of the Caribbean region, for example, meet every other year to discuss, among other things, issues brought up in this article. This author, a sympathetic American outsider, is honored to be included in their number. See http://caribbeantheologytoday.net/

The World in the Theology of Joseph Ratzinger/Benedict XVI

Tracey Rowland

A TABLOID CARICATURE OF Joseph Ratzinger/Benedict XVI is that he has imbibed too much of the thought of St. Augustine, leaving him with a neo-Manichean stance of hostility to the world. A related caricature draws Catholics into two camps: the camp of the grace sniffers and the camp of the heresy sniffers, with the former Prefect of the Congregation for the Doctrine of the Faith presented as the captain of the latter. A third caricature is that Joseph Ratzinger was so shocked by the student demonstrations at the University of Tübingen in 1968 that he has developed a pathological fear of "the world" ever since. These various caricatures are not only simplistic, but they fail to engage with Ratzinger/Benedict's actual academic work on the issue of the relationship between the church and the world, and the church and the cultures of modernity and post-modernity. Contrary to these caricatures, a number of scholars who are not necessarily in agreement with Ratzinger's general theological framework, nonetheless agree that Ratzinger's theology does exhibit a quality of consistency over the decades and is not reacting one way or another to events in world history. In other words, the argument is that Ratzinger/Benedict's theology is *not* driven by his emotional response to world events. Joseph A. Komonchak, for example, has written that "from Ratzinger's *Introduction to Christianity* (1968) down to the homily he delivered on his installation as Pope Benedict XVI, a distinctive and consistent approach has been visible."[1] Similarly, Francis Schüssler Fiorenza, a former student of Ratzinger, wrote at the time of Ratzinger's election to the papacy, that "the negative slogans are wrong, the personal descriptions are true, and the biographical explanations are, in general, misleading. They overlook that Ratzinger has from early days had a consistent theological vision."[2] Finally, Lieven Boeve and Gerard Mannion have

---

[1] Joseph A. Komonchak, "The Church in Crisis: Pope Benedict's Theological Vision," *Commonweal* (3 June 2005): 11-14. Note: This paper was submitted to the editor in the final week of the papacy of Benedict XVI.
[2] Francis Schüssler Fiorenza, "From Theologian to Pope: A Personal View Back, Past and Public Portrayals," *Harvard Divinity Bulletin* 33 (2005).

concluded that "Ratzinger's theological insights have not fundamentally changed, but have rather demonstrated a firm internal consistency throughout more than fifty years."[3]

The purpose of this article is, therefore, to situate the work of Joseph Ratzinger/Benedict XVI in the context of early twentieth century German Augustinian studies, which was far removed from earlier German Protestant appropriations of the thought of St. Augustine. Further, the article presents a summary of Ratzinger's theological understanding of the concept "the world" in the context of rival interpretations of *Gaudium et spes*, the Pastoral Constitution of the Second Vatican Council on the Church in the Modern World.

The young Joseph Ratzinger's appropriation of the thought of St. Augustine was mediated through the scholarship of Fritz Hofmann, Erich Przywara, Romano Guardini, Gottlieb Söhngen and Henri de Lubac.[4] Hofmann was a professor of Theology at the University of Würzburg, and in 1933 he published a seminal work on the ecclesiology of St. Augustine which the young Ratzinger read in preparation for his own doctoral dissertation on the concepts of the People of God and the House of God in the works of St. Augustine. In this publication, Hofmann paid particular attention to the role of grace and the Holy Spirit in the life of the church. Hofmann's treatment of Augustinian ecclesiology was followed in 1940 by another Augustinian reflection, this time the "God is Love" theme, which was later to become the title of Benedict XVI's first encyclical.[5]

In the inter-bellum period, the Jesuit Erich Przywara (1889-1972) was also publishing material on Augustine and was one of the most influential German-speaking Jesuits of the twentieth century. He was a teacher of both Karl Rahner and Hans Urs von Balthasar and a spiritual director of the Carmelite-martyr, Jewish-convert, and philosopher, Edith Stein. Przywara was also for a time the editor of the influential journal *Stimmen der Zeit* and one of those responsible for having the works of John Henry Newman translated into German. In all, he wrote some 60 books and 600 articles including *Crucis myste-*

---

[3] Lieven Boeve and Gerard Mannion, ed., *The Ratzinger Reader* (London: Continuum, 2010), 12. Nonetheless, Boeve and Mannion do observe that Ratzinger's *tone of writing* became more polemical after 1968.
[4] Erich Przywara, "St. Augustine in the Modern World," in *A Monument to Saint Augustine*, ed. Martin D'Arcy (New York: Sheed & Ward, 1930); Fritz Hofmann, *Der Kirchenbegriff des hl. Augustinus in seinen Grundlagen und in seiner Entwicklung* (Munich: Max Hueber, 1933); Gottlieb Söhngen, "Wissenschaft und Weisheit im augustinischen Gedankengefüge," *Einheit in der Theologie* (München: Verlag, 1952); Romano Guardini, *Die Bekehrung des Aurelius Augustinus: Der innere Vorgang in seinen Bekenntnissen* (Münich: Grünewald, 1945), published in English translation as *The Conversion of St. Augustine* (Chicago: Regnery, 1966); Henri de Lubac, *Corpus Mysticum: L'Eucharistie et l'Église au moyen âge* (Paris: Aubier, 1944).
[5] Fritz Hofmann, *Gott ist die Liebe: die Predigten des. Hl. Augustinus über den 1. Johannesbrief* (Freiburg im Breisgau: Herder, 1940).

rium: Das christliche Heute (1939), a work which was later praised by Ratzinger, and *Humanitas: der Mensch Gestern und Morgan* (1952). For Przywara, the most perfect reincarnation of Augustinianism in the modern world was to be found in the writing of John Henry Newman. Przywara concluded that Newman "settles accounts with the Reformation more thoroughly than Hegel and Kierkegaard," and "he prophetically anticipated the conviction, born of the fiascos of Lausanne, Stockholm and Malines, that the Reformation cannot be overcome by 'negotiations' of any kind, but only by a thoroughgoing reversal of 'first principles'."[6] There was, in short, nothing remotely Protestant about Przywara's appropriation of Augustine.

The same can also be said of the Augustinian appropriations of Romano Guardini (1885-1968) who was a professor at the University of Munich from 1948-1962 and thus an important figure during the years when Ratzinger was a seminarian. Karl Rahner described Guardini as a "Christian humanist who led Germany's Catholics out of an intellectual and cultural ghetto and into the contemporary world."[7] Von Balthasar said of Guardini that he believed that "it is not Christ who is in the world, but the world is in Christ" and further that the "immensity of this reversal" was "the very basis" of Guardini's thought.[8] Guardini was also highly critical of the extrinsicist account of the relationship between nature and grace. In his 1939 work *Welt und Person*, which predated Henri de Lubac's *Surnaturel* by seven years, he wrote:

> Seen in the fullness of its energy as Paul proclaimed it and Augustine unfolded it, grace means something that is, not added on to the nature of man for his perfection, but rather the form that man definitely is. Of course, this presupposes that we understand by the term "man" what once again Paul and Augustine mean: not some being artificially let loose in a "pure nature," but rather that human being whom God intends and of whom Scripture speaks.[9]

In his later work *Freedom, Grace and Destiny*, Guardini suggested that the ultimate character of the world is not "Nature" but "History."[10] Since it proceeds from an act of God, nature exists *within* the world; it is a reality constructed in accordance with certain principles without consciousness or liberty, which has to operate in conformity

---

[6] Erich Przywara, "St Augustine and the Modern World," in *A Monument to Saint Augustine*, 280.
[7] Robert. A. Krieg, *Romano Guardini: The Precursor of Vatican II* (Indiana: University of Notre Dame, 1997).
[8] Hans Urs von Balthasar, *The Theology of Karl Barth* (San Francisco: Ignatius, 1992), 330.
[9] Romano Guardini, *Welt und Person* (Würzburg: Werkbund, 1939), 186-7.
[10] Romano Guardini, *Freedom, Grace, Destiny* (London: Harvill, 1961), 120-1.

with these principles. But nature is not synonymous with the world.[11] Moreover, Guardini wrote:

> The God of revelation is the same God who created the world and therefore the relation between revelation and the world is not merely one of difference. The Creator ordinated the world towards revelation, and this fundamental reality of existence has not been suppressed by sin. Scattered throughout the world are premonitions from which, in themselves, no single detail of revelation could be deduced but, once revelation has taken place, the Logos, as John declares, "without whom was made nothing that was made" comes "unto his own" and created being remains His property, even though it has turned against Him in sin and "his own received Him not" (John 1, 3-11). Thus a light is cast by revelation also on the things of the world. The paradox is in fact true that the real significance of these worldly things issues not from the things themselves but in the first instance, from revelation.[12]

Alongside Guardini, another prominent teacher of the young Joseph Ratzinger was Gottlieb Söhngen (1892-1971). Söhngen was a professor of fundamental theology at the University of Munich who supervised both of Ratzinger's theses, the doctoral dissertation on Augustine's ecclesiology and the *habilitationsschrift* on St. Bonaventure's theology of history. It was also under Söhngen that Ratzinger studied Newman's *Grammar of Assent*. Söhngen's rise to academic prominence was boosted by his publication of a two volume work on the *analogia fidei* in 1934, which was favourably reviewed by Karl Barth, although Barth doubted that Söhngen's approach was strongly representative of the Catholic position. It was nonetheless a position which was more Augustinian in the priority it gave to faith than some of the more rationalist currents which Barth detected in the typical Catholic theology of the era. Ratzinger's former Prefect of Studies, Alfred Läpple, said of Söhngen:

> [He] usually never gave damning judgments on any author. He never refused *a priori* any contribution, from wherever it came. His method was to pick up and improve the good that could be found in any author and in every theological perspective, to weave the new things into the Tradition and then go ahead, indicating the further development that could follow.... [I]n Söhngen Ratzinger also saw a willingness to rediscover Tradition understood as the theology of the Fathers. And a willingness to do theology by going back to the great

---

[11] Guardini, *Freedom, Grace, Destiny*, 121.
[12] Guardini, *Freedom, Grace, Destiny*, 101.

sources: from Plato to Newman, via Thomas, Bonaventure, Luther, and obviously Saint Augustine.[13]

At Söhngen's funeral, Ratzinger described his former teacher as "a radical and critical thinker" and a "radical believer."[14]

While a student at the Theology Faculty in Munich, Alfred Läpple also introduced the young Ratzinger to the works of Henri de Lubac, including his *Catholicism* of which Ratzinger was later to write that it was perhaps de Lubac's most significant work. Ratzinger also described *Catholicism* as "a key reading event" which gave him "not only a new and deeper connection with the thought of the Fathers but also a new way of looking at theology and faith as such."[15] Following *Catholicism,* Ratzinger read de Lubac's *Corpus Mysticum,* which helped him to "enter into the required dialogue with Augustine."[16]

The significant point about this genealogy from Hofmann, through Pryzwara, Guardini and Söhngen to de Lubac is that not one of these authors who had engaged with the thought of St. Augustine in the first half of the twentieth century had neo-Manichean, Lutheran or Calvinist inclinations or otherwise negative attitudes to the "world." Their fundamental dispositions were toward some form of Christian humanism, and they were all enlisting St. Augustine in this enterprise because of the value of his theological anthropology. Augustine wrestled with themes which were resurfacing among the early to mid-twentieth century existentialist philosophers. As Ratzinger has remarked, in the works of St. Augustine, "the passionate, suffering, questioning man is always right there, and one can identify with him."[17]

An extensive analysis of the various theological treatments of the concept of the "world" can be found in an essay by Cardinal Charles Journet, entitled "Les trois cités: celle de Dieu, celle de l'homme, celle du diable."[18] Journet sub-divides his presentation into the treatments of the concept in the Old Testament, the New Testament, and the works of St. Augustine. In the section on the New Testament meanings, he cites Jacques Maritain's observation that the world cannot be

---

[13] Alfred Läpple, "That New Beginning that Bloomed Among the Ruins," *30 Days* (January 2, 2006): www.30giorni.it/articoli_id_10125_l3.htm.
[14] Joseph Ratzinger, Beim Requiem in Köln am 19, November, 1971. "Söhngen war ein radikal und kritisch Fragender. Auch heute kann man nicht radikaler fragen, als er es getan hat. Aber zugleich war er ein radikal Glaubender."
[15] Joseph Ratzinger, *Milestones: Memoirs 1927-1977* (San Francisco: Ignatius, 1998), 98.
[16] Ratzinger, *Milestones*, 98.
[17] Joseph Ratzinger, *Salt of the Earth: The Church at the End of the Millennium: An Interview with Peter Seewald* (San Francisco: Ignatius, 1996), 61.
[18] Charles Journet, "Les trois cités: celle de Dieu, celle de l'homme, celle du diable," *Nova et Vetera* 33 (1958): 25-48.

neutral in relation to the kingdom of God. Either the world aspires to be the kingdom of God and is vivified by it, or it fights against it and exists in a relation of separation and of conflict.[19] The world is thus simultaneously an object of redemption and a city of evil. In his treatment of the concept in Augustine, Journet not only cites Augustine's comment in the *City of God* that the universe is more admirable than miracles, but he also draws attention to a lesser known statement from St. Augustine to the effect that the world is for God a kind of vast poem whose beauty unravels like a grandiose song. Journet also noted that one of St. Augustine's pastoral outreach audiences, the Donatists, did not want the world to include the church. However, contrary to the Donatists, Augustine was of the view that to say that the world can be reconciled to God and saved by Christ is to say that the world means the church, who alone, reconciled to God by Christ, is saved.[20] Journet sums up the position with the statement: "The damned world persecutes; the reconciled world is persecuted, it is the Church, *mundus damnatus, quidquid praeter Ecclesiam; mundus reconciliatus, Ecclesia.*"[21] With reference to the same phrase, Ernest Fortin, in his Saint Augustine Lecture of 1971, wrote: "The Church is not an entity distinct from the world but the world reconciled unto itself and unto God: *mundus reconciliatus ecclesia.*"[22]

This way of understanding the church-world relationship is also evident in von Balthasar's exegesis on Christ's words: "As the Father has sent me, so I send you into the world." Von Balthasar wrote:

> As Christ fulfils the will of the Father precisely by going away from the Father and so remains one with the Father, so too the Church fulfils the will of Christ in her going into the world and so remains one with Him. Indeed, this "going away" has its ultimate source and justification in the intra-divine "going away" of the Son from the Father himself, in the eternal *missio* in which all missions in salvation history are rooted.[23]

As a consequence of this reading, von Balthasar observes that the church, in her being sent out to the world, "is herself fundamentally a part of the world, just as Christ as man was a part of the world."[24] Moreover, "the Church walks in the path of redemption by plunging

---

[19] Jacques Maritain, *On the Philosophy of History* (New York: Scribner, 1957), 136.
[20] St. Augustine, *Ad donatistas post collationem*, ch. VIII.11, cited in Journet, "Les trois cités," 44 n. 4.
[21] Journet, "Les trois cités,"45.
[22] Ernest Fortin, "Political Realism and Christianity in the Thought of St. Augustine," The Saint Augustine Lecture 1971 (Villanova University, 1972), 25.
[23] Hans Urs von Balthasar, "The Father, the Scholastics, and Ourselves," *Communio* 24 (Summer 1997): 362.
[24] Balthasar, "The Father," 363.

with determination into the world and becoming herself the tool of this redemption, the *instrumentum redemptionis*."[25]

The contrary tendency to think of the church and the world dualistically has arisen apace with the emergence of the concept of the "secular" as a distinct ontological realm. Several authors have mapped this development, including Oliver O'Donovan and John Milbank. They both make the observation that initially the concept of the *saeculum* or secular order referred to time, not space. The *saeculum* was the time between Christ's resurrection and return in glory; it had nothing to do with social spheres.[26] As S. Joel Garver has explained the notion:

> Ecclesial order and civil order do not occupy two different spaces, but two different times: the church having an eternal end, rooted in God's past saving acts in Christ, made present now in word and sacrament; the civil order having a temporal function within the present *saeculum*, ordained to continually pass away, though its treasures are carried in the bosom of the church into the eternal kingdom.[27]

However, an Augustinian understanding of the relationship between the church and the world, such as it was expressed in von Balthasar's exegesis above, did not provide the theological infrastructure for *Gaudium et spes*. The infrastructure was the subject of much discussion and debate and the inevitable compromises which follow when there is little consensus about the best way to proceed.

In his *Principles of Catholic Theology*, first published in 1982, Ratzinger lamented that "despite many attempts to clarify it in section two of *Gaudium et spes*, [the concept of the world] continues to be used in a pre-theological stage."

> By "world" the Council means the counterpart of the Church. The purpose of the text is to bring the two into a relationship of cooperation, the goal of which is the "reconstruction of the 'world'." The Church cooperates with the world in order to build up the world—it is thus that we might characterise the vision that informs the text. It is not clear, however, whether the world that cooperates and the world that is to be built up are one and the same world; it is not clear what meaning is intended by the word "world" in every instance. In any event, we can be sure that the authors, who were aware that they spoke for the Church, acted on the assumption that they themselves were not the world but its counterpart and that they had up to then

---

[25] Balthasar, "The Father," 363.
[26] Oliver O'Donovan, *The Desire of the Nations- Rediscovering the Roots of Political Theology* (Cambridge: Cambridge University, 1996); John Milbank, *Theology and Social Theory: Beyond Secular Reason* (Oxford: Blackwell, 1990).
[27] Joel S. Garver, "There is another *King*: Gospel as Politics," www.*joelgarver*.com/-writ/phil/politics.htm.

had a relationship to it that was, in fact, unsatisfactory where it existed at all. To that extent, we must admit, the text represents a kind of ghetto mentality. The Church is understood as a closed entity, but she is striving to remedy the situation. By "world", it would seem, the document understands the whole scientific and technical reality of the present and all those who are responsible for it or who are at home in its mentality.[28]

Thus defined, the "world" comes across as a concept embracing all those social institutions in which the church has little or no influence, and the document sounds like a plea from the ghetto to be offered the occasional invitation into the hallowed halls of secular academies. As E. Michael Jones remarked, the Council occurred at the high noon of the Catholic inferiority complex. It occurred at a moment in history when Catholic intellectuals, tired of being regarded as reactionary and anti-intellectual, "lusted after modernity."[29]

Operating within the church-world dualism in *Gaudium et spes* there was also a church-humanity dualism. Ratzinger lamented the use of the term *genus humanum* to refer to the church's dialogue partner in the modern world. The church herself, he claimed, was part of the *genus humanum* and cannot be contradistinguished from it:

> The Church meets its *vis-a-vis* in the human race.... But it cannot exclude itself from the human race and then artificially create a solidarity which in any case is the Church's lot. The lack of understanding shown in this matter by those who drafted the text can probably only be attributed to the deeply-rooted extrinsicism of ecclesiastical thought, to long acquaintance with the Church's exclusion from the general course of development and to a retreat into a special little ecclesiastical world from which an attempt is then made to the speak to the rest of the world.[30]

At the foundation of the "deeply-rooted extrinsicism" was a tendency to think of the church canonically or bureaucratically, not mystically—to presume an ecclesiology based more on the Tridentine era theology of St. Robert Bellarmine than the multi-dimensional outlook one finds in de Lubac and von Balthasar and upon which the post-Conciliar Communio theology was built. Both de Lubac and von Balthasar tried to steer away from a narrowly juridical ecclesiol-

---

[28] Joseph Ratzinger, *Principles of Catholic Theology* (San Francisco: Ignatius, 1987), 379-80.
[29] E. Michael Jones, *Living Machines: Bauhaus Architecture as Sexual Ideology* (San Francisco: Ignatius, 1995), 42.
[30] Joseph Ratzinger, "The Dignity of the Human Person," in *Commentary on the Documents of the Second Vatican Council,* ed. Herbert Vorgrimler (London: Burns and Oates, 1969), 119.

ogy and instead presented the church as a symphonic interplay of different spiritual missions and relationships. The relations within the Trinity were of primary importance, but also important were the typological relationships found in the Scriptures, the sacramental relationships and the historical relationships between the Old and New Testaments.

With reference to the typographical relationships, de Lubac pointed out that the church is at once Mt. Sion (St. Basil), Noah's Ark (St. Augustine), the paradise in the midst of which Christ, the Tree of Life, is planted (St Irenaeus), and a foreigner, a slave and even a harlot. On the one hand, we see "an assembly of sinners, a mixed herd, wheat gathered with the straw... on the other, the unspotted virgin, mother of saints, born on Calvary from the pierced side of Christ."[31]

In his treatment of typology, von Balthasar referred to a "Christological constellation" of characters, each representing a different spiritual mission in the life of the church. For example, the Johannine mission (typified by St. John) is one of contemplative love and prayer; the Jacobite mission (typified by St. James) is one of preserving the tradition uncorrupted; the Petrine mission (typified by St. Peter) is one of ecclesial governance, and the Pauline mission (typified by St. Paul) is one of prophetic movement and utterance. Each mission is dependent on the others and operates in a symphonic harmony.

With reference to the notion of sacramental relations, de Lubac emphasised that the sacramental form of relationality is one that ties together the church, as the mystical body of Christ, with the church as the historical people of God. The church not only links the visible with the invisible, time with eternity, but also the universal and the particular, the Old and New Covenants. This link between the invisible and visible elements of ecclesial communion constitutes the church as the sacrament of salvation.

The conclusion to be drawn from this Communio ecclesiology, which Ratzinger has long argued was one of the great advances of the Second Vatican Council, is that any assessment of the relationship between the church and the world requires something much more theologically complex than a merely juridical understanding of the church and a merely sociological understanding of the world. In the early years of the 1960s, however, the Communio ecclesiology was still in its infancy and those responsible for drafting *Gaudium et spes* struggled to articulate a coherent analytical framework for a subject as large and complex as the church's relationship to the world.

In his introduction to his commentary on *Gaudium et spes* published in 1969, Ratzinger noted that Article 2 of the Zurich text of the document had attempted to justify the whole notion of the church's

---

[31] Henri de Lubac, *Catholicism and the Common Destiny of Man* (San Francisco: Ignatius, 1988), 69.

dialogue with "the world" by means of the scriptural reference to reading the signs of the times (Matt 16:3 and Luke 12:56). This earlier draft regarded epochs as a sign and a voice to the extent that they involve God's presence or absence; and consequently it was argued that the voice of the age must be regarded as the voice of God. However, Ratzinger observed that this idea was, quite correctly, criticized:

> To link the Roman proverb on time as the voice of God with Jesus' eschatological warning against the blindness of his nation which, though on the look-out for signs, was not able to interpret him, God's eschatological sign to that age, or his message, was considered not only exegetically unacceptable but of doubtful validity in itself. Since Christ is the real "sign of the time," is he not the actual antithesis to the authority of *chronos* expressed in the proverb "*vox temporis vox Dei*"?[32]

The idea that "Christ is the sign of the time" and that Christ is the "Light of the Nations," and thus that the Conciliar documents should be read with a Christocentric accent, was not the dominant reading of the documents in the 1960s. Instead the central message of the Council was often taken to be a general "openness to the world," however defined. This openness was then taken up by the correlationist theologians, of whom Edward Schillebeeckx was the most prominent, who sought to correlate the faith to the culture of the times. The correlationists also gave priority to the first sections of *Gaudium et spes* which were addressed to people of good will or "the world" at large. Walter Kasper and others have noted that there is a tension between the first sections of the document which are merely theistically hued and were directed to all peoples of good will regardless of faith traditions and the later sections which foster a Trinitarian Christocentric anthropology and thereby presuppose belief in Christian revelation.[33]

Ratzinger agrees with Kasper that a major problem with *Gaudium et spes* is that those responsible for its drafting never resolved the inherent tension between a merely theistically hued account of the human person and an explicitly Trinitarian account. The Trinitarian account, he said, "fell victim to the tendency to simplify."[34] Speaking directly of the treatment of human person in Article 12, Ratzinger complained that "there was not a radical enough rejection of a doctrine of man divided into philosophy and theology." The text was "still based on a schematic representation of nature and the super-

---

[32] Ratzinger, "The Dignity of the Human Person," 115.
[33] Walter Kasper, "The Theological Anthropology of *Gaudium et spes*," *Communio* 23 (1996): 129-40; David L. Schindler, "Christology and the Imago Dei: Interpreting *Gaudium et spes*," *Communio* 23 (1996): 156-84.
[34] Ratzinger, "The Dignity of the Human Person," 116.

natural viewed far too much as merely juxtaposed." To the mind of the critics of Article 12, it "took as its starting-point the fiction that it is possible to construct a rational philosophical picture of man intelligible to all and on which all men of goodwill can agree, the actual Christian doctrines being added to this as a sort of crowning conclusion. The latter then tends to appear as a sort of special possession of Christians, which others ought not to make a bone of contention but which at bottom can be ignored."[35] This approach thereby prompted the question of "why exactly the reasonable and perfectly free human being described in the first articles was suddenly burdened with the story of Christ."[36] Ratzinger went on to say that this criticism (the idea that the first section of *Gaudium et spes* seems to imply that the second section is a mere optional extra for Catholics who want to take it) was the basis of the protest against the "optimism" of the schema, not some "pessimistic view of man" or "an exaggerated theology of sin" more typically Lutheran than Catholic.[37]

At the end of this analysis Ratzinger noted that at the foundation of the *Gaudium et spes* conundrum was not only the relationship between nature and supernature but also the relationship between faith and understanding. He was then critical of the habit of positing a strong division between philosophy and theology, a habit he associated with the Thomist tradition, though without naming any particular branches of the tradition or acknowledging the internal debates within that tradition that had, for example, flared in French Thomist circles in the 1940s.[38] He merely concluded that the juxtaposition had gradually been established but "no longer appears adequate" and that "there is, and must be, a human reason in faith; yet, conversely, every human reason is conditioned by a historical standpoint so that reason pure and simple does not exist."[39] In other words, he was critical of the tendency to read "reason" as Kantian reason.

Lest this statement be discredited as the "low point" of Ratzinger's "theological teenager" period, he reiterated his stance against "pure reason" in his 1996 address to the bishops of Mexico. In that address

---

[35] Ratzinger, "The Dignity of the Human Person," 119.
[36] Ratzinger, "The Dignity of the Human Person," 120.
[37] Ratzinger, "The Dignity of the Human Person," 120.
[38] For an account of these debates see: Gregory B. Sadler ed./trans., *Reason Fulfilled by Revelation: The 1930s Christian Philosophy Debates in France* (Washington, DC: The Catholic University of America, 2011). This book sets out the players in the 1930s Christian Philosophy debates in France and places them into the categories of: Neo-Thomist Opponents of Christian Philosophy, Thomist Proponents of Christian Philosophy, and Non-Thomist Proponents of Christian Philosophy. For a more general account of the different approaches to the relationship between faith and reason in the Thomist tradition which is not restricted to the French contributions to the debate, see Fergus Kerr, *After Aquinas: Versions of Thomism* (Oxford: Blackwell, 2002).
[39] Ratzinger, "The Dignity of the Human Person," 120.

he said that "neo-scholastic rationalism failed in its attempts to reconstruct the *preambula fidei* with wholly independent reasoning, with pure rational certainty."[40] Karl Barth, he said, was "right to reject philosophy as the foundation of faith, independent of faith," since if that were so, "our faith would be dependent from the beginning to the end on changing philosophical theories."[41] Nonetheless he rejected Barth's idea of faith as a pure paradox that can only exist against reason and totally independent of it. As Aidan Nichols has argued, Ratzinger/Benedict's account of the faith and reason relationship sounds "highly Gilsonian" (according to whom the relationship is intrinsic), and it also "made *some* movement towards *bautainisme*, which, owing to its inheritance from traditionalism, considered faith to be an indispensable auxiliary to reason if reason were ever to attain fundamental truths."[42] Nichols also draws attention to affinities between Ratzinger's account of the faith and reason relationship and that of Franz Jacob Clemens and Paul Tillich. In general, Nichols observes that Benedict tends to unite "philosophy and theology in a single, internally differentiated but also internally cohesive, intellectual act," and thus, what one finds in Benedict's many publications is a "convergence of the mainly philosophical disclosure of logos with the chiefly theological revelation of love."[43] "Love and Reason," Benedict writes, are the "twin pillars" of reality. This in turn gives rise to a quintessentially Augustinian theological anthropology which pays equal attention to the head and the heart, to objectivity and affectivity. As Paige E. Hochschild observed in her work *Memory in Augustine's Theological Anthropology*, for St. Augustine, "the two problems of knowledge and love cannot be separated, given that one determines the object for the other."[44]

At the time of the drafting of *Gaudium et spes*, however, there was still a strong habit of thinking of faith and reason extrinsically. This was due, at least in part, to the influence of the first paragraph of Chapter Two of the document *Dei Filius* of Vatican I. The much quoted "anathema" sentence reads:

> If anyone says that the one, true God, our creator and lord, cannot be known with certainty from the things that have been made, by the natural light of human reason, let him be anathema.

---

[40] Joseph Ratzinger, "The Current Situation of Faith and Theology," *L'Osservatore Romano* (November 6, 1996): 6.
[41] Ratzinger, "The Current Situation," 6.
[42] Aidan Nichols, *Faith and Reason: From Hermes to Benedict XVI* (Leominster: Gracewing, 2009), 228-30.
[43] Nichols, *Faith and Reason*, 228, 193.
[44] Paige E. Hochschild, *Memory in Augustine's Theological Anthropology* (New York: Oxford University, 2012), 139.

That particular paragraph was drafted at a moment in time when the Catholic Church was under attack from rationalist philosophers and thus her champions were focused on defending the rationality of the faith.

Precisely how it is to be interpreted in the light of later debates and magisterial documents, especially the "Catholic philosophy" debates of the 1940s, the Conciliar document *Dei Verbum*, and John Paul II's encyclical *Fides et Ratio* (which scholars have argued was at least implicitly Gilsonian), remains a subject of academic dispute.[45] Fergus Kerr has noted that "it remained unsettled at Vatican I whether the natural light by which reason can attain knowledge of God should be equated with the prelapsarian light enjoyed by Adam in the Garden of Eden or the light in which someone in a state of grace might exercise his reasoning powers, or the light which someone might supposedly have independently of the effects of sin and grace."[46] Moreover, Kerr observes that, while the First Vatican Council (1869-70) decreed that for Catholics it is a dogma of faith that we can have certain knowledge of God by the natural light of reason, it was only in the Anti-Modernist Oath (1910) that this knowledge was defined as rationally demonstrable by cosmological arguments.

Similarly, Noel O'Sullivan has suggested that what is interesting about *Dei Filius* is "not so much what it says but rather what it doesn't say," and in particular "one is struck by the absence of a Trinitarian dimension in the definition of 1870."[47] In a manner which is consonant with Ratzinger's criticisms, O'Sullivan observes:

> The key difficulty that arises from this overly rationalistic approach is that a separation arises between creation and salvation. In this perspective creation is seen as primarily concerned with the world and the universe, while the human being is only considered on a secondary level, as a being in the world. The human is treated as of primary concern only in the context of salvation. The act of creation is antecedent to humanity and is of no significance where revelation and salvation history is concerned. Creation is just a neutral shell where salvation history is acted out. Even God is looked on differently, depending on whether the perspective is that of creation or salvation. From the perspective of creation taken in isolation, God is the first cause of everything that exists: there is an immensurable gap between Creator and creature. From the perspective of salvation alone,

---

[45] Kenneth L Schmitz reads *Fides et Ratio* as implicitly Gilsonian, and John Milbank has suggested that *Fides et ratio* is at least open to a Gilsonian interpretation even though other interpretations are also possible.

[45] Fergus Kerr, "Knowing God by Reason Alone: What Vatican I Never Said," *New Blackfriars* 91 (May 2010): 222.

[46] Kerr, "Knowing God by Reason Alone," 222.

[47] Noel O'Sullivan, *Christ and Creation: Christology as the Key to Interpreting the Theology of Creation in the Works of Henri Lubac* (Oxford: Peter Lang, 2009), 139.

God is a personal being in relationship with humanity. As a result of this manner of viewing creation and salvation in such distinct categories, an opposition between faith and reason develops. Faith is seen as concerned with the salvific action of God and not connected to the creative action of God.[48]

On Ratzinger's reading, Article 21 of *Gaudium et spes* represents a kind of immature compromise between the rationalist interpretation of *Dei Filius* and some of the criticisms of extrinsicism which began in the works of Maurice Blondel and flowed into the French Thomist debates in the 1940s. Thus he wrote:

> The term "ratio" was simply meant to recall in abbreviated form the well-known definitions of Vatican I, and by the addition or retention of *"experientia"* the aim was to limit the neo-scholastic rationalism contained in the formula of 1870 and to place its over-static idea of *"ratio naturalis"* in a more historical perspective. The text dictates... that the possibilities of reason in regard to knowledge of God should be thought of less in the form of a non-historical syllogism of the *philosophia perennis* than simply as the concrete fact that man throughout his whole history has known himself confronted with God and consequently in virtue of his own history finds himself in relation with God as an inescapable feature of his own existence.[49]

The Conciliar document that dealt with these issues more to Ratzinger's liking was *Dei Verbum*. As Gregory Baum has argued, while *Dei Filius* did not address the issue of *how* knowledge of the true God based on human reason is related to the saving actions of God revealed in Christ, the "profounder understanding of revelation" offered by *Dei Verbum* "introduces a new theological epistemology."[50] Baum summarises this epistemology in the following paragraph:

> Vatican I affirms that "God, the beginning and end of all things, can be known with certainty from created reality by the light of human reason." In accordance with Vatican II, we can now say that if God allows Himself to be found – across whatever distance – through the works of His creation as understood by human reason, this does not take place because of an independent or sovereign act of man, but rather because of the appeal which the gracious God through His creation makes to the mind and heart of men. The "natural" knowledge of God is related to the history of salvation appointed for the whole human family, which is revealed once and for all in Jesus Christ.[51]

---

[48] O'Sullivan, *Christ and Creation*, 139-40.
[49] Ratzinger, "The Dignity of the Human Person," 153.
[50] Gregory Baum, "Vatican II's Constitution on Revelation: History and Interpretation," *Theological Studies* 28, no. 1 (March 1967): 62.
[51] Baum, "Vatican II's Constitution," 64.

In short, *Dei Verbum* emphasises that the structure of revelation is Trinitarian, and this "profounder understanding" is something of a solvent for rationalist interpretations of *Dei Filius*. This deeper theological epistemology was not however integrated into *Gaudium et spes*, and notwithstanding the addition of the concept of "experiential" which was a move in an anti-rationalist direction, Ratzinger regarded Article 21 as an inadequate response to atheism.

He suggested that in order to address the concerns of atheists, God's invisibility is something that has to be taken into account:

> [Christianity] cannot be taken seriously if it acts as if reason and revelation present a smooth, plain certainty accessible to everyone; in that case atheism could only be a matter of evil will. In that case, too, the atheist could not consider that he was being taken seriously. He would feel little inclination to engage in discussion when his cause is declared from the start to be contrary to plain reason and he is treated merely as a sick man worthy of pity, the causes of whose malady are being inquired into so that he may be cured.[52]

Taken as a whole, Ratzinger regarded Article 21 as offering no advance in regard to the problem raised at Vatican I.

He thought the mere addition of "*experientia*" to "*ratio*" would not solve the problems and that the whole article fails to engage with contemporary theological reflections, especially those fostered by Karl Barth's criticisms of the doctrine of the *analogia entis*:

> The Council passed over the essentials of the *theologia negativa*. It took no account of Augustine's epistemology, which is much deeper than that of Aquinas, for it is well aware that the organ by which God can be seen cannot be a non-historical "ratio naturalis" which just does not exist, but only the *ratio pura*, ie. *purificata* or, as Augustine expresses it echoing the gospel, the *cor purum* ("Blessed are the pure in heart, for they shall see God"). Augustine also knows that the necessary purification of sight takes place through faith (Acts 15:9) and through love, at all events not as a result of reflection alone and not at all by man's own power. By ignoring these approaches, the opportunity was lost of manifesting the positive service to faith performed by atheism.[53]

Against Barth however, Ratzinger applauded the fact that the article does at least emphasise that faith "cannot remain inaccessible to a reason which is ready to listen."[54] Ratzinger is not a Barthian, but he

---

[52] Ratzinger, "The Dignity of the Human Person," 154-5.
[53] Ratzinger, "The Dignity of the Human Person," 155.
[54] Ratzinger, "The Dignity of the Human Person," 155.

shares Barth's aversion to rationalism and Barth's linkage of rationalism with secularism.

Notwithstanding his specific judgements about the inadequacy of the Conciliar engagement with the phenomenon of atheism, Ratzinger nonetheless approved of the general orientation of a small sub-commission consisting of Cardinal König, Cardinal Šeper, Henri de Lubac and Jean Daniélou which decided to deal with the question of atheism as an anthropological (not a narrowly epistemological) issue. These committee members understood that atheism "does not simply express a metaphysical failure or a breakdown in epistemology, but draws its inspiration from an authentic desire for a true humanism."[55] Further, Ratzinger asserted that "atheism is a question which can only be understood on the level of existence; a philosophy of pure essences cannot cope with it."[56] He suggested that the fundamental question is: Is God merely a projection of man or is it God who makes it possible for man to be human?[57]

The language used by Ratzinger for describing how to combat atheism was that of "showing the face of God to the world." This he said had nothing to do with a "one-sided activism." Rather, an important component of it is "participation in the spirituality of the Cross," and indeed, Ratzinger noted that martyrdom is the clearest exposition of the face of God. He concluded:

> The real answer to atheism is the life of the Church, which must manifest the face of God by showing its own face of unity and love. Conversely this includes the admission that the disunity of Christians and their consent to systems of social injustice, hide the face of God. It also implies the realisation that knowing God is not a question of pure reason alone, that there is an obscuration of God in the world produced by guilt, which can only be removed by penance and conversion.[58]

Reading this passage in the first week of Lent 2013, that is, during the final week of the pontificate of Benedict XVI, is quite a sobering exercise. One senses that Ratzinger/Benedict's decision to resign from the papacy represents an exchange of a Petrine mission for a Johannine mission. Jean Daniélou, one of those *periti* Ratzinger praised for understanding that atheism is fundamentally an anthropological rather than epistemological issue (although he would no doubt agree that there is an epistemological dimension to the anthropological problem), wrote the following words:

---

[55] Ratzinger, "The Dignity of the Human Person," 146
[56] Ratzinger, "The Dignity of the Human Person," 146.
[57] Ratzinger, "The Dignity of the Human Person," 146.
[58] Ratzinger, "The Dignity of the Human Person," 157.

> Our Lord has told us that souls are to be won away from the Devil first by fasting and vigils, and that the great battle is fought in the heart of the desert, in the depth of solitude, on the summit of Carmel, before it is fought through the ministry of preachers, on the great highways and in the villages....We must tear souls away from Satan first of all through prayer, penance and sacrifice.[59]

Benedict XVI's decision to retire and pray for the church appears to have been the adoption of precisely this approach to the problem of contemporary unbelief, both within and without the church. Just as John Paul II died on the stage of the world bearing witness to a Christian understanding of death with dignity, Benedict XVI leaves the stage of the world bearing witness to the truth that prayer and fasting is sometimes the only way to triumph over extreme evil.

A core element of any anthropology is that of its understanding of freedom. Here it is highly significant that of all Ratzinger's criticisms of *Gaudium et spes*, his most acidic comments are directed against the treatment of freedom in Article 17. It was "one of the least satisfactory of the whole document;" it "cannot stand up to either theological or philosophical criticism;" philosophically, "it by-passes the whole modern discussion of freedom;" it "shut itself out from the factual situation of man whose freedom only comes into effect through a lattice of determining factors, theologically speaking it leaves aside the whole complex of problems which Luther, with polemical one sidedness, comprised in the term *'servum arbitrium'*." Moreover, "the whole text gives scarcely a hint of the discord which runs through man and which is described so dramatically in Rom 7:13-25. It even falls into downright Pelagian terminology when it speaks of man *'sese ab omni passionum captivitate liberans finem suum persequitur et apta subsidia... procurat'*."[60] He concluded:

> If optimism in John XXIII's sense means readiness for today and tomorrow, if it means abandoning nostalgia for the past for a spirituality of hope in the midst of each particular present moment, then it does not in any way impose the platitudes of an ethics modeled on that of the Stoa. Here it would have been possible to learn from Marxism about the extent of human alienation and decadence. Not to take them seriously does not mean to think highly of man, but to deceive him about the gravity of his situation.[61]

Positively, however, Ratzinger noted that the Council Fathers were keen to affirm man's freedom against the variety of determinisms which so characterized early twentieth century history. Although no

---

[59] Jean Daniélou, *The Salvation of the Nations*, trans. Angeline Bouchard (New York: Sheed & Ward, 1950), 43.
[60] Ratzinger, "The Dignity of the Human Person," 138.
[61] Ratzinger, "The Dignity of the Human Person," 138.

specific examples were given, the racist determinism of the Nazi ideology, the class determinism of the Marxist ideology, and the hormonal or sex-drive determinism of Freudian psychology were all likely to have been in the thoughts of the Council Fathers.

While the Council Fathers may have been so focused on rejecting these various determinisms that they failed to analyze in any depth the limitations on human freedom, the whole pontificate of John Paul II can be read as a theo-dramatic study on this very topic. Against the backdrop of the Cold War, many of John Paul II's publications dealt with critiques of Pelagian-liberal conceptions of freedom on the one side and Marxist conceptions on the other. As he remarked in an address to the scholars of Lublin University in 1987 in the dying days of the Communist regime, "the human person must stave off a double-temptation: the temptation to make the truth about himself subordinate to his freedom and the temptation to subordinate himself to the world of objects: he has to refuse to succumb to the temptation of both self-idolatry and of self-subjectification."[62] The first temptation is the liberal temptation; the second is the Marxist. Both are erroneous because, as he was later to express the problem poetically, "the human person is a pillar that has a crack to be sealed within."[63] Only grace can seal the crack, and grace is not part of the conceptual framework of the liberal or the Marxist.

In addition to the lack of clarity regarding the relationship of anthropology to Christology or, more specifically, of a merely theistically coloured account of creation to an explicitly Trinitarian account, there is the further problem of the interpretation of Article 36 of *Gaudium et spes*. This article speaks of a *terrenarum rerum autonomia*, which is normally rendered in English (including in the official Holy See English translation) as "the legitimate autonomy of earthly affairs." With reference to this particular phrase David L. Schindler has argued that "the root meaning of the '*legitima autonomia*' finds its proper meaning in an analogy of being based on the descent of God into the world" and, further, that "the organic relation between the Trinity and the creature established in Jesus Christ does not reduce creaturely autonomy but rather grants it a new and expanded meaning."[64] The paragraph is capable of a non-secularising interpretation, especially if it is read by persons who have studied theology. However a "plain person" reading the phrase "a legitimate autonomy of earthly affairs" is likely to interpret the expression quite differently

---

[62] Karol Wojtyła, "Address to the Scholars of Lublin University," *Christian Life in Poland* (November 1987), 51.
[63] See the poem *La Libertá* written by John Paul II and recorded as a song by Placido Domingo.
[64] David L. Schindler, "Trinity, Creation and the Order of Intelligence in the Modern Academy," *Communio* 28 (Fall 2001): 407.

from a professional theologian. Cardinal Angelo Scola has noted that there is a "latent ambiguity" around the interpretation of the principle of the autonomy of earthly affairs.[65] Scola reads Article 36 as an acknowledgement that there is a realm of life which is the responsibility of the laity. He does not read it as authority for the proposition that there might be aspects of life which have no intrinsic relationship to the Creator and thus that there might be social provinces in which theological insight has nothing to contribute.

Consistent with such an interpretation, in an essay on the contributions of Cardinal Joseph Frings to the Conciliar debates, Ratzinger drew attention to Frings' speech of October 27, 1964 in which he warned that earthly advances do not transfer directly to the kingdom of God. As Ratzinger expressed his argument:

> The three stages of creation, incarnation, and Passover must be seen each in their dynamic relation, each with its own weight and each in relation to the others. Literally, his [Frings'] formulation was, "For the Christian life in the world three revealed truths are always to be kept before us: creation, which teaches us to love the things of the world as God's work; the Incarnation, which spurs us on to dedicate to God all the things of the world; cross and resurrection, which leads us in the imitation of Christ to sacrifice and continence with regard to the things of the world."[66]

What Scola identified as a latent ambiguity in *Gaudium et spes* 36 may be identified as a concrete example of the problems which arise when interpreters of the Conciliar documents approach them with a lopsided focus on creation at the expense of the incarnation and Paschal mysteries.

Writing in 1965 but without directly mentioning the recently promulgated *Gaudium et spes*, Romano Guardini observed that "the whole modern view of the autonomy of the world and of man... seem to rest ultimately on the notion which made of God the 'other'."[67] The end result of this mentality is that the world becomes an idol. Guardini concluded that this concept of autonomy "is a kind of tetanus in which the world suffocates."[68] One of Guardini's colleagues at the University of Munich, Michael Schmaus, who was actually Ratzinger's adversary when it came to the presentation of his *habilitationsschrift*, was equally critical of the notion of the world's autonomy understood in any popular or plain-meaning sense. Refer-

---

[65] Angelo Scola, "El Peligro de una Falsa 'Autonomia'," *Humanitas: Revista de Antropología y Cultura Christianas* 66 (Otono 2012): 299.
[66] Joseph Ratzinger, "Cardinal Frings's Speeches during the Second Vatican Council: Apropos of A. Muggeridge's *The Desolate City*," *Communio* 15, no. 1 (1988): 143-4.
[67] Guardini, *The World and the Person*, 204.
[68] Guardini, *The World and the Person*, 204.

ring to St. Paul's Letter to the Colossians, he noted that when Paul speaks of our having "being" because of Christ, he implies that nature is something given as a gift:

> That we even exist at all is based on Christ, since we could only exist as people who are called in Christ to be saved and healed. He is the One from whom and toward whom the universe exists at all…The world, accordingly, does not possess a completely autonomous order that is ultimately self-subsistent and self-sufficient. Its order is in fact taken up into that order whose ground is Christ.[69]

In addition to all these various problems of interpretation relating to theological anthropology and the church-world relationship, there is the problem (more of a linguistic and sociological nature) that although there are many references to the modern world and modern man to be found in *Gaudium et spes*, at the time of the document's drafting by predominately Francophone theologians, there was very little scholarship available on "modernity as a cultural formation" (aside from a few scattered works in German and English).

The Canadian philosopher Kenneth Schmitz has observed that in the 1960s very few Catholic scholars had any understanding of what sociologists now mean by the concept of modernity:

> Had we been more perceptive we might have guessed that the foundations of modernity were beginning to crack under an increasingly incisive attack. But we had no such cultural concept as modernity: all we had instead was the historical category: modern philosophy.[70]

In his autobiographical work, *A Theologian's Journey*, Thomas F. O'Meara suggested that "much conflict would have been avoided if [Romano Guardini's] perspectives on modernity had been read by the Vatican."[71] That they were not was probably due to the rigidity of the seminary curricula of the time which was not designed for the kind of inter-disciplinary analysis required of what is now called the theology of culture. Pre-Conciliar Thomism prided itself on being "above history," not on its intellectual analysis of transient historical cultural phenomena. It is striking that those Catholic scholars who were interested in modernity as a cultural formation were predominately members of the laity, for example, Georges Bernanos and Christopher Dawson.

---

[69] Michael Schmaus, *Katholische Dogmatik II*, 4th ed. (München: Verlag, 1949), 52, cited in Balthasar, *The Theology of Karl Barth*, 331.
[70] Kenneth L. Schmitz, "Postmodernism and the Catholic Tradition," *American Catholic Philosophical Quarterly* LXXIII.2 (1999): 235.
[71] Thomas F. O'Meara, *A Theologian's Journey* (Boston: Paulist, 2002), 218.

Today, however, some five decades later, most post-Conciliar generation scholars are familiar with the many critiques of modernity from theological and sociological perspectives. There is, for example, the Alasdair MacIntyre reading of modernity as the *severance* of the classical-theistic synthesis, the Charles Taylor reading as a *mutation* of the same synthesis, the Hans Blumenberg reading as the *re-occupation* of defunct Christian concepts with a new non-Christian substance, the Eric Voegelin thesis of modernity as *neo-gnosticism*, and the "Radical Orthodoxy" reading represented by Catherine Pickstock and John Milbank, as the *heretical re-construction* of the classical-theistic synthesis. Regardless of the differences in nuance between severance, mutation, re-occupation, neo-gnosticism, and heretical reconstruction, in each of these accounts of the culture of modernity there is a common agreement that this culture developed in opposition to the medieval theological (especially Thomistic) synthesis and the culture which embodied its principles. Theologians such as von Balthasar would add that the severance of the relationship between the true, the beautiful, and the good was a central pathological feature of the new culture.

Tragically, in the 1960s and beyond, Catholic theologians who interpreted the Council, especially *Gaudium et spes*, as a call to make the Catholic faith more compatible with the culture of modernity were often unaware of just how far *behind the times* such thinking really was. As Augustine Di Noia has noted: "The Post-Conciliar interpretation of John XXIII's vision of *aggiornamento* as updating theology is, from the perspective of post-modern eyes, a project which has never really caught up, while conceived more grandly as modernization, it is already far behind."[72]

The remedy of both Blessed John Paul II and Benedict XVI to the correlationist interpretations of *Gaudium et spes*, which often resulted in the teachings and practices of the church being expressed in the language of liberal modernity and which today now sound so dated as to be almost incomprehensible to those born after the 1970s, was to emphasise the Christocentric sections of the document, in particular Article 22. By making Article 22 the hermeneutical lens through which the rest of the document is read, many of the problems which Ratzinger, Kasper, Scola and others have identified, can be overcome.

Ratzinger has suggested that the merit of *Gaudium et spes*, notwithstanding its unresolved inner tensions and tendency to use ambiguous language, is that it offered a "daring new theological anthropology," albeit one that was not well expressed in the actual document. As he wrote:

---

[72] Augustine Di Noia, "American Catholic Theology at Century's End: Postconciliar, Postmodern and Post Thomistic," *The Thomist* 54 (1990): 518.

Article 22 thus returns to the starting-point, Article 12, and presents Christ as the eschatological Adam to whom the first Adam already pointed; as the true image of God which transforms man once more into likeness to God. The attempt to pursue discussion with non-believers on the basis of the idea of "*humanitas*", here culminates in the endeavour to interpret being human Christologically and so attain the "*resolutio in theologiam*" which, it is true, also means "*resolutio in hominem*" (provided the sense of "homo" is understood deeply enough). We are probably justified in saying that here for the first time in an official document of the magisterium, a new type of completely Christocentric theology appears.[73]

In Article 22, the idea of the "*assumptio hominis*" is first touched upon it its full ontological depth. The human nature of all men is one; Christ's taking to himself the one human nature of man is an event which affects every human being; consequently human nature in every human being is henceforward Christologically characterised... This outlook is probably also important because it opens a bridge between the theology of the incarnation and that of the cross. A theology of the incarnation situated too much on the level of essence, may be tempted to be satisfied with the ontological phenomenon: God's being and man's have been conjoined...But since it is made clear that man's being is not that of a pure essence, and that he only attains his reality by his activity, it is at once evident that we cannot rest content with a purely essentialist outlook. Man's being must therefore be examined precisely in its activities.[74]

Herein lies an important point of convergence between Ratzinger/Benedict and Wojtyła/John Paul II. They are both interested in relationality or that dimension of the human person which is determined by their relations with other persons, including each of the Persons of the Trinity, in time and history. As Michael Schmaus expressed the principle: "Nature cannot come to its fulfilment in the antechambers of God's love and glory, but only in the inner chamber of his Trinitarian divine life."[75] Michael Hanby made the same point in his *Augustine and Modernity*, when he wrote that at issue within the culture of modernity is the Trinity itself and specifically whether the meaning of human nature and human agency are understood to occur within Christ's mediation of the love and delight shared as *donum* between the Father and the Son, or beyond it.[76]

Among Benedict's many papal homilies and documents, one can find numerous criticisms of the culture of modernity from a Trinitarian Christocentric perspective. One of the most sustained criticisms

---

[73] Ratzinger, "The Dignity of the Human Person," 159.
[74] Ratzinger, "The Dignity of the Human Person," 160.
[75] Schmaus, *Katholische Dogmatik II*, 200.
[76] Michael Hanby, *Augustine and Modernity* (London: Routledge, 2003), 73.

is found in his second encyclical *Spe Salvi* which some commentators have described as his "antidote" to the secularist renderings of poorly drafted passages in *Gaudium et spes*. Although this is probably an accident (not something he intended), Article 22 of *Spe Salvi* resonates strongly with the Christocentricism of Article 22 of *Gaudium et spes*. Here he wrote:

> A self-critique of modernity is needed in dialogue with Christianity and its concept of hope. In this dialogue Christians too, in the context of their knowledge and experience, must learn anew in what their hope truly consists, what they have to offer to the world and what they cannot offer. Flowing into this self-critique of the modern age there also has to be a self-critique of modern Christianity, which must constantly renew its self-understanding setting out from its roots. On this subject, all we can attempt here are a few brief observations. First we must ask ourselves: what does "progress" really mean; what does it promise and what does it not promise?...If technical progress is not matched by corresponding progress in man's ethical formation, in man's inner growth (cf. Eph 3:16; 2 Cor 4:16), then it is not progress at all, but a threat for man and for the world.

In the following paragraph, Pope Benedict was critical of notions of rationality "detached from God," and he argued that "if progress, in order to be progress, needs moral growth on the part of humanity, then the reason behind action and capacity for action is likewise urgently in need of integration through reason's openness to the saving forces of faith, to the differentiation between good and evil. Only thus does reason become truly human."

This means that the great Enlightenment project, severing faith from reason and then, with a much reduced rational capacity, setting about building political utopias based on nothing more than this faith-less rationality, was not going to foster the very freedom it desired. Hence, there is Benedict's judgment in *Spe salvi* 24 that "the right state of human affairs, the moral well-being of the world can never be guaranteed simply through structures alone, however good they are:"

> Since man always remains free and since his freedom is always fragile, the kingdom of good will never be definitively established in this world. Anyone who promises the better world that is guaranteed to last for ever is making a false promise; he is overlooking human freedom. Freedom must constantly be won over for the cause of good. Free assent to the good never exists simply by itself. If there were structures which could irrevocably guarantee a determined—good— state of the world, man's freedom would be denied, and hence they would not be good structures at all.

Particularly in Article 25 of *Spe salvi*, Benedict concluded that Francis Bacon and those who followed in the intellectual current of modernity that he inspired were wrong to believe that man would be redeemed through science.

Nothing in these paragraphs however should be construed as a Christian call to withdraw from the world. Earlier in *Spe Salvi*, at Article 15, Benedict explicitly rejected the idea that the church's endorsement of the monastic vocation has something to do with a "contempt for the world" mentality. He suggested that if we take "a more or less randomly chosen episode from the Middle Ages," the monastic movement of St Bernard of Clairvaux, St Bernard was not encouraging youth to treat monasteries "as places of flight from the world (*contemptus mundi*) and of withdrawal from responsibility for the world, in search of private salvation." Rather, St. Bernard's monks were performing "a task for the whole church and hence also for the world."

In the later paragraphs of *Spe Salvi* (Arts. 34, 35 and 36), Benedict exhorted Catholics to "keep the world open to God":

> We can open ourselves and the world and allow God to enter: we can open ourselves to truth, to love, to what is good. This is what the saints did, those who, as "God's fellow workers", contributed to the world's salvation (cf. 1 Cor. 3:9; 1 Thess. 3:2). We can free our life and the world from the poisons and contaminations that could destroy the present and the future. We can uncover the sources of creation and keep them unsullied, and in this way we can make a right use of creation, which comes to us as a gift, according to its intrinsic requirements and ultimate purpose....
>
> We know that this God exists, and hence that this power to "take away the sin of the world" (Jn. 1:29) is present in the world. Through faith in the existence of this power, hope for the world's healing has emerged in history.

In the final analysis, the conflict over the correct interpretation of the church's relationship to the world is not between grace sniffers and heresy sniffers, or between those who want to plunder the spoils of the Egyptians, the "open to the world" types, or those who want nothing whatsoever to do with Egyptians, the "closed to the world" types, but between those who think that human nature can or cannot come to fulfilment in the antechambers of God's love and glory. Ratzinger's Augustinianism was not a neo-Protestant Augustinianism fixated on the theology of the Cross, but a classically Catholic Trinitarian Christocentric Augustinianism for which the Incarnation is the fulcrum of history, presupposing creation and looking forward to the final renewal of the cosmos. M

Mapping a Method for Dialogue: Exploring the Tensions between Razian Autonomy and Catholic Solidarity as Applied to Euthanasia

Amelia J. Uelmen

IN THE MIDST OF polarizing culture wars, many long not only for a peaceful truce, but also for a glimpse of the way forward—some indication of a path to help us communicate across our deep differences and articulate a common commitment to building a more humane and just society. It is in this spirit that theologian, bioethicist and law professor Cathleen Kaveny endeavors to construct a "bridge" between secular liberal legal theory and the Catholic intellectual tradition.[1]

In *Law's Virtues: Fostering Autonomy and Solidarity in American Society*, Kaveny chooses the work of Joseph Raz as her primary conversation partner as he sets out a theory of "liberal perfectionism" in *The Morality of Freedom* (1986).[2] Those who appreciate the broad framework of Catholic social thought might find much that is attractive in Raz's 1986 analysis. Raz's rhetoric of simultaneous respect for human freedom and a shared concern for social good resonates deeply with Catholic perspectives on human fulfillment and social life.

But for the project of constructing a bridge between profoundly different systems of thought, it can be problematic to work with a text that remains at an extremely high level of abstraction. As legal theorist Jeremy Waldron critiqued, when it comes to understanding exactly "what makes an option or an individual's conception of the good repugnant or immoral," *The Morality of Freedom* says "almost nothing."[3] To make the conversation even more complex, recent scholarship in which Raz articulates a vigorous defense of a broad

---

[1] Cathleen Kaveny, *Law's Virtues: Fostering Autonomy and Solidarity in American Society* (Washington, DC: Georgetown University, 2012), 27.
[2] Joseph Raz, *The Morality of Freedom* (New York: Oxford University, 1986).
[3] Jeremy Waldron, "Autonomy and Perfectionism in Raz's *Morality of Freedom*," *Southern California Law Review* 62 (1988-1989): 1130.

right to voluntary euthanasia reveals striking disjunctions between his theory and the Catholic intellectual tradition.[4]

This article takes the complexity implicit in Kaveny's efforts as a springboard for reflection on methods of dialogue when conversation partners seek to understand each other across profound cultural and intellectual differences. The first part of the analysis sketches a description of Kaveny's project with an appreciative eye for the aspects of Razian autonomy that may be attractive to those who locate themselves within the Catholic intellectual tradition. The second part tests the strength of the project by probing the disjunction between the theoretical descriptions of autonomy in Raz's abstract analysis as compared with his recent argument in favor of the legal right to voluntary euthanasia. The third part opens out some of the methodological questions that emerge from observations about these disjunctions. The fourth part explores some of the methodological implications of what I see as the powerful driver for Kaveny's chapters on euthanasia—a personal narrative in which a bishop of the Catholic Church describes his spiritual journey with cancer—and considers against this backdrop the role of narrative in the larger project of bridging deep differences.

KAVENY'S BRIDGE BETWEEN RAZIAN AUTONOMY AND CATHOLIC SOLIDARITY

In the opening chapter of *Law's Virtues*, Cathleen Kaveny is critical of the extent to which liberal theory has perpetuated individualistic interpretations of the role of liberty which have resulted in what she perceives to be distorted perspectives on communal responsibility. She rejects as too negative and individualistic Joel Feinberg's subjectivist account of value in which goods are "valuable because they are sought after and valued."[5] Such theories, she notes, fail "to acknowledge a social component to both the exercise and protection of autonomy," and suffer the limitation of construing autonomy "only in a way that places it in opposition to tradition, community and culture."[6]

Hoping to identify a more promising conversation partner within the liberal tradition, Kaveny gravitates toward "liberal perfectionism," which she considers to be a corrective internal to liberalism.[7]

---

[4] See Joseph Raz, "Death in Our Life," *Journal of Applied Philosophy* 30 (February 2013): 1-11. A draft version of this lecture was posted to the Social Science Research Network on May 29, 2012.

[5] Kaveny, *Law's Virtues*, 22.

[6] Kaveny, *Law's Virtues*, 25.

[7] Kaveny, *Law's Virtues*, 23. Compare Loren E. Lomasky, "But Is It Liberalism?" *Critical Review* 4, nos. 1-2 (1990): 86-105, esp. 86-7. Lomasky argues that Raz's rejection of standard liberal linchpins such as neutrality, rights, equality, anti-perfectionism,

As bioethicist Craig Peterson explains, in contrast to "anti-perfectionists" who argue that it is not the role of the state "to enforce deep or substantive conceptions of what constitutes the 'good life' upon its citizens,"[8] perfectionist liberals "argue that it is necessary to focus on a substantive theory of the good—the key values that are truly constitutive of human well-being. Those values are perfectionist, for it is the very pursuit of them that truly makes life fulfilling and rewarding."[9]

Further, as Denise Meyerson defines, state perfectionists hold that the state is "legitimately concerned with the moral character of its citizens."[10] Raz, for example, "believes that there is nothing wrong in principle with the state encouraging citizens to lead good lives, provided that the state's judgments are sound."[11] Thus for Raz the moral ends of choices and actions are not indifferent. Raz explains: "The morally good person is he whose prosperity is so intertwined with the pursuit of goals which advance intrinsic values and the well-being of others that it is impossible to separate his personal well-being from his moral concerns."[12]

As Kaveny highlights, much in Raz's theory of liberal perfectionism seems to track principles and projects that are also of concern to Catholic social thought. For Raz "human freedom is not value-free but is oriented toward enabling and supporting human beings in living morally valuable ways of life."[13] Kaveny explains how in contrast to subjectivist liberal theories, for Raz:

> The ultimate point of negative freedom is positive freedom; the agent's freedom from the restrictions and requirements of others only bears fruit when the agents grab hold of that opportunity in a positive way to help shape their own identities and place their imprints upon the circumstances under which they will live.[14]

Further, Raz also appreciates the extent to which commitments are socially embedded: "Our projects and relationships depend on

---

subjective preference and individualism, in favor of an effort to enshrine autonomy as the core value of a justifiable liberalism, ultimately founders as a liberal structure.

[8] Craig Paterson, *Assisted Suicide and Euthanasia: A Natural Law Ethics Approach* (Burlington: Ashgate, 2008), 155. Paterson notes as examples the work of Ronald Dworkin and John Rawls.

[9] Paterson, *Assisted Suicide and Euthanasia*, 165. See also Peter de Marneffe, "Liberalism and Perfectionism," *American Journal of Jurisprudence*, 43 (1998): 99-116. Paterson discusses the relation between liberalism and perfectionism according to varying understandings of both terms.

[10] Denise Meyerson, "Three Versions of Liberal Tolerance: Dworkin, Rawls and Raz," *Jurisprudence* 3 (2012): 38.

[11] Meyerson, "Three Versions," 38.

[12] Raz, *Morality of Freedom,* 320. See also Kaveny, *Law's Virtues*, 27.

[13] Kaveny, *Law's Virtues,* 23.

[14] Kaveny, *Law's Virtues,* 23.

the form they acquire through social conventions."[15] As Kaveny summarizes, in contrast to other liberal theories, Razian autonomy points to "a richer vision of the person situated in and interacting with a community in order to develop an identity that draws equally upon his internal, unique talents and motivations as well as those opportunities provided by the broader society."[16]

Against this backdrop, Kaveny traces the parallels between Raz's articulation of the value of personal autonomy and the concerns of Catholic social thought. For Raz, individual autonomy has three fundamental requirements: "1) the raw mental capacity to make and carry out choices; 2) freedom from attempts at manipulation as well as from coercion on the part of other people; and finally, 3) a range of morally worthwhile choices from which to choose. Options cannot exist outside the creative and constructive social context of a group."[17]

As Kaveny explains, the components of the virtue of solidarity as articulated in the Catholic intellectual tradition "correspond to and supplement Raz's conditions for true human autonomy in ways that are very illuminating."[18] Like Razian autonomy, solidarity also rests on the premise of 1) meeting basic needs; 2) recognizing the nature of each person as essentially social; and 3) providing vehicles through which all persons can contribute to the community.[19]

In light of these parallels, the heart of Kaveny's thesis is that in cultures such as that of the contemporary United States,

> the law needs to teach and support two virtues particularly appropriate to our time and place: autonomy (understood in Joseph Raz's terms) and solidarity (understood in terms of Catholic social teaching). Without denying the existence of significant tensions between these two realms of thought, I nonetheless believe that bringing Catholic social thought into conversation with the work of perfectionist liberal legal theorists such as Joseph Raz highlights ways in which both are mutually necessary.[20]

---

[15] Raz, *Morality of Freedom*, 383. See also Kaveny, *Law's Virtues*, 24.
[16] Kaveny, *Law's Virtues*, 27.
[17] Kaveny, *Law's Virtues*, 25.
[18] Kaveny, *Law's Virtues*, 28.
[19] Kaveny, *Law's Virtues*, 28.
[20] Kaveny, *Law's Virtues*, 33. It would be interesting to further explore Kaveny's characterization of autonomy as a *virtue*, and the potential disjunction with Raz's own descriptions. See Joseph Raz, "Facing Up: A Reply," *Southern California Law Review* 62 (1988-1989): 1153-1236, at 1228. Raz is discussing Jeremy Waldron's critique of Raz's argument that an autonomous, demeaning, bad, or worthless life is worse than a non-autonomous life which is bad, demeaning, or worthless in similar ways. Raz responds: "Waldron's objection is based on an analogy with virtue. But autonomy is not a virtue but a property of a life. The question is, does that property contribute to the value of the life. The answer, to which we both agree, is that it does

Kaveny is not the first to recognize the potential affinity between liberal perfectionism and the Catholic intellectual tradition. For Paterson, a natural law theorist, "[w]hat is refreshing in perfectionist accounts of liberalism is the need to embrace and found state concerns on what is necessary for the promotion of human well-being. Only by embracing and promoting values can we begin to legitimize the exercise of state power in a way that credibly respects the nature of persons."[21]

Especially for pluralistic democratic societies, Raz's version of perfectionist liberalism seems to support the kind of social harmony that fosters commitment to the good despite profound difference. As Kaveny highlights, Raz "holds that the rationale for protecting freedom stems from the recognition that there are a number of mutually incompatible but objectively morally worthwhile ways of living one's life, all of which deserve protection precisely because they are objectively morally worthwhile."[22]

Given these profound conceptual parallels with the Catholic intellectual tradition, it does not seem to be too much of a stretch to explore how Raz's version of secular liberal theory might be an important conversation partner.[23] As Kaveny's analysis in *Law's Virtues* moves through various applications, from abortion to the use of genetic information, from euthanasia to voting, her nuanced and tightly woven arguments seem to present a convincing case for a fruitful dialogue between Razian autonomy and Catholic solidarity.

EUTHANASIA: RAZIAN AUTONOMY
BETWEEN THEORY AND APPLICATION

Raz is a good conversation partner for Catholic social thought so long as his part of the analysis remains abstract and conceptual. But when Raz gets down into the weeds of a specific application, significant disjunctions between his system of thought and the Catholic intellectual tradition emerge. This section explores Raz's concept of autonomy in light of his May 2012 lecture, "Death in Our Life." It argues that his analysis in favor of a strong "respect-based right" to

---

so only if the life is spent in valuable pursuits." See also Waldron, "Autonomy and Perfectionism," 1127.

[21] Paterson, *Assisted Suicide and Euthanasia*, 165. Kaveny's project also runs parallel to progressive efforts to move beyond the spent sterility of an exclusive focus on procedural justice toward a more robust conversation in legal theory to develop categories of "normative jurisprudence." For example, see Robin West, *Normative Jurisprudence: An Introduction* (New York: Cambridge University, 2011), 10. West argues for a "rejuvenated normative jurisprudence that centralizes, rather than marginalizes, the concept of individual, common, social and legal good and the varying accounts of human nature that might inform such understandings."

[22] Kaveny, *Law's Virtues*, 23. See Raz, *Morality of Freedom*, 396.

[23] Kaveny, *Law's Virtues*, 27.

voluntary euthanasia makes it difficult to imagine a sustainable bridge between his system of thought and the Catholic intellectual tradition.

Raz summarizes his perspective on the right to euthanasia as a function of personal autonomy. He states his focus clearly: "We are concerned with a right to euthanasia because the ability to choose how and when one's life will end is valuable in itself."[24] For Raz, the capacity for rational agency is the basis of a duty to respect those who have it, and in particular to respect the choices that people make about how to lead their lives. Rational agents should be able to exercise their autonomy in order "to determine when and how to end one's life."[25] He explains: "Having that option is valuable, and therefore it is protected by the right to euthanasia. The right to life protects people from the time and manner of their death being determined by others, and the right to euthanasia grants each person the power to choose themselves that time and manner."[26]

This concrete application clarifies exactly what Raz means by his definition of autonomy as "the capacity to be 'part-author' of one's own life by making a successive series of choices that form a more or less coherent narrative."[27] For Raz, "the ideal of personal autonomy is the vision of people controlling, to some degree, their own destiny, fashioning it through successive decisions throughout their lives."[28] Control over one's life is a pervasive and expansive core value in his work. As he explained in a 1997 essay:

> My life is mine to the extent that I am in charge of it. It is not mine if I lose control, if urges and emotions invade me which are out of my control. When they are under my control they are intelligible to me. I understand them, and why I have them.... Reason makes us intelligible to ourselves. Through it we direct our lives, we are in control.[29]

For Raz, when control is not present, it as if we are held hostage by an intruder. He explains: "Some thoughts we have, emotions we feel, some of our beliefs, desires and actions are experienced as not really ours. It is as if we lost control, as if we were taken over, possessed by a force which is not us."[30]

In light of this feature of his thought, it is not surprising that in making an argument for the normative power to choose the time and

---

[24] Raz, "Death in Our Life," 8.
[25] Raz, "Death in Our Life," 8.
[26] Raz, "Death in Our Life," 8.
[27] Kaveny, *Law's Virtues*, 53.
[28] Raz, *Morality of Freedom*, 369. See also Kaveny, *Law's Virtues*, 153.
[29] Joseph Raz, "The Active and the Passive," *Aristotelian Society Supplementary Volume* 71 (June 1997): 226-7.
[30] Raz, "The Active and the Passive," 227.

manner of one's death,[31] Raz considers the capacity to control the time and manner of one's death to be an enrichment to one's life. He argues: "Inevitably shaping one's dying contributes to giving shape, contributes to the form and meaning one's life has. Those who reflect, plan, and decide on the manner of their dying make their dying part of their life. And if they do so well then by integrating their dying into their life they enrich their life."[32] This sense of control, according to Raz, could be the door to alleviate the fear of death that pervades our life:

> The main way in which making death a part of our life by giving us greater control over its time and manner changes our life is not, however, by its impact on specific attachments or pursuits. The main impact is likely to be more pervasive and diffuse. Consciousness of death and fear of dying—a separate factor, to be sure, but one which in our life is hard to separate from knowledge of our mortality—have a way of colouring much of our life, and the changing attitude I am envisaging will likewise affect our life, real and imaginative, in multifarious and diffuse ways.[33]

Thus the value of a "broad right to euthanasia," he argues, is "not only the option to escape certain undesirable conditions at the end of one's life, but also and primarily to protect an option to shape the way one's life ends, by deciding on its time and manner."[34]

For Raz, seizing power over this aspect of one's life is a door to freedom from helplessness, terror and alienation. He argues:

> So, while the power to decide the time and manner of one's death, when wisely used, will contribute to the value of various episodes in one's life, the main positive effect I have in mind is the full, guiltless acceptance of the power itself. It can transform one's perspective on one's life, reduce the aspects of it from which one is alienated, or those that inspire a sense of helplessness and terror. It is a change that makes one whole in generating a perspective, a way of conceiving oneself and one's life free from some of those negative aspects.[35]

The Meaning of Razian Autonomy
in Light of his Analysis of the Right to Euthanasia

In *Law's Virtues*, Kaveny admits that there are "significant tensions" between the aspects of Razian autonomy she discusses and Catholic social thought.[36] These tensions are even more evident in

---

[31] Raz, "Death in Our Life," 1.
[32] Raz, "Death in Our Life," 9.
[33] Raz, "Death in Our Life," 10.
[34] Raz, "Death in Our Life," 9.
[35] Raz, "Death in Our Life," 10.
[36] Kaveny, *Law's Virtues*, 33.

light of his analysis in "Death in Our Life." Raz's lecture was available online a few months prior to the publication of *Law's Virtues*, but I appreciate that it appeared too late on the scene to be integrated into Kaveny's analysis. The discussion that follows intends not to critique Kaveny's work, but to ask a forward looking question: In light of "Death in Our Life," how should theorists of Catholic social thought evaluate Kaveny's argument that Razian autonomy is an important complement to Catholic solidarity?

When it comes to this specific application, it would certainly be an understatement to describe Raz's views as in "significant tension" with the net prohibition of euthanasia as articulated by Catholic moral theology. As Kaveny notes, in the Catholic theological tradition, "It is wrong to perform any action with the aim of taking innocent life, whether one's own or that of another."[37] As John Paul II explained in *Evangelium vitae*: "Euthanasia is a grave violation of the law of God, since it is a deliberate and morally unacceptable killing of a human person."[38] While this teaching does not mean that one is obligated to try to prolong one's life with any means, it does lead to a clear rejection of euthanasia and physician assisted suicide.[39] Beyond this disjunction in the normative analysis, it is also interesting to note how Raz's concrete application dramatically undercuts the seeming parallels between his version of perfectionist liberalism and the Catholic intellectual tradition.

First, recall Kaveny's rejection of Feinberg's subjectivist account of value in which goods are "valuable because they are sought after and valued."[40] Raz's concrete analysis of the exercise of autonomy at the end of one's life is fraught with similar tensions. Objective considerations about "quality of life" all but disappear, because such matters should be assessed according to the subjective perspective of each rational agent. Raz explains: "When it comes to rational agents, the duty to respect their rational powers, and protect their ability to use them, modifies the implications of quality of life considerations: they become matters to be considered by each person regarding their own lives."[41] In fact, in this application to euthanasia, the exercise of autonomy looms so large that it seems to overshadow all other considerations. Raz submits:

> Contemporary claims for a right to euthanasia are claims to this rights-based approach. They recognise that there are quality of life reasons for ending life, but take them to be matters over which each

---

[37] Kaveny, *Law's Virtues,* 146.
[38] John Paul II, *Evangelium vitae,* 65 (1995). See *Catechism of the Catholic Church* (Vatican: Libreria Editrice Vaticana, 1994), nos. 2276-7.
[39] Kaveny, *Law's Virtues,* 146; *Catechism,* nos. 2278-9.
[40] Kaveny, *Law's Virtues,* 22.
[41] Raz, "Death in Our Life," 9.

person has sovereign power to decide his or her course. And if nothing else then that sovereignty means that the right can be exercised for a variety of reasons, and also for presumed reasons that are either no reasons at all, or not adequate to justify ending one's life.[42]

Second, recall that Raz seemed to be an attractive conversation partner for Catholic social thought because at least in theory he acknowledges "a social component to both the exercise and protection of autonomy," in contrast to a construal of autonomy "only in a way that places it in opposition to tradition, community and culture."[43] In theory, Razian autonomy "is also social in both its inception and its goals."[44]

On the surface, one might say that Raz's "respect-based right" to euthanasia does include "other regarding" concerns. Probing deeper, the application of this theory to the question of end-of-life decision-making reveals a vision of human experience which is strikingly isolated and atomistic. Factors include:

1) Sparing the effort and distress that looking after ailing people causes those who are personally involved in looking after them;

2) Preventing one's savings from being used up on medical and other forms of care in order to have more to leave by one's will;

3) Saving the public the expense of providing medical, nursing, and other publicly provided care;

4) Preventing the memory of a person one cares about as being one of someone in decline.[45]

In light of these factors, Raz's definition of "social" might be summarized as the right to maintain an image of isolated individual control, posing neither a bother nor an expense to family, friends and the public.

Finally, in theory, Raz seems to point the way forward for the complexities of pluralistic democratic societies in which we may encounter deep disagreement on the definition of the good. Perfectionist liberalism seems to offer a path for negotiating some of the "mutually incompatible but objectively morally worthwhile ways of living one's life, all of which deserve protection precisely because they are objectively morally worthwhile."[46] In theory, Razian autonomy poses

---

[42] Raz, "Death in Our Life," 9.
[43] Kaveny, *Law's Virtues,* 25.
[44] Kaveny, *Law's Virtues,* 129.
[45] Raz, "Death in Our Life," 10-11.
[46] Kaveny, *Law's Virtues,* 23. See Raz, *Morality of Freedom,* 396.

limits based on moral and social ends: "No society is required to make morally objectionable options available to individuals; his observation can be extended to assert that no society has to make available morally objectionable means to achieve those options."[47]

When Raz argues for legalizing voluntary euthanasia, he leaves precious little room for debate about what is "morally objectionable." As indicated by a "small point, illustrating the direction of travel,"[48] if voluntary euthanasia were to be legalized, then in Raz's view there should be "widespread consequences for professional and occupational opportunities," which "cannot be objected to."[49] Because "no one has an unconditional right to be a medical practitioner," and such right is conditioned on being "able and willing to perform the duties that go with jobs for which medical skills are needed,"[50] the duty to assist a patient in this regard should be considered part of the job if voluntary euthanasia were legalized. Period.

In theory, Raz seems to champion the social harmony that could be the result of "moral pluralism," which "claims not merely that incompatible forms of life are morally acceptable but that they display distinct virtues, each capable of being pursued for its own sake."[51] In his application to euthanasia, Raz argues that space for doctors who are conscientious objectors to exercise their distinct visions of the good should be shut down completely. If voluntary euthanasia were to be legalized, it would generate "a conflict of reasons in which the conscientious objectors lose."[52]

The Elusive Harm Principle

Are there other principles of liberal theory that might pose limits to the expansive role that autonomy plays in Raz's system of thought? For example, the "harm principle" allows the exercise of state power over individuals for the purpose of preventing harm to others. This could help to flesh out the definition of what is "morally objectionable."[53] In *The Morality of Freedom*, Raz explains how the harm principle connects with his account of perfectionist liberalism. It is "derivable from a morality which regards personal autonomy as an essential ingredient of the good life, and regards the principle of auton-

---

[47] Kaveny, *Law's Virtues*, 129.
[48] Raz, "Death in Our Life," 2.
[49] Raz, "Death in Our Life," 3.
[50] Raz, "Death in Our Life," 3.
[51] Raz, *Morality of Freedom*, 396.
[52] Raz, "Death in Our Life," 3.
[53] John Stuart Mill, *On Liberty*, ed. E. Rappaport (Indianapolis: Hackett, 1978), 9. See Neil M. Gorsuch, "The Right to Assisted Suicide and Euthanasia," *Harvard Journal of Law & Public Policy* 23 (2000): 666.

omy, which imposes duties on people to secure for all the conditions of autonomy, as one of the most important moral principles."[54]

For Raz, disregard for the harm principle can lead to a violation of autonomy:

> First, it violates the condition of independence and expresses a relation of domination and an attitude of disrespect for the coerced individual. Second... there is no practical way of ensuring that the coercion will restrict the victims' choice of repugnant options but will not interfere with their other choices.[55]

Thus, "[a]utonomy based duties never justify coercion when there is no harm."[56]

But how does one define "harm"? In *The Morality of Freedom*, Raz admits that the concept of "causing harm" is a "normative concept acquiring its specific meaning from the moral theory within which it is embedded. Without such connection to a moral theory the harm principle is a formal principle lacking specific concrete content and leading to no policy conclusions."[57] John Safranek draws out the implications of this link:

> Even if ascriptive autonomy does not require an individualistic view of human beings, it entails a profound dilemma. The principle of autonomy or liberty requires a "harm" principle to justify prohibiting certain types of autonomous acts, but whether an act is specified as harmful or harmless will depend on the preferred theory of the good. Therefore the normative use of the principle of autonomy is performatively self-refuting: when scholars proscribe certain autonomous acts in the name of harm, or defend other autonomous acts judged harmless, they impose an axiology and subvert autonomy.[58]

Considering the specific problem of assisted suicide, Safranek concludes: "The debate over assisted suicide is a conflict between competing theories of the good, and not a dispute between proponents of autonomy and the sanctity or dignity of life."[59]

In light of such different ways of defining what is "objectively morally worthwhile," what is "social," and what is "harm," can Razian autonomy be in dialogue with Catholic solidarity? When such terms were considered in the abstract it was hard to tell whether potential differences would be innocuous or devastating. In light of

---

[54] Raz, *Morality of Freedom*, 415.
[55] Raz, *Morality of Freedom*, 418-19.
[56] Raz, *Morality of Freedom*, 415.
[57] Raz, *Morality of Freedom*, 414.
[58] John P. Safranek, "Autonomy and Assisted Suicide: The Execution of Freedom," *Hastings Center Report* 28 (July-August 1998): 33.
[59] Safranek, "Autonomy and Assisted Suicide," 35.

Raz's specific application to the law and policy of euthanasia, it turns out that the disjunctions are indeed devastating.

Mapping a Method for Dialogue

When analyzing the relationship between *The Morality of Freedom* (1986) and "Death in Our Life" (2013), one could argue that Raz left the normative questions open when he wrote the earlier analysis. On that basis, it would be fair to take his abstract analysis of the functions of autonomy to places where, at least in light of his more recent work, Raz himself would not go. This leads to an approach in which one attempts to bring the particular abstract concepts from different systems into dialogue in order to illuminate a practical application. This raises a number of methodological questions.

First, one might consider the extent to which we need to account for a linguistic mismatch. The problem is not only finding a way to communicate when the same words have different meanings within different systems of thought. The deeper problem is that the meaning of those words may remain so opaque that we cannot engage the differences or similarities in a substantive way. Even if we are using the same words to describe concepts within differing thought systems—e.g., "good" and "harm"—the substantive content given to those words within one's own thought system may differ to such a degree that it is difficult to draw working comparisons. In W.B. Gallie's turn of the phrase, we face the interpretive problems inherent in "essentially contested concepts."[60]

A second and related risk is that when one draws on abstract principles from a thought system that is not one's own, the meaning one gives to those principles may be distorted by projections of one's own thought system, and thus become disconnected from the meaning that the author may have originally intended. For example, the concept of "perfectionist liberalism" holds a certain attraction for Catholic social thought theorists because of a shared concern about social ends and the good, and a seemingly shared readiness to put the brakes on the whims of subjective personal choice. So long as definitions of "good" or "harm" remain undefined and without context, we can imagine that we are on the same page. But as evident from the discussion above, when we enter into the complexity of comparisons between normative analyses of concrete applications, it is often there that we see more clearly what we mean by the words we say, and realize how far apart we are in what we mean.

A third risk in bringing abstract concepts from different systems into dialogue regarding practical applications is that severe distortions can emerge due to the failure to account for the role that a giv-

---

[60] See generally W.B. Gallie, "Essentially Contested Concepts," *Procedures of the Aristotelian Society* 56 (1955-56): 167-98.

en concept plays within the distinct thought system as a whole. Within any system of thought, concepts function as part of a larger weave, and are often balanced and tempered by their interaction with other concepts or principles. For example, within the Catholic social thought system, it is difficult to understand the full texture of solidarity without an appreciation for how it interacts with subsidiarity, participation, dignity, and other principles, depending on the context.[61]

A particular challenge of the dialogue between Razian autonomy and Catholic solidarity is that within his own system Razian autonomy looms so large that it seems to swallow up other concepts that would hold an important parallel function within the Catholic social thought system. Is Razian autonomy simply too big to share the stage with any other balancing factor? Would Razian autonomy still be Razian if it were not allowed the space to overpower other more "objective" considerations? If one does not account for the role and weight that a particular concept carries within a thought system and how it interacts with other elements of the system, is the comparison doomed to distortion?[62]

For those familiar with debates within Catholic social thought, questions about how to apply the abstract concepts from Raz's *Morality of Freedom* in light of his practical analysis of euthanasia in "Death in Our Life," might bring on an odd sense of *déjà vu*. Catholic social thought debates are often fraught with the tensions that arise when conversation partners of different political stripes agree on broad abstract principles but are unable to resolve their discord over how those principles should be applied in practical circumstances.[63] Consider, for example, Raz's description of self-authorship: "The autonomous person is a (part) author of his own life. The ideal of personal autonomy is the vision of people controlling, to some degree, their own destiny, fashioning it through successive decisions throughout their lives."[64] When read through a certain lens, one may

---

[61] See, e.g., Pontifical Council for Justice and Peace, *Compendium of the Social Doctrine of the Church* (Vatican: Libreria Editrice Vaticana, 2004), no. 162. The *Compendium* explains the importance of analyzing the principles of the Church's social doctrine "in their unity, interrelatedness and articulation."

[62] See, for example, Paterson, *Assisted Suicide and Euthanasia*, 165-6. Paterson notes that liberal perfectionists and natural law theorists disagree not on the elements at stake but on the extent to which autonomy should be recognized as "a master good," potentially at the expense of recognizing other goods.

[63] See, for example, Amelia J. Uelmen, "*Caritas in veritate* and Chiara Lubich: Human Development from the Vantage Point of Unity," *Theological Studies* 71 (March 2010): 29-30. I discuss the heated debates about the interpretation of *Caritas in veritate*.

[64] Raz, *Morality of Freedom*, 369 (see also 201). See generally Jeremy Waldron, "Moral Autonomy and Personal Autonomy," in *Autonomy and the Challenges to Liberalism*, ed. John Christman and Joel Anderson (New York: Cambridge University, 2005), 307.

find, as Kaveny described, deep parallels with Catholic notions of personal responsibility, and the consequent commitments to support social structures that facilitate personal responsibility in the ordinary lives of citizens. But as discussed above, when one probes the overarching structure of Raz's thought system as applied to euthanasia, it becomes clear that "part author" suggests, at least to Raz, the "full, guiltless acceptance"—or seizure—of power and control over one's own life and death.[65] Personal autonomy means assertion of control over boundaries which many religious traditions, including the Catholic intellectual tradition, maintain belong to a creator God.

Similarly, aspects of solidarity as defined within Catholic social thought may sound attractive to people from a variety of backgrounds, as they resonate with aspects of liberal theory. But when one probes the theological roots of this concept, questions emerge about the process for translating the ideas into secular terms. For example, Pope John Paul II locates the roots of solidarity in a profoundly Christian vision of humanity under the common fatherhood of God, as brothers and sisters in Christ, illuminated by the life of the Holy Spirit.[66] But how far would a vision of solidarity—as understood within Catholic social thought—go without this transcendent root? Can the notion be framed in secular terms without losing the characteristic "thickness" that it has in the context of Catholic social thought?

More broadly, can a framework which is rooted in and bound to a transcendent point of reference be in meaningful conversation with a secular framework? For example, as discussed below, the concept of Catholic solidarity is firmly embedded within the weave of a transcendent point of reference in which the ultimate relinquishment of autonomy and control can even be perceived and experienced as an ultimate good, part of the divine order, in full harmony with a positive notion of freedom. In what ways might this transcendent point of reference make the concept of solidarity in some sense inaccessible to secular understanding and discourse?

In light of current cultural tensions and political polarization, I appreciate the attraction of finding some common conceptual ground, even and especially across profound differences in perspective. I also appreciate that, as Kaveny herself noted, the development of a comprehensive jurisprudence centered on Razian autonomy and solidarity was beyond the scope and audience of the *Law's Virtues*

---

[65] Raz, "Death in Our Life," 10.
[66] John Paul II, *Sollicitudo rei socialis* (1987), no. 40. John Paul II discusses the theological lens which provides a "new criterion" for discerning "in the light of faith a new model of the unity of the human race, which must ultimately inspire our solidarity. This supreme model of unity, which is a reflection of the intimate life of God, one God in three Persons, is what we Christians mean by the word 'communion'."

project.⁶⁷ Nonetheless, I think it is important to acknowledge that the method of choosing abstract principles as prime material for building a bridge across different systems of thought poses some serious and perhaps insurmountable obstacles—including the risk that the points of seeming agreement will be at best opaque, and at worst, manipulative of one or both systems.

The scholarship of legal theorist Robert Cover illuminates this point. Asked to reflect upon the relationship between Judaism and human rights, he confessed: "The first thought that comes to mind is that the categories are wrong. I do not mean, of course, that basic ideas of human dignity and worth are not powerfully expressed in the Jewish legal and literary traditions. Rather, I mean that because it is a legal tradition Judaism has its own categories for expressing through the law the worth and dignity of each human being. And the categories are not closely analogous to 'human rights'."⁶⁸

Cover proceeds to explain the "myths," or "fundamental stories" that give force to the key words within the different systems—for rights, the story of social contract; and for obligation or "mitzvah," the myth of Sinai.⁶⁹ Each is grounded in a particular history and social context. Each allows for interpretive variation. As revealed by a discussion of particular applications, each has a differing "loaded evocative edge"—for mitzvah the rhetorical advantage is in assignment of responsibility and the definition of communal entitlements;⁷⁰ for rights the rhetorical advantage is in the area of political participation.⁷¹ The different systems solve certain problems "rather naturally," and encounter in others "conceptual difficulties of the first order."⁷² Cover emphasizes that it is not "that particular problems cannot be solved, in one system or the other—only that the solution entails a sort of rhetorical or philosophical strain."⁷³

Cover does not suggest that we need to choose. As he puts it, in the struggle for universal human dignity and equality "we can use as many good myths in that struggle as we can find. Sinai and social contract both have their place."⁷⁴ But he does conclude his analysis

---

⁶⁷ See, for instance, Kaveny, *Law's Virtues,* 82.
⁶⁸ Robert Cover, "Obligation: A Jewish Jurisprudence of the Social Order," *Journal of Law & Religion* 5 (1987-1988): 65.
⁶⁹ Cover, "Obligation," 66.
⁷⁰ Cover, "Obligation," 72.
⁷¹ Cover, "Obligation," 73.
⁷² Cover, "Obligation," 70.
⁷³ Cover, "Obligation," 71. For an interesting analysis of similar tensions between human rights discourse and currents of Christian Orthodox thought, see Aristotle Papanikolaou, *The Mystical as Political: Democracy and Non-Radical Orthodoxy* (Notre Dame: University of Notre Dame, 2012), 87-130.
⁷⁴ Cover, "Obligation," 73. See John Courtney Murray, *We Hold These Truths* (New York: Sheed & Ward, 2005), 39. Murray notes that a civilized structure of "dialogue"

on a personal note, with a personal question: What speaks to me? He confesses "the rhetoric of obligation speaks more sharply to me than that of rights."[75]

What I find attractive about Cover's method is that it maintains a strong connection between the words that we use and the "fundamental stories" which give these words their thickest meaning. The "loaded evocative edge" of the differing rhetorical systems is determined by an analysis of concrete applications, which then helps to further flesh out the meaning of abstract principles within a given system. And one does not exclude the other—potentially illuminating comparisons and contrasts unfold from the depth and breadth of this context.[76]

Lessons from the Methods of Interreligious Dialogue

Cover's method also brings to mind some important lessons learned in the course of the Roman Catholic Church's encounter with people of different religious traditions. Especially since the Second Vatican Council's declaration of the relation of the Church to non-Christian religions, *Nostra aetate*,[77] the Catholic intellectual tradition has been greatly enriched by reflection on this interaction. Speaking specifically about Jewish-Christian relations, Cardinal Walter Kasper distinguished the practices of "dialogue" from "syncretism" and "relativism:"

> Dialogue lives from mutual respect for the otherness of the other. Dialogue takes differences seriously and withstands their difficulties.... [Dialogue], when it is serious and honest, cannot be always harmonious and easy.... To bear with [misunderstandings and tensions] is not a setback to the Second Vatican Council or a betrayal of the dialogue; they are—when confronted with mutual respect—the reality of dialogue. Only when we take seriously the other in his/her otherness can we learn from each other and can we be what we should be: a blessing for each other.[78]

---

would be "no less sharply pluralistic, but rather more so, since the real pluralisms would be clarified out of their present confusion."

[75] Cover, "Obligation," 73.

[76] See Gallie, "Essentially Contested," 193. Gallie recognizes that "essentially contested concepts" may be of "permanent potential critical value" and raise the level of quality of arguments in a dispute.

[77] See, for example, *Nostra aetate*, no. 2. "The Catholic Church rejects nothing which is true and holy in these religions. She looks with sincere respect upon those ways of conduct and of life, those rules and teachings which, though differing in many particulars from what she holds forth, nevertheless often reflects a ray of that Truth which enlightens all men."

[78] Quoted in Robert Bonfil, "Jewish Memory, History and Vision," in *Nostra Aetate: Origins, Promulgation, Impact on Jewish-Catholic Relations*, ed. Nelville Lamdan, Alberto Melloni (Munster: LIT Verlag, 2007), 106.

Especially in initial stages, interreligious gatherings often include time for a shared meal, reflection, and exchange. The opportunities to encounter one another as human beings, to hear one another's stories and to enter, in some way, the world of the other's perspective is essential to building authentic relationships of trust and to opening channels of communication.[79] Working together on concrete social projects that serve local or international communities provides another vehicle to experience the transformative power of shared goals and commitments. Much of this exchange and work proceeds regardless of the systematic development of shared concepts or shared language, at least initially. Proceeding in this manner, conversations that otherwise would not have occurred due to disagreement over abstract tenets of belief can gradually build the kind of trust and understanding that eventually allows for a mutually illuminating exchange even across marked difference in conceptual beliefs and modes of expression.[80]

How might this analogy inform conversation between Catholic social thought and liberal theory, such that the method for dialogue respects profound differences while at the same time builds mutual understanding even across profound divergence in normative assessments? One possibility is to explore the place and the role of narrative, and the extent to which this genre may help to generate a space in which those with differing perspectives might illustrate for their conversation partners the reasons and experiences which have led to their approach to contested issues, and open themselves to the reasons and experiences that have led the other to adopt a different position.

In law as in interreligious encounters, narratives or "stories" can function as a kind of connective tissue between people with different worldviews. As Robin West describes, stories "expand our knowledge not only of objective history, but also of what is unaccessible, the subjective life of the other. We learn what it is to walk in another's shoes, to experience another's pain, to anticipate another's pleasures, and by so learning we enlarge our individual humanity and our society's sense of inclusion."[81]

---

[79] See, for example, Amelia J. Uelmen, "Reconciling Evangelization and Dialogue through Love of Neighbor," *Villanova Law Review* 52 (2007): 317. This essay discusses Chiara Lubich's description of the process of listening which allows people of different religious traditions to "open up, reveal themselves to us, express and explain themselves."

[80] See generally, Chiara Lubich, *Essential Writings: Spirituality, Dialogue, Culture* (Hyde Park: New City, 2007), 337ff. Lubich describes a method for interreligious dialogue and its initial results.

[81] Robin West, *Narrative, Authority and Law* (Ann Arbor: University of Michigan, 1993), 425.

Robert Cover's scholarship is helpful on this point as well. In his essay "*Nomos* and Narrative," like Kaveny, he uses the image of a bridge, but in his case, also to describe law itself: "Law may be viewed as a system of tension or a bridge linking a concept of reality to an imagined alternative—that is, as a connective between two states of affairs, both of which can be represented in their normative significance only through the devices of narrative."[82] Thus he defines a "*nomos*" as "a present world constituted by our system of tension between reality and vision."[83]

For Cover, what is the role of narrative in the creation of legal meaning? "Because the *nomos* is but the process of human action stretched between vision and reality, a legal interpretation cannot be valid if no one is prepared to live by it…. The transformation of interpretation into legal meaning begins when someone accepts the demands of interpretation and, through the personal act of commitment, affirms the position taken."[84] For example, in discussing civil disobedience, personal commitment is what builds a bridge between current law and the hope for change: "Our lives constitute the bridges between the reality of present official declarations of the law and the vision of our law triumphant (a vision that may, of course, never come to fruition)."[85]

Of course, narrative cannot be the only or the last word in the political process of developing law and policy—but it is an important complement. Robin West explains the dynamic interplay:

> A regime of rights that is unsupported and uncomplemented by narratives that explain the source of those rights does indeed give rise to an excessively legalistic and alienating community, while a society bound by stories and unresponsive to claims of individual right does risk excessive authoritarianism in the name of communitarian necessity or harmony.[86]

An additional feature of narrative, both West and Cover observe, is that it often surfaces when we want to assign or deny responsibility for some event.[87] Cover explains: "Creation of legal meaning entails, then, subjective commitment to an objectified understanding of a demand. This objectification of the norms to which one is committed frequently, perhaps always, entails a narrative—a story of how the law, now object, came to be, and more importantly, how it came to

---

[82] Cover, "*Nomos* and Narrative," 9.
[83] Cover, "*Nomos* and Narrative," 9.
[84] Cover, "*Nomos* and Narrative," 45.
[85] Cover, "*Nomos* and Narrative," 47.
[86] West, *Narrative, Authority and Law*, 426.
[87] West, *Narrative, Authority and Law*, 426.

be seen as one's own. Narrative is the literary genre for the objectification of value."[88]

I believe that all of these features of narrative can serve as a methodological starting point that may help dialogue partners to render the meaning of their "essentially contested concepts" more transparent to each other. Disagreements may remain, but it may be more likely that they can be worked out on the basis of a deeper appreciation and understanding of the sources and driving motivations of those values. As West describes the argument for narrative: "Stories, not rights talk, enable us to break down barriers between persons from radically different backgrounds, to reclaim and honor the traditions of our past, to empathize with others, and to actually build upon, rather than simply rest upon, the bonds of community."[89]

NARRATIVE IN THE ANALYSIS OF END-OF-LIFE CARE

As may be evident from the earlier discussions, I am not sanguine about the extent to which the concept of Razian autonomy may be helpful for our discussions about an approach to law and legal systems that accord with my hopes for justice and the common good. Interestingly, when it comes to the law and policy of euthanasia, I do not think Kaveny herself is all that sanguine either.

The two chapters that Kaveny devotes to discussion of euthanasia in *Law's Virtues* actually engage Raz's work very little other than to admit that when it comes to facing suffering in the process of dying, Razian autonomy seems to have met its match. As she explains, for Raz "suffering is a wrenching experience because it disintegrates previously autonomous persons, cleaving them from the plans and purposes with which they have defined themselves as part-authors of their own lives."[90] In Kaveny's two chapters, a Christian narrative of solidarity takes center stage, and it seems expansive enough on its own to speak to important concerns regarding patient autonomy as defined through a Christian lens. As Kaveny explains, one of the arguments against legalizing euthanasia is the concern that it will substantially increase the risk that "patients will be coerced or manipulated into making that fateful choice for the benefit of third parties."[91]

From a methodological perspective, how does Kaveny illustrate what Cover might describe as the "loaded evocative edge" of Catholic solidarity? For me, the driver of this part of the book is the personal narrative of the spirit in which Cardinal Joseph Bernardin, the Arch-

---

[88] Cover, "*Nomos* and Narrative," 45.
[89] West, *Narrative, Authority and Law*, 425.
[90] Kaveny, *Law's Virtues*, 153.
[91] Kaveny, *Law's Virtues*, 165. Kaveny notes, "There is reason to worry that legalization would in fact pose certain threats to autonomy by increasing the danger of coercion of the risk of manipulating vulnerable patients to 'choose' death prematurely" (180).

bishop of Chicago, lived his own illness and death, and his relationships with those who were caring for him. Just two weeks before he died, he finished *The Gift of Peace,* a book of reflections on his personal experience of illness and suffering. It is above all through the power of this narrative that Kaveny demonstrates the substance of Catholic solidarity and the layers of what the Catholic intellectual tradition means by the "socially conditioned" nature of autonomy.[92]

In sharp contrast with Raz's emphasis on the importance of control, Bernardin felt that the events of his later life had called him "to let go of his own views of the proper course of his life and to grow ever more radical in his trust in Jesus Christ."[93] As Kaveny explains, for a Christian facing the reality of death, "the appropriate model is not one of dominion but of stewardship."[94] When Bernardin placed his own life into the context of the grand narrative and participation in the life, death, and resurrection of Jesus, he discovered "the freedom to let go, to surrender ourselves to the living God, to place ourselves completely in his hands, knowing that ultimately he will win out!"[95] Aiming to eradicate oneself would be "to fail to appreciate life's goodness and to fail to trust in God's goodness and mercy."[96] An attempt at "dominion" or control would be a net-negative because it would transgress the limits set by a loving creator-God.[97]

Thus Cardinal Bernardin's spiritual journey at the end of his life could be summed up as "learning to subordinate his own will to God's will"—an act of submission rather than self-assertion.[98] In this context, Bernardin was able to overcome the human urge to "fix" the situation.[99] As he explained: "It is precisely in letting go, in entering into complete union with the Lord, in letting him take over, that we discover our true selves. It's in the act of abandonment that we experience redemption, that we find life, peace and joy, in the midst of physical, emotional, and spiritual suffering."[100]

How he lived his terminal illness became an extension of his priesthood and an opportunity to model the discovery of a coherent narrative in the process of letting go. In dying, he perceived a "task to accomplish," not only for himself but for the people of his Archdiocese.[101] Walking among other terminally ill patients, he saw himself as "priest first, a patient second," with a capacity to offer "words and

---

[92] Kaveny, *Law's Virtues,* 165.
[93] Kaveny, *Law's Virtues,* 141.
[94] Kaveny, *Law's Virtues,* 145.
[95] Kaveny, *Law's Virtues,* 146.
[96] Kaveny, *Law's Virtues,* 147.
[97] Kaveny, *Law's Virtues,* 148.
[98] Kaveny, *Law's Virtues,* 149.
[99] Kaveny, *Law's Virtues,* 156.
[100] Kaveny, *Law's Virtues,* 156.
[101] Kaveny, *Law's Virtues,* 146.

deeds with a special credibility and power to comfort."[102] In fact, within this dynamic of giving and receiving love, to have cut short the process of dying would have denied others the "gift" of being able to give and minister to him.[103] Most strikingly, Kaveny reflects:

> Cardinal Bernardin writes simply and movingly of how he was sustained in difficult times by the support of his friends, family, and fellow priests. He cannot but have known how much that opportunity to care for him meant to them.[104]

The narrative quality of Bernardin's experience helps to reveal a logic which is strikingly different from Raz's analysis in support of legalizing euthanasia and assisted suicide. More than any conceptual analysis, Bernardin's narrative provides a substantive definition of Christian solidarity. Bernardin's sense that if he had not allowed others to care for him, he would have denied them a "gift" was not a euphemism. It was an expression of the witness at the heart of the Christian experience—to love and be loved, and to experience how suffering itself is transformed within the supportive relationship of mutual love.[105] Bernardin's concern that he may have denied others the "gift" of being able to care for him may sound strange to some liberal ears, but it brings to life what has deep roots in the tradition of Catholic social thought.

As Pope John Paul II explained in the 1980 document on the nature of mercy:

> In reciprocal relationships between persons merciful love is never a unilateral act or process. Even in the cases in which everything would seem to indicate that only one party is giving and offering, and the other only receiving and taking (for example, in the case of a physician giving treatment, a teacher teaching, parents supporting and bringing up their children, a benefactor helping the needy), in reality the one who gives is always also a beneficiary. In any case, he too can easily find himself in the position of the one who receives, who obtains a benefit, who experiences merciful love; he too can find himself the object of mercy.[106]

Narrative is also a primary figure in Kaveny's description of the role of those who are accompanying another person in the process of

---

[102] Kaveny, *Law's Virtues*, 149.
[103] Kaveny, *Law's Virtues*, 149.
[104] Kaveny, *Law's Virtues*, 149.
[105] See John Paul II, *Dives in misericordia* (1980), no. 14. "An act of merciful love is only really such when we are deeply convinced at the moment that we perform it that we are at the same time receiving mercy from the people who are accepting it from us."
[106] John Paul II, *Dives in misericordia*, no. 14.

dying. Kaveny suggests that such relationships can be the key to helping one who is dying in the effort to reinterpret and reframe the narrative of one's purposes and commitments: "If suffering involves disintegration of one's self-identity, then overcoming suffering involves finding a way forward toward reintegration, toward a new life that somehow also incorporates a narrative about the old."[107]

The effort to truly understand those who are suffering, why they are suffering, and what their values and life projects are, can "offer those who are suffering ways of reinterpreting their past purposes that will allow them some continuity, even in circumstances—such as chronic illness or disability—that have significantly changed for the worse."[108] In the current legal landscape, Kaveny discerns a clear and imperative task to all who endorse the Catholic tradition's rejection of assisted suicide and euthanasia: "By standing with those who suffer, we can potentially help them reconstruct their identities, find a new wholeness in their lives, and ultimately transcend the loss of their previous integrity."[109]

In Cover's terms, Bernardin's *life* was the bridge between "vision and reality," and his narrative a sign of the possibility of a personal commitment that illustrates how the virtue of solidarity might inform society's approach to law in this area.[110] More than any conceptual sparring, Bernardin's example is what calls into deep question Raz's list of the concerns that would substantiate a robust right to voluntary euthanasia.[111] Further, the lives and examples of those who accompanied Bernardin in his illness are a bridge to envision the social commitment required to weave the virtue of solidarity into law and policy regarding end of life care.

But if we take narrative as a methodological starting point for conversation across different thought systems, it would also be important to probe some of the particularistic limitations of Bernardin's story. For example, it might have been a little bit easier for a beloved bishop to live out the process of dying in the context of a reciprocal experience of giving and receiving love—both as part of his ministry and as part of his community leadership role.

Narrative can also serve a critical function—for example, helping to flesh out what might have been Raz's fears and concerns when he generated his list of factors.[112] As a methodological starting point, narrative could help to illuminate the complex situations of patients whose families or caretakers do experience care as a burden, whose

---

[107] Kaveny, *Law's Virtues*, 155.
[108] Kaveny, *Law's Virtues*, 156.
[109] Kaveny, *Law's Virtues*, 172-3.
[110] Cover, "*Nomos* and Narrative," 45-7.
[111] Raz, "Death in Our Life," 10-11.
[112] Raz, "Death in Our Life," 10-11, and discussion *supra* at note 45.

economic resources are stretched to the breaking point by an illness in the family, and who are already mourning the loss of the person that they once knew because this person is no longer present to them due to the course of disease or degeneration.

Many of these elements are illustrated in *Bouvia v. Superior Court*, a case in which the California Court of Appeals analyzed a 28-year-old disabled woman's request for removal of a nasogastric tube. The factual background of the case describes Elizabeth Bouvia's state of dependence due to severe cerebral palsy from birth and to other factors:

> She is intelligent, very mentally competent. She earned a college degree. She was married but her husband has left her. She suffered a miscarriage. She lived with her parents until her father told her that they could no longer care for her. She has stayed intermittently with friends and at public facilities. A search for a permanent place to live where she might receive the constant care she needs has been unsuccessful. She is without financial means to support herself and, therefore, must accept public assistance for medical care.[113]

In concluding that the state's interest in preserving life did not outweigh Bouvia's right to refuse treatment, the court reasoned:

> Her condition is irreversible. There is no cure for her palsy or arthritis. Petitioner would have to be fed, cleaned, turned, bedded, toileted by others for 15-20 years! Although alert, bright, sensitive, perhaps even brave and feisty, she must lie immobile, unable to exist except through physical acts of others. Her mind and spirit may be free to take great flights but she herself is imprisoned and must lie physically helpless subject to the ignominy, embarrassment, humiliation and dehumanizing aspects created by her helplessness. We do not believe it is the policy of this state that all and every life must be preserved against the will of the sufferer.[114]

From a methodological perspective, what I find especially interesting about the use of narrative for probing these kinds of concerns is that it leaves the space to open out beyond itself. For example, Paul Longmore's contextual study of the case fleshes out some of the details, including abuses on the part of agencies administering funds for in-home supportive services, refusal on the part of a local hospital to make a reasonable accommodation which would have allowed Bouvia to complete her field work for a Master's in Social Work, and how she had been caught in a bureaucratic Catch-22 in which disability

---

[113] *Bouvia v. Superior Court*, 179 Cal. App. 3d 1127, 1136 (1986).
[114] *Bouvia*, 1144.

benefits were contingent on not working.[115] These additional layers show how at various junctures in Bouvia's story, social prejudice may have fostered an extreme experience of isolation and depression, leading Longmore to query to what extent Bouvia's expression of the desire to die was an expression of her "autonomous choice" and to what extent a result of the kind of isolation due to society's short-sighted prejudices.

In light of these examples, what are the benefits of narrative as a methodological starting point in the dialogue between profoundly different thought systems? As the Bernardin and Bouvia stories indicate, narrative can help to render more transparent the values at stake and the meaning of those values within a given thought system. Bernardin's experience pushes the envelope on what solidarity and autonomy mean when reciprocal love is the defining quality of one's relationships, and when the categories of a broader religious narrative function as a lens through which to interpret one's personal story. For some, Bernardin's "personal act of commitment" in a Coverian sense will be an inspirational literary key for interpreting the law and policy of end of life care.[116]

The *Bouvia* narratives foster transparency in a different yet also crucially important sense: They help to flesh out the extent to which interpretation of the law and a person's encounter with the legal system and social structures may be infected with social prejudice and economic injustice. Here the Coverian "personal act of commitment" that might inform legal interpretation and law formation is essentially critical—provoking the kind of reflection that helps us to consider all of the ways in which the *Bouvia* narrative signals significant failures in the ideals of solidarity and respect which should have informed her social experience and that of many others.

Both narratives help to flesh out for legal discourse important elements of social context, the presence or lack of community and sustaining relationships, the impact of social prejudice, as well as important concerns about economic resources and economic justice. Both narratives help us to access the fears, needs and hopes of people in vulnerable circumstances. If, as Cover submits, "Creation of legal meaning entails, then, subjective commitment to an objectified understanding of a demand,"[117] narrative—both inspirational and critical—might help to sustain the initial steps on the path to common commitments.

---

[115] Paul K. Longmore, "Elizabeth Bouvia, Assisted Suicide and Social Prejudice," *Issues in Law & Medicine* 3 (1987): 153-4.
[116] Cover, "*Nomos* and Narrative," 45.
[117] Cover, "*Nomos* and Narrative," 45.

CONCLUSION

Scholarly work at the intersection of Catholic social thought and legal theory poses formidable challenges, especially if one hopes to move beyond critique toward constructive proposals and models. This article has explored only a narrow slice of Cathleen Kaveny's path breaking contributions to this field. It is largely thanks to the groundwork of her scholarship that we can begin to sort through the methodological questions about the dialogue. While I have significant doubts that a dialogue between Catholic solidarity and Razian autonomy can be sustained on the topic of euthanasia, I nonetheless very much agree with Kaveny's core insight—that we can reach across the profound differences in our systems of thought in order to appreciate the questions and the concerns that give shape to a different way of looking at the world and that this empathetic exchange is the best foundation for a constructive dialogue about how to build a more humane and just society.[118]

---

[118] I am grateful to Robin West, Gregory M. Klass, and participants in the Georgetown Law School Fellows Collaborative for a workshop discussion of a draft which transformed my approach to the article; and also for helpful comments, suggestions and critique from John Borelli, Lisa Cahill, William Gould, John Haughey, S.J., Gregory A. Kalscheur, S.J., Patricia A. King, Howard Lesnick, Thomas Masters, Michael P. Moreland, and Aristotle Papanikolaou.

REVIEW ESSAY

Locating the Church in the World: Ethnography, Christian Ethics, and the Global Church

Christopher P. Vogt

THIS REVIEW ESSAY will focus on the work of two groups of theologians who have begun to collaborate and produce scholarship. Their work should be of interest to anyone in the field of moral theology and more specifically to those working on the relationship between the church and the world. In the review, I will discuss first the literature that speaks to the importance of ethnographic research for moral theology and ecclesiology. Second, I will turn to the growing movement of Catholic moral theologians who are consciously seeking to do their work in the context of the "world church."

ETHNOGRAPHY, ECCLESIOLOGY, AND MORAL THEOLOGY

In his introduction to the inaugural book in Eerdmans' new series, "Studies in Ecclesiology and Ethnography," Pete Ward asks why more theologians do not engage in fieldwork that might help them find out what is going on in the church and in the world. At a time when theologians profess to be very interested in practices and the embodiment of religious doctrines, why don't theologians spend more time observing the actual practice of faith?[1] Eerdmans' new series is the fruit of recent conversations and collaborations among theologians—primarily ecclesiologists, ethicists, and practical theologians—who share an interest in ethnographic research and reflecting upon its theological significance. They believe that the church should be understood as both a theological and social/cultural entity, and therefore to understand the church it is necessary to employ theological and social scientific tools simultaneously.[2] The contributors to

---

[1] Pete Ward, "Introduction," in *Perspectives on Ecclesiology and Ethnography*, ed. Peter Ward (Grand Rapids: Eerdmans, 2012), 1.
[2] Ward, "Introduction," 2.

the volumes in this series are sensitive to the criticism that there is a risk that the use of social scientific tools can lead to a reductionist understanding of the church—one that essentially robs the church of its theological significance by seeing it as a strictly human invention. On the contrary, these authors insist that theological concerns are driving their research. They believe that you cannot come to an adequate theological understanding of the church without ethnography. Ward explains that he and his colleagues seek to employ a method in which there is "a constant interaction between theories and principles generated from the theological tradition, and careful participative observation of the particularities of an ecclesial situation."[3] He notes that the interaction should work both ways. What we observe and how we understand what we are observing are always deeply informed by a theological understanding of the church; likewise, those beliefs, generalizations, categories, etc. can ultimately be reshaped by what is learned via the observational research.

It is clear that these theologians are not motivated to turn to social science by some kind of inferiority complex about our discipline. They are not embracing ethnography and the tools of ethnography to justify their place in the academy. They are undertaking this turn for theological reasons. Ward offers a Christological basis for an approach to ecclesiology that is deeply informed by ethnographic research. He proposes the image of Christ as the one in whom all things hold together and simultaneously "the head of the body, the church" (Col 1:18). Christ is at the same time the firstborn of creation, in whom all things have their origin and in whom all things are reconciled (Col 1:15-20). Thus to study the church is to study something created through Christ, held together by Christ, and deeply linked to Christ as its head. Obviously, these theological claims cannot be demonstrated through observational research. Ward and his colleagues make no apologies for the fact that the starting point of their inquiry into the church is not a blank slate. Rather, "we see our situated understanding as itself arising from a traditioned ecclesial expression. This expression includes a doctrinal and liturgical canon that forms us as we set about trying to understand the church."[4] These authors make it clear that the turn to ethnography does not require setting aside theological categories that help us to understand what is "really going on" when we observe what takes place in church.

This is not to say that there isn't a temptation to remove the theological dimension of ethnographic research on the church. In the series' first volume, John Swinton offers a very helpful discussion of hermeneutics, epistemology, and ethnographic research. He

---

[3] Ward, "Introduction," 2.
[4] Ward, "Introduction," 3

acknowledges that "[t]he temptation to collapse theology into ethnography in order to please audiences beyond the church seems irresistible in terms of 'relevance' and 'effective communication' between church and the world."[5] This temptation largely arises from a desire to have research published in secular journals that have a very specific notion of what constitutes "unbiased" research, one that excludes specifically Christian theological categories. There are some forms of ethnographic research on the church in which all theology has been made invisible and that makes perfect sense without any reference to God, but that does not mean all ethnographic research must be that way. Several contributors to this volume make the point that rather than attempting to work in the field of ethnography and publishing on terms entirely set by that field, theologians should seek to use ethnography *as theologians* in their own research.

Drawing largely upon Hans-Georg Gadamer's model of a fusion of horizons, Swinton explains how ethnographic research might be "sanctified" (by which he means "blessed and set aside for a special purpose") in a way that makes it theologically helpful. He points out that any "ethnographic look" (i.e., any observation that is derived from ethnographic research) is always value-laden. There is no neutral mode of mere observation in which one sees what is really going on without any act of interpretation. Ethnography always entails hermeneutics. Although this fact might be obvious to most readers of this journal, it is a fact worth repeating because it goes unacknowledged by some natural and even social scientists. For example, in his description of the nature of ethnographic research, John Brewer writes that data must be collected through observation of people in naturally occurring settings "in a way that meaning is not imposed on them from the outside."[6] On the surface this sounds quite reasonable and necessary; however, it turns out to be impossible in the sense that one's framework for understanding what is being observed is never neutral. Offering a strictly phenomenological or psychological explanation for what one observes might seem neutral but in fact such a move reflects a very specific (likely empiricist) epistemological and philosophical point of view. Swinton notes that the question is not *whether* to use a value-laden framework of analysis; that is inevitable. The only question is whether a researcher will acknowledge the hermeneutical nature of observation and speak openly about what he or she brings to the task of interpretation or will he/she pretend that framework does not exist.[7] Thus theologians should acknowledge the

---

[5] John Swinton "Where is Your Church? Moving toward a Hospitable and Sanctified Ethnography," in *Perspectives on Ecclesiology and Ethnography*, ed. Ward, 86.
[6] John Brewer, *Ethnography* (Buckingham: Open University, 2000), 18. Cited in Swinton, "Where is Your Church," 78.
[7] Swinton, "Where is Your Church," 81-2.

very complex, rich theological categories they bring to their observations of the church, and they should make the argument that these categories are essential for a true understanding of the church and Christian practices.

Even if ethnographic research can be theologically legitimate, we might still ask why it is important or even essential specifically for *moral* theology. *Why* is the turn toward ethnography a move that moral theologians should be aware of and begin to integrate into their own work? And *how* might ethnographic research be helpful for theological ethics? Several essays in the first two volumes of the Studies in Ecclesiology and Ethnography series offer some helpful answers to both of those questions.

Liturgy and the church have become focal points for a lot of work in theological ethics largely due to the influence of Stanley Hauerwas and his considerable body of work on the church, virtue, and Christian practice. The church, in Hauerwas's theology, occupies a central place as a community that bears witness to the truth of the gospel. The church shows the world what it is by offering a contrast—a living example of what the world would look like if in fact the gospel is true.[8] Liturgy in turn plays a defining role in the life of the church and its task of bearing witness. It is at worship that Christians are formed and their characters reshaped so that they can hear, understand, and enact the gospel story.[9] According to Hauerwas, "Through liturgy we are shaped to live rightly the story of God, to become part of that story, and are thus able to recognize and respond to the saints in our midst."[10] It is worth noting that this point of view is not unique to Hauerwas, but is widely shared by scholars who write on liturgy and ethics today.[11] Hauerwas and many like-minded theologians claim that if we are to understand the meaning of Christianity and if we are to develop a theologically informed understanding of

---

[8] Stanley Hauerwas, *With the Grain of the Universe: The Church's Witness and Natural Theology* (Grand Rapids: Brazos, 2001), 214.
[9] Stanley Hauerwas, "The Gesture of a Truthful Story: The Church and 'Religious Education'," *Encounter* 43, no. 4 (1982): 325.
[10] Stanley Hauerwas, *Christian Existence Today*. Cited in Christian B. Scharen, "Introduction," in *Explorations in Ecclesiology and Ethnography*, ed. Christian B. Scharen (Grand Rapids: Eerdmans, 2012), 1.
[11] For example, the late Mark Searle wrote of liturgy as a "rehearsal room" in which actions are repeated over and over again until participants have identified with the part assigned to them as actors in the church and the world. See Mark Searle, "Serving the Lord with Justice," in *Vision: The Scholarly Contributions of Mark Searle to Liturgical Renewal*, ed. Anne Y. Koester and Barbara Searle (Collegeville: Liturgical, 2004), 19. Similarly, Don Saliers writes that good liturgy is a kind of "deliberate rehearsal" of bringing all aspects of our character into harmony with God's will for us. See Don E. Saliers, "Liturgy and Ethics: Some New Beginnings," in *Liturgy and the Moral Self: Humanity at Full Stretch before God*, ed. E. Byron Anderson and Bruce T. Morrill (Collegeville: Liturgical, 1998), 34.

how we should live in the world, our primary theological task is to turn to the church and observe its practices. Rowan Williams reflected this point of view when he wrote in the introduction to his *On Christian Theology* that we learn the meaning of the word God by "watching what the community does... when it is acting, educating, or 'inducting', imagining and worshipping."[12]

Nicholas Healy has pointed out that even if we accept this approach to theology (i.e., that we should understand God and the meaning of Christianity by watching the church) this task is not as straightforward as the model implies. We must decide what exactly should be the focus of our attention—should it be the church as a whole or just part of it? We must decide how the church is to be observed—a data-driven approach, historical analysis, doctrinal, etc.[13] Healy goes on to complain that, despite their arguments about the importance of "watching" the church, Williams and Hauerwas spend very little time observing actual church life and practice.[14] Instead (in Healy's view), both Williams and Hauerwas reflect upon what a very limited group of select Christians have done and written.

Healy goes on to question whether it is even possible to make claims about the practices and life of the church as a whole. Here Healy would get support from Robert P. Jones who writes that "any reference to some ideal, monolithic 'witness of the church' is problematized immediately by the conflicting witnesses of multiple churches on any concrete issue. The question is not just what Athens has to do with Jerusalem but what the United Church of Christ has to do with Southern Baptists."[15] Even beyond denominational differences, Healy asks whether we would be justified in speaking of a unified witness even within a given congregation. There is often a diversity of styles of worship, considerable difference of opinion on some important matters of doctrine, and no uniform view regarding what exactly are the implications of faith for living a moral life.[16]

Christian Scharen offers some criticisms that are in line with Healy's. He maintains that the idealized description of church and of worship offered by Hauerwas, Millbank, and others is quite far re-

---

[12] Rowan Williams, *On Christian Theology* (Oxford: Blackwell, 2000), xii. Cited in Nicholas M. Healy, "Ecclesiology, Ethnography, and God: An Interplay of Reality Descriptions," in *Perspectives on Ecclesiology and Ethnography*, ed. Ward, 182.
[13] Healy, "Ecclesiology, Ethnography, and God," 183.
[14] Healy, "Ecclesiology, Ethnography, and God," 183.
[15] Robert P. Jones, "Ethnography as Revelation: Witnessing in History, Faith, and Sin," in *Ethnography as Christian Theology and Ethics* (London: Continuum, 2011), 120.
[16] Healy, "Ecclesiology, Ethnography, and God," 185-7. Healy develops an alternative approach to ecclesiology at length in his book *Church, World and the Christian Life* (Cambridge University, 2000).

moved from the actual beliefs and practices of worshipers.[17] Scharen is in agreement with Hauerwas regarding the theological importance of the church, but he believes that a vague or naïve reference to "the church" is inadequate. As Harald Hegstad argues in the series' second volume, there is a need for actual data about church belief, practice, and worship.[18]

An example from my own recent work may illustrate what I see to be a valid critique of work in liturgy and ethics in the vein of Hauerwas, Williams, and company. For a volume commemorating the publication of *Economic Justice for All* (a pastoral letter on the economy by the United States Conference of Catholic Bishops), I contributed an essay entitled "Liturgy, Discipleship, and Economic Justice" that addresses the importance of liturgy for the personal and social transformation that would be necessary to move the United States toward a more just economy.[19] Drawing extensively on contemporary theological writing on liturgy and justice as well as the work of Virgil Michel, the essay analyzes how some fundamental Christian beliefs about human dignity, social equality, God's special concern for the poor, etc. are deeply inscribed in the Eucharistic liturgy. The essay also discusses how liturgy can be vital for forming people in these beliefs and motivating them to act to bring about a more just world. It paints a very attractive portrait of the liturgy and makes many connections between the Eucharist and the understanding of justice put forward in *Economic Justice for All*. I will not pretend that I didn't think it was a good essay, and yet after reading the work of Ward, Scharen, Healy, et. al. I have come to see that it has a very serious deficiency in that I did not bother to try to measure the liturgy's actual impact on the beliefs of people nor did I endeavor to find out how the Eucharistic liturgy is received by believers. Do the people of God experience the liturgy as I described it? Are they able to make the connections that I so carefully described? Does the liturgy ever change the way people think about solidarity and justice? Can you really write an essay on liturgy and formation without providing evidence that people are actually formed in the way that is described?[20]

---

[17] Scharen, "Introduction," in *Explorations in Ecclesiology and Ethnography*, 1.
[18] Harald Hegstad, "Ecclesiology and Empirical Research on the Church," in *Explorations in Ecclesiology and Ethnography*, ed. Scharen, 41.
[19] Christopher P. Vogt, "Liturgy, Discipleship, and Economic Justice," in *The Almighty and the Dollar: Reflections on Economic Justice for All*, ed. Mark Allman (Winona: Anselm Academic, 2012), 242-62.
[20] I am at least consoled by the fact that I am not alone in my omissions. For example, in *Self and Salvation*, David Ford follows a similar path. In his analysis of that book, Christian Scharen complains that even though Ford's theoretical framework should lead him to a close and careful study of the formation of a particular religious community, Ford turns instead to Scriptural analysis. See Christian Scharen, "Ecclesiology 'From the Body': Ethnographic Notes toward a Carnal Theology," in *Perspec-*

Christian Scharen helpfully explains why a theological analysis of the words of the liturgy alone is inadequate. Sometimes the congregation totally misses the point. This was the case in Corinth where the Eucharist became a source of division and scandal rather than unity and justice (1 Cor 11:17-22). A more recent example that explains why it is necessary to examine the formative effects of the liturgy as well as how it is received comes from an ethnographic study of worship in Ireland by Siobhán Garrigan. She observed that none of the congregants in any of the Catholic churches she studied received communion under both forms. She wanted to find out why there was a universal refusal to take the cup despite persistent encouragement from the Irish bishops. In her study she found that there was a widespread perception among the laity: "The Protestants, they receive the wine. We do not." Some held the corresponding view, "If we received the wine, we'd be just like the Protestants." Further study revealed that the reluctance was also deeply entwined with Irish history, especially with the British stereotype of the Irish as drunkards.[21] In effect, despite clear ecclesiastical instruction about full participation in the Eucharistic liturgy, local history and social practices are profoundly formative and perhaps more clearly instructive in the celebration of the Mass. Without careful ethnographic research like Garrigan's there may be no way of knowing what kinds of formative practices are operative. Thus, it is insufficient to explain the meaning of the Eucharist without any reference or investigation into how the liturgy is actually celebrated and understood by particular people. Moral theologians working on liturgy and ethics need to attend to this and similar challenges uncovered by our colleagues studying ecclesiology and ethnography.

CATHOLIC THEOLOGICAL ETHICS IN THE WORLD CHURCH

Over four hundred Catholic ethicists from around the globe gathered in the Italian city of Padua in 2006 for what was billed as the "First Cross-cultural Conference on Catholic Theological Ethics."[22] The purpose of the gathering was "to appreciate the challenges of pluralism; to dialogue from and beyond local culture; and to interconnect within a world church not dominated solely by a northern

---

tives on Ecclesiology and Ethnography, ed. Ward, 55. David F. Ford, *Self and Salvation: Being Transformed* (New York: Cambridge University, 1999).

[21] Sibohán Garrigan, *The Real Peace Process: Worship, Politics, and the End of Sectarianism* (London: Equinox, 2010), 122. Cited in Scharen, "Ecclesiology 'From the Body'," 60-1.

[22] James F. Keenan, S.J., ed., *Catholic Theological Ethics in the World Church: The Plenary Papers from the First Cross-cultural Conference on Catholic Theological Ethics* (New York: Continuum, 2007). For select papers from concurrent, applied ethics sessions, see Linda Hogan, ed., *Applied Ethics in a World Church: The Padua Conference* (Maryknoll: Orbis, 2007).

paradigm."²³ The organizers of the conference believed that even in an age of international electronic communication and publication an actual gathering of theologians was vital in order to allow participants to get to know one another, to learn to be together and to share ideas with one another. By spending a few days together in Italy what they achieved was "more than simply a sharing of ideas; it was a meeting of persons."²⁴ The theologians who gathered in Padua judged the conference to have been a success and wanted more.²⁵ A planning committee was formed to take on the formidable logistical and fund-raising work necessary to hold a similar event.²⁶ Four years later (July 24-27, 2010), the "Catholic Theological Ethics in the World Church" (CTEWC) group held a second international conference in Trent (Trento, Italy). The second gathering was even more successful than the first if the number of participants is any indicator, drawing over six hundred theologians from nearly 75 countries (compared to four hundred theologians from 67 countries at Padua).

In a retrospective article, James F. Keenan, S.J. (a central figure in planning both conferences who together with Linda Hogan now co-chairs the CTEWC planning committee) called Trento 2010 "a defining moment in church history."²⁷ That is a very strong claim. While it is always dangerous to judge whether events are "historic" as we live through them, there are good reasons to believe that a genuine and significant movement has grown out of the conferences in Trent and Padua.²⁸ The work presented at those conferences has been published widely and in many translations, but perhaps more importantly the group has begun to organize itself in such a way that it no longer functions merely as a planning body for international conferences. The Catholic Theological Ethics in the World Church (CTEWC) organization is becoming a network of scholars committed to building up professional ties among theologians across the globe and to promoting a specific set of priorities for doing moral theology in the twenty-first century. Among other things, the group has established a monthly forum that publishes short theological reflections from contributors recruited from Africa, Asia, North Amer-

---

[23] Keenan, *Catholic Theological Ethics in the World Church*, 3.
[24] Keenan, *Catholic Theological Ethics in the World Church*, 3.
[25] For a helpful analysis of the first conference and the work presented there, see Christopher Steck, S.J., "Catholic Ethics as Seen from Padua," *Journal of Religious Ethics* 39, no. 2 (2011): 365-90.
[26] For a full account of the planning of the second conference and what transpired there see James F. Keenan, "What Happened at Trento 2010?" *Theological Studies* 72 (2011): 131-49.
[27] Keenan, "What Happened at Trento," 131.
[28] I wish to make clear that my perspective on this organization is not that of a neutral bystander, but an active, invested participant. I presented work at both conferences, and I currently serve on the North American Regional Committee of CTEWC.

ica, and South America, and has sponsored regional events in Nairobi, Bangalore, and Berlin, which complement the global gatherings held in the past.[29]

In what follows, I explain and assess what this group is proposing regarding the proper shape of moral theology today. I do so by analyzing some of the work that emerged from the Padua and Trento conferences and by looking at the group's stated goals and plans. It will become clear below that a specific theology of the church and the world plays an important role in shaping the mission and self-understanding of this group. Its agenda and approach to moral theology emerge from a sense that it is imperative for theologians and indeed the church itself to locate themselves within the world. Given the large number of theologians who have participated in these conferences and the growing engagement of theologians with CTWEC's new initiatives, consideration of the publications and plans of this organization will have a significant impact on how people in our field understand the church and their place in it, and how they engage "the world."

Sometimes explicitly and other times implicitly, the CTEWC group sets forth a particular understanding of how moral theologians should do their work and why. The group is offering an agenda both in terms of what questions should be taken up and how they should be analyzed theologically. I will highlight three overlapping priorities or qualities of the work that have come out of the CTEWC conferences. Together, these three aspects illuminate a discernible agenda and a way of doing moral theology: 1) the importance of being a "listening church" and reading the signs of the times, 2) the central importance of dialogue for theological ethics, and 3) a simultaneous insistence on the importance of the contextual and the possibility of a universal ethic. Along the way, I also uncover important beliefs about the church and the world that are embedded in this approach to moral theology.

Perennial questions facing moral theologians pertain to our research agendas: What should we write about? Should we dig deeply into Augustine or Aquinas? Should we put ourselves into dialogue with moral philosophers? Should we focus on complicated quandaries or provide a simple vision of how to pursue discipleship in everyday life? Of course, moral theologians are doing all of these things and more, but at the same time choices are always being made about what papers to include in conference programs, what books to publish, what topics should be the focus of an issue of a journal, and so on. Thus, the question of priorities is very real. It is worthwhile to be attentive to the priorities being promoted by the CTEWC group and

---

[29] For more on the group's organizational structure, mission, newsletters, forum, etc., see www.catholicethics.com.

others in the field and to assess whether they are worthy of being promoted.

The CTEWC group clearly supports the point of view that "the world" should be granted a very substantial role in setting the research agenda for moral theologians. The very first plenary session in Padua was devoted to the question: "How Can Theological Ethicists Respond to the World's Needs?" Antonio Papisca's response to that question asked ethicists to attend to issues of human rights—to expound upon the basis of such rights, but more importantly to develop practical proposals regarding how human rights can be protected and promoted via programs, public policies, and individual actions.[30] Adela Cortina pointed to the importance of theological work on economic justice and economic systems "because they affect people's lives and the sustainability of nature."[31] In her view, the economy must be on the agenda for moral theologians because of its enormous impact on the lives of all people and also because there are teleological questions and choices always at play in the economic realm. Although Cortina recognizes that "theological ethicists cannot resolve… economic problems" they must commit themselves to working with specialists in business, economics, and social sciences to understand the goals of economic activity and how that activity should be shaped to create a good society.[32] For both authors, theologians must find ways to move people toward a clearer understanding of justice, meaning or purpose (e.g., help answering the question "what is the economy for?"), but also to craft practical solutions to problems that cause human suffering or impede human flourishing.

James Keenan's essay introducing the Trento conference shares a similar view of the sort of questions moral theologians should be investigating. He writes that "[ethicists] are needed because things are not as they could be. As the critics and reformers of society and church, we seek to practically bridge the gulf between who we are and who we can be. Thus, we always begin with the premise that there is a deficit in our location, and therefore, we need to work together to find a way to remedy it."[33] Although Keenan's description still emphasizes action, his view of the task of moral theology is more textured than merely "responding to the world's needs." He highlights the importance not only of social criticism and practical action, but also the development of good character. Furthermore, Keenan

---

[30] Antonio Papisca, "The Needs of the World and the Signs of the Times: The Challenge of Human Rights," in *Catholic Theological Ethics in the World Church*, 11-19.
[31] Adela Cortina, "Challenges of Economic Activity in a Global World," in *Catholic Theological Ethics in the World Church*, 20-8 at 22.
[32] Cortina, "Challenges," 20-1.
[33] James F. Keenan, "Introduction: The Trento Conference," in *Catholic Theological Ethics Past, Present, and Future: The Trento Conference*, ed. James F. Keenan (Maryknoll: Orbis, 2011), 6.

clearly sees that the agenda of moral theology goes beyond practical problem-solving. There is room for fundamental moral questions as well. Writing on the agenda at Trento and also the agenda for the field as a whole, Keenan explains:

> We could go to Trento to share fundamental insights and claims, to reflectively and respectfully consider the needs of today within the context of a world church and its evolving and constantly emerging traditions. But we could also explore ways that for the next twenty-five years we too could dispute about authority, conscience, sin, gender, sustainability, health, economy, natural law, history, the right to food, the need to love, family, the emotions, and yes, even the traditions themselves.[34]

Thus while attending to the needs of the world is an important feature of the agenda of this movement, it is not advocating "applied ethics" at the expense of fundamental moral theology. Clearly there is an emphasis on the former, but there is room and a need for both.

Endeavoring to hear the needs of the world is not the only way in which "listening" is emphasized by participants in this movement. Including a variety of voices is also important. The conferences were designed in a way that emphasized the importance of dialogue and organizers paid very careful attention to issues of "voice." Keenan writes of how the organizers sought to bring specific groups of individuals into the conversation: members of the hierarchy, "new" or young scholars, women theologians, and scholars from the global South. It should be noted that the desire to include these groups was followed through with action in the form of invitations to archbishops to participate in two plenary addresses and financial support for young scholars and for theologians (especially women) living in the global South. These decisions are in line with the group's desire to be aware "of those not heard, rejected, oppressed, or abandoned," but also reflect an understanding of the church and the place of theologians in it.[35] Here the model is very inclusive and collaborative. The hierarchy must be included, but it seems only as one voice among others.[36]

The model for doing moral theology put forward by CTEWC at their conferences and in the events that they have planned for the

---

[34] Keenan, "Introduction," *Catholic Theological Ethics Past, Present, and Future*, 1-2.
[35] Keenan, "Introduction," *Catholic Theological Ethics Past, Present, and Future*, 7.
[36] Christopher Steck notes that one certainly did not find at Padua the model of theological scholarship practiced in which the bishops teach and theologians strive to provide good reasons to believe what is taught. However, the theologians participating in the Padua conference did move "within the linguistically and theologically bounded world of Catholicism," where "official Church pronouncements, not recent theological scholarship, are the guides and touchstones for their scholarly thinking." See Steck, "Catholic Ethics as Seen from Padua," 370.

future is decisively marked by dialogue. There is an insistence that theologians must be in dialogue with the Magisterium, with each other, and perhaps most importantly with "the world." This model of theological engagement was fully in evidence at the opening session of the Trento conference. Whereas Padua began by encouraging theologians to listen to the needs of the world, the opening plenary in Trento began with the theme of "Ethics and Interreligious Dialogue in a Globalized World." Before an audience of Catholic theological ethicists, a Roman Catholic archbishop (Bruno Forte), a Protestant theologian (Mercy Amba Oduyoye), and an Islamic scholar (Ahmad Syafi Ma'arif) from three different continents (Europe, Africa, and Asia) were called upon to discuss the nature of ethics in a globalized world.

This session not only modeled the importance of dialogue, three scholars also offered varying but interwoven reasons *why* an interreligious, theological dialogue about ethics and the problems of the contemporary world is essential. Mercy Oduyoye offered perhaps the most basic reason: No community can solve problems in today's world on its own, and therefore we must learn to diagnose and solve problems together.[37] Ahmad Syafi Ma'arif spoke more specifically to why the world actually needs theological analysis in order to understand the contemporary situation rightly and therefore needs to be in dialogue with theologians. He locates the problems of the twentieth and twenty-first centuries ultimately in secularism and anthropocentrism—in an intentional attempt to forget God. Secularism and an excessive focus on the human person led to an exaggeration of the scope of human freedom and to a forgetfulness about transcendence.[38] Bruno Forte focused primarily on identity in providing reasons for the imperative of dialogue across many boundaries. The church has no choice but to engage the world because the church can never be entirely separated from the world. The identity of the people who make up the church (including moral theologians) is always informed by multiple sources.[39] As Archbishop Forte put it very pointedly in his opening address, "The illusion of purity of identity and

---

[37] Mercy Amba Oduyoye, "A Protestant Perspective," in *Catholic Theological Ethics Past, Present, and Future*, ed. Keenan, 19.

[38] Ahmad Syafi Ma'arif, "A Muslim Perspective," in *Catholic Theological Ethics Past, Present, and Future*, 28-30.

[39] Drawing upon Kathryn Tanner's work, Vincent Miller makes the case that this is true, not only for contemporary Christians, but throughout Christian history. "Syncretism and cultural mixture mark [Christianity] from the beginning." Vincent J. Miller, *Consuming Religion: Christian Faith and Practice in a Consumer Culture* (New York: Continuum, 2004), 25. See Kathryn Tanner, *Theories of Culture: A New Agenda for Theology* (Minneapolis: Fortress, 1997).

race is pure folly."⁴⁰ People today have plural or "mixed identities," informed simultaneously by multiple belongings. Individuals, institutions (even the church), and cultures are engaged in a mixing and mingling interchange. According to Forte, if a culture or institution is to remain alive, it must be able to enter into a process of dialogical exchange.

Miguel Ángel Sánchez Carlos provides a similar reading of the theological significance of the fluidity of identity and culture. He notes that in many urban contexts today, culture is often a hybrid formed from multiple sources and adds that Christianity is no longer at the forefront of the production of culture. Instead the church is more likely to be shaped by culture rather than the other way around.⁴¹ Aloysius Cartagenas makes a similar point later in the Trento volume where he notes that the church has lost the privileged socio-political location it once enjoyed. It no longer sits on the same plane as leaders of nation-states in public discourse. Furthermore, the bodies that once served as social carriers of Catholicism into the public sphere (Catholic charities, Catholic social groups, reform movements, etc.) have also substantially declined.⁴² One lesson that must be learned by the church and theological ethicists from these facts of life is the inescapability of collaboration and partnerships when addressing the moral issues of our day. Sánchez Carlos concludes that "we should seriously question the quality of life in our cities and look for ways to collaborate with others who from different mystical and logical perspectives are working to build more humane cities, especially for the impoverished or excluded majorities around them."⁴³

The nature of identity today and the church's location in the world also has an impact on what sort of argumentation should be put forward by theological ethicists. Sánchez Carlos and many other theologians who presented at the CTEWC conferences believe that theologians and the church more generally must come forward with ethical proposals that are understandable and reasonable to an audience who is shaped simultaneously by multiple traditions of mean-

---

[40] Bruno Forte, "A Catholic Perspective," in *Catholic Theological Ethics Past, Present, and Future*, 13.
[41] Miguel Ángel Sánchez Carlos, "Urban Life, Urban Ethics," in *Catholic Theological Ethics Past, Present, and Future*, 168. Here Sánchez Carlos is drawing insight from the 2007 gathering of the Bishops of Latin America and the Caribbean in Aparecida, Brazil. See *Aparecida, Concluding Document: Fifth General Conference of the Bishops of Latin America and the Caribbean, May 13-31, 2007* (Washington, DC: USCCB, 2008), www.rcpos.org/v2.0/downloads/Concluding%20Document%20CELAM%20Aparecida.pdf.
[42] Aloysius Cartagenas, "The Abuse of Power in the Church: Its Impact on Identity, Reciprocity, and Familial Relations," in *Catholic Theological Ethics Past, Present, and Future*, 240-1.
[43] Sánchez Carlos, "Urban Life, Urban Ethics," 169.

ing. This mode of argumentation is important not only for dialogue with people outside of the church, but also when writing for the people who make up the church today. Sánchez Carlos is arguing that to write for the church is not to write to a monolithic audience who is shaped only or even primarily by Christian sources. Instead, even members of the church itself have been affected by "cognitive contamination"—the result of a process by which people open up their worldview by seeing similarities and connections between their own beliefs and those of others. The result of this cognitive contamination is that Christians do not have a purely Christian worldview; instead they keep in mind simultaneously multiple worldviews.[44] For such an audience, Sánchez Carlos believes that theological ethics must embrace a mode of discourse that is concrete and multi-disciplinary in order to be effective.

Even in the midst of all of this emphasis on multiple belongings, diversity of voices, local context and so on, the third important characteristic of the CTWEC organization is its aspiration to a universal ethic of some sort. This comes out most clearly in the notion of universal human rights that is defended in several essays and assumed in others. Of course exactly how you can emphasize particularity and universality at the same time is not always clear. This problem remains one of the great philosophical and theological challenges of our day: the task of finding a way to recognize the importance of culture and context without giving up on the belief that all human beings share some fundamental things in common (which in turn have universal ethical implications). It is clear that this group believes that the way forward is to cultivate scholarship that is deeply rooted in a particular context, but in productive dialogue with an international audience.

LINKING THESE TWO DEVELOPMENTS

The CTEWC movement and theologians engaging in ethnographic research are both pointing to the importance of lived human experience as a source of theology. The level of importance and authority attached to experience varies considerably as do the methods by which individual theologians connected with each of these groups bring data about human experience into dialogue with other theological sources. On the one hand, some theologians like Denise Ackerman insist that without field work and close attention to lived human experience theological analysis is worthless.[45] Others take a more

---

[44] Sánchez Carlos, "Urban Life, Urban Ethics," 170. The concept of "cognitive contamination" actually comes from Peter Berger.
[45] She says that "[t]heology done at arm's length from the reality of the context in which we seek to speak theological words is not worth the paper it is written on." Denise Ackerman, "From Mere Existence to Tenacious Endurance: Stigma,

measured stand such as Emily Reimer Barry who is adamant about the importance of "listening" and ethnographic research for theology and the church but who also recognizes that "one need not live in a war zone to critique the horrors of war" and there are valid forms of doing theology that do not take ethnographic research as their starting point.

The rise of ethnographic research in theology and the prominent place of "voice" and local reflection in the CTEWC movement point to the need for moral theologians to continue to debate and study how experience functions as a source of moral insight. It is necessary not only to learn to listen, but to be able to explain more systematically and theologically why it is important to do so. In a similar vein, more systematic methods are needed for bringing lived experience into productive dialogue with the Catholic moral tradition and contemporary magisterial teaching. This will take more than assembling the right "voices" for a conference or for a book. Undoubtedly the question of experience and how a global context should inform the way theologians everywhere do their work will be on the agenda of a newly formed CTSA interest group, "Beyond Trento: North American Moral Theology in a Global Church." As they move forward in their endeavors, theologians connected with the conferences, interest-groups and publications of CTEWC would do well to be attentive to the important work being published in the Studies in Ecclesiology and Ethnography series where theologians are grappling with some of the same questions about the status of the world, the importance of experience, how to engage in interdisciplinary research and so on. The growing strength of these two movements bodes well for our field. M

HIV/AIDS, and a Feminist Theology of Praxis," in *African Women, Religion, and Health: Essays in Honor of Mercy Amba Ewudziwa Oduyoye*, ed. Isabel Apao Phiri and Sarojini Nadar (Maryknoll: Orbis, 2006), 239. Cited in Emily Reimer Barry, "The Listening Church: How Ethnography Can Transform Catholic Ethics," in *Ethnography as Christian Theology and Ethics* (London: Continuum, 2011), 116.

CONTRIBUTORS

William T. Cavanaugh is Senior Research Professor and Director of the Center for World Catholicism and Intercultural Theology at DePaul University. His degrees are from Notre Dame, Cambridge, and Duke. He has published numerous articles and five books, most recently *The Myth of Religious Violence* (Oxford, 2009) and *Migrations of the Holy* (Eerdmans, 2011). His books have been published in French, Spanish, Polish, and Norwegian.

David Clairmont is Associate Professor of Theological Ethics in the Department of Theology, University of Notre Dame. He is the author of *Moral Struggle and Religious Ethics: On the Person as Classic in Comparative Theological Contexts* (Wiley-Blackwell, 2011) and co-editor (with Don S. Browning) of *American Religions and the Family: How Faith Traditions Cope with Modernization and Democracy* (Columbia University Press, 2007). His articles on comparative theological ethics and the traditions of Catholic spirituality have appeared in the *Journal of the Society of Christian Ethics*, the *Journal of the American Academy of Religion*, and the *Journal of Religious Ethics*.

Laurie Johnston is Assistant Professor of Theology and Religious Studies at Emmanuel College in Boston where she directs the Peace Studies program. She has published essays on topics such as just war, peacebuilding, reconciliation, and health care ethics. She serves on the Steering Committee for the Catholic Peacebuilding Network.

David M. Lantigua is Assistant Professor of Moral Theology and Ethics at The Catholic University of America. With Darrell Fasching and Dell deChant he is co-author of *Comparative Religious Ethics: A Narrative Approach to Global Ethics,* 2nd Edition (Wiley-Blackwell, 2011). He is co-editor and co-translator with Lawrence A. Clayton for *The Essential Bartolomé de las Casas: A Brief History with Documents* (Bedford/St Martin's Press, forthcoming). He is a contributor to *Hispanic American Religious Cultures* (ABC-CLIO) and *The Oxford Handbook of Christianity in Latin America* (forthcoming).

Ramón Luzárraga is Assistant Professor of Theology and a member of the founding faculty of Benedictine University in Mesa, Arizona. He serves on the board of the Academy of Catholic Hispanic Theologians of the United States, co-convenes the Latino/a ethics group in the Society of Christian Ethics, co-convenes the Latino/a theology consultation of the Catholic Theological Society of America, and is a member of Caribbean Theology Today, a group of Catholic theologians from the Caribbean region. He has written articles for reference works and book reviews concerning ethics, Latino theology, Caribbean theology, and systematic theology.

Tracey Rowland is Dean of the John Paul II Institute for Marriage and Family in Melbourne, Australia and a Permanent Fellow of the Institute in Political Philosophy and Continental Theology. She is the author of *Culture and the Thomist Tradition: After Vatican II* (Routledge, 2003), *Ratzinger's Faith: the Theology of Pope Benedict XVI* (Oxford, 2008), and the *Benedict XVI* volume in T & T Clark's *Guides for the Perplexed* series. She is also a member of the editorial board of the English language edition of *Communio: International Catholic Review*, a journal co-founded by Joseph Ratzinger, among others, in 1972.

Amelia J. Uelmen is a Lecturer at Georgetown Law School where her scholarship and teaching focus on religious values and legal practice and Catholic social thought. She is the co-author of *Focolare: Living a Spirituality of Unity in the United States* (New City Press, 2011) and *Education's Highest Aim: Teaching and Learning through a Spirituality of Communion* (New City Press, 2010). In progress is a doctoral thesis on the common law "no-duty to rescue" seen through the lens of relational ethics and Trinitarian theology.

Christopher P. Vogt is Associate Professor and Chair of the Department of Theology & Religious Studies at St. John's University in New York. He is the author of *Patience, Compassion, Hope, and the Christian Art of Dying Well* (Rowman & Littlefield, 2004). His recent publications include "Liturgy, Discipleship, and Justice," in *The Almighty and the Dollar*, ed. Mark Allman (Anselm, 2012), and "Catholic Social Thought and Creation," in *Green Discipleship*, ed. Tobias Winright (Anselm, 2011). "Business, Capabilities Theory, and the Virtue of Justice" will be published in *The Handbook of Virtue Ethics and Business*, ed. Alejo Sison (Springer, forthcoming).

Claire E. Wolfteich is Associate Professor at Boston University School of Theology, where she also co-directs the Center for Practical Theology. She is the immediate past President of the International Academy of Practical Theology. Her most recent book project is the forthcoming edited volume, *Invitation to Practical Theology: Catholic Voices and Visions* (Paulist, 2014). Other publications include *Sabbath in the City: Sustaining Urban Pastoral Excellence*, co-authored with Bryan Stone (Westminster John Knox Press, 2008), *Lord, Have Mercy: Praying for Justice with Conviction and Humility* (Jossey Bass, 2006), *Navigating New Terrain: Work and Women's Spiritual Lives* (Paulist, 2002), and *American Catholics Through the Twentieth Century: Spirituality, Lay Experience, and Public Life* (Crossroad, 2001).

JOURNAL OF MORAL THEOLOGY

Upcoming Issues

Virtue
Volume 3, Number 1 (January 2014)
Editors: David Cloutier
and William C. Mattison III

Environment and Creation: Non-Human Animals
Volume 3, Number 2 (June 2014)
Editor: John Berkman, Charles Camosy,
and Celia Deane-Drummond

Technology, Human Community and Being Human
Volume 4, Number 1 (January 2015)
Editors: James F. Caccamo
and David Matzko McCarthy

Open to all Submissions
Volume 4, Number 2 (June 2015)
Editor: David McCarthy

Articles and information about
the JMT are available at:

www.msmary.edu/jmt

> The
>
> *Journal of Moral Theology*
>
> is proudly sponsored by the
>
> Fr. James M. Forker Professorship
> of Catholic Social Teaching
>
> *and the*
>
> College of Liberal Arts
>
> *at*
>
> Mount St. Mary's University

www.ingramcontent.com/pod-product-compliance
Lightning Source LLC
Chambersburg PA
CBHW071456150426
43191CB00008B/1367